THE WRITINGS OF DANIEL BERRIGAN

Ross Labrie

UNIVERSITY
PRESS OF
AMERICA

Lanham • New York • London

Copyright © 1989 by

University Press of America,® Inc.

4720 Boston Way
Lanham, MD 20706

3 Henrietta Street
London WC2E 8LU England

British Cataloging in Publication Information Available

Library of Congress Cataloging-in-Publication Data

Labrie, Ross.
The writings of Daniel Berrigan / by Ross Labrie.
p.   cm.
Bibliography: p.
Includes index.
1. Berrigan, Daniel—Criticism and interpretation.
2. Social problems in literature.   I. Title.
PS3503.E734Z77   1989   811'.54—dc20   89–33138 CIP

ISBN 0–8191–7495–5 (alk. paper)

All University Press of America books are produced on acid-free paper.
The paper used in this publication meets the minimum requirements of American
National Standard for Information Sciences—Permanence of Paper for Printed Library
Materials, ANSI Z39.48–1984.   ∞

for Mary Reilly

Acknowledgements

Grateful acknowledgement is made to Daniel Berrigan for permission to quote from his published and unpublished writings and from the following publishers for permission to quote from the following works by Daniel Berrigan:

- to the Macmillan Publishing Co. for permission to quote from *Time Without Number, They Call Us Dead Men, No One Walks Waters, Consequences: Truth and..., Night Flight to Hanoi, and False Gods, Real Men.*
- to Harper & Row for permission to quote from *The Mission: A Film Journal.*
- to Crossroad Publishing Co. for permission to quote from *Portraits: Of Those I Love.*
- to Doubleday & Co. for permission to quote from *The Dark Night of Resistance.*
- to the Putnam Publishing Group for permission to quote from *The Bow in the Clouds.*

CONTENTS

Daniel Berrigan
(Photo by Michael A. Fager)

Preface

In addition to a full life of social activism Daniel Berrigan has produced an impressive literary corpus amounting to over thirty volumes. The present study considers these writings - which are largely autobiographical - from the point of view of both the immediate and long-term effects of the life upon the writings. For this reason, although a number of Berrigan's writings are given extended formal and thematic analysis, there is much more biographical background provided than is customary in a study of this kind. The method followed is fundamentally chronological, beginning with the early years of Berrigan's life as a priest and theologian, followed by the tumultuous period of the Vietnam War, and finally by Berrigan's defiant challenging of the pronouncements of both church and state regarding the morality of war in general and the deployment of nuclear armaments in particular.

What makes Berrigan interesting and significant as a writer is his straddling of the roles of priest, artist, and activist. While this division of effort might theoretically seem to have been unpromising, Berrigan passed easily and productively between these separate callings. If his variegated life fertilized his consciousness as a writer, the writing in turn clarified his sense of direction as both priest and activist. The result has been a distinctive and articulate record in both poetry and prose of a man of conscience embattled with the contemporary state and with many of the cultural assumptions underlying it.

I am indebted to Daniel Berrigan for allowing me to look through the extensive collection of his manuscripts at Cornell University and for his helpful answers to my questions. I would also like to thank James Tyler of the Rare Books department of the Olin Library at Cornell and Phillip Runkel of the Marquette

University Library for their patient and generous assistance. I am grateful to those of Daniel Berrigan's friends and relatives who offered information and advice, especially Jerome Berrigan, Jim Forest, Dan and Linda Finlay, Jack Lewis, Bob Keck, and James and Shelley Douglass. I would also like to thank the General Theological Union Library at Berkeley for providing copies of many otherwise unobtainable articles by and about Berrigan. Finally, I should like to thank the Social Sciences and Humanities Research Council of Canada for the grant that enabled me to travel to Cornell in order to carry out research on the book.

Ross Labrie

University of British Columbia

Chapter One

EARLY PROSE

Although less immediately keyed to events in his life than would be the case with his later writings, Daniel Berrigan's prose writings in the 1950s and early 1960s nonetheless clearly mirrored his early life and experience. While these writings were theological studies for the most part, they incorporated an aggressive historical view of the social mission of the church that was unusual in American Catholicism prior to the impact of the Second Vatican Council in the 1960s. This view resulted largely from Berrigan's childhood experiences at home and from his studies in France in the early 1950s.

Born in Virginia, Minnesota, on May 9, 1921, Daniel Berrigan was the fifth of six sons born to Thomas and Frida Berrigan. Thomas Berrigan was a fervent trade union supporter and organizer, who had fallen away from the practice of his religion as a young man because of the American Catholic church's lack of support for unionism at the turn of the century. While living in Minnesota, he met and married Frida Fromhart, a devout and gentle Catholic girl who as a child had been brought to the United States from Germany. Frida's piety brought her husband back to the church, but her relationship with her volatile and demagogic husband was a long-suffering one.

In 1927 Thomas Berrigan and his family moved to Syracuse, New York, primarily because of his desire to be reunited with his numerous relations there.   In Syracuse he obtained a position as a maintenance man at a Catholic orphanage, and moved into a sixty-year-old farmhouse on a hilltop in Galesville, a few miles west of Syracuse.   Daniel Berrigan remembers his father espousing a "near religion of labor," his presence impinging on them all like the "whirr of an emory wheel on a blade."[1]   Daniel was of slighter build and less robust health than the others, and so was given a lot of the housework to do in the company of his mother.   The arrangement led to the closest of bonds between himself and his mother as well as to a bitter estrangement between his father and himself.   If in his father's eyes he frequently perceived the fire of anger, however, he also saw there an extraordinary capacity to "look closely at the fabric of life; to weigh and touch and lay one's hand along its length and breadth. Not to be taken in."[2]   This was a look with which the son would identify as he took the measure of his society and of his church in the years to come.

In retrospect Daniel Berrigan has marvelled at the emotional survival of his mother, just as, paradoxically, he has lamented the absence of a vivid memory of her physical presence. She had borne her suffering for all of them - a passive role on the surface, he has observed, "but, in reality, a life that, like impeded streams, found its own way - around, under."[3] If Berrigan inherited a zeal for activity from his father, it was his mother who showed him the still depths of the contemplative life from his earliest years.

Berrigan has recalled two impressions of home that were especially positive and formative. First of all, he has noted, both of his parents lived their lives "as though nobody owned them."[4] Secondly, although they were poor, they shared what they had. Throughout the 1930s Berrigan remembers his parents feeding an endless stream of the unemployed and the poor with the hard-won fruits of the farm, inviting sometimes the most forbidding-looking men into the house and seating them at the family table. One such man, having been lavished with Frida Berrigan's hospitality, turned out to be an escaped convict, and when the authorities came looking for him she blandly sent them in the wrong direction, an incident that was to foreshadow Berrigan's own later dealings with the law.

Berrigan remembers his childhood home being amply supplied with reading - Hardy, Scott, Trollope, Dickens - books lugged home from the city library by his mother at his father's behest. Apart from this solid grounding, Berrigan remembers the weekly appearances of *The Catholic Worker*, a newspaper started by Dorothy Day which supported trade unionism, pacifism, and the care of the urban poor and homeless. The paper, which sold for a penny a copy, was welcomed by Berrigan's father, who had become a leader in the electrical workers union in Syracuse during the 1930s. Dorothy Day, journalist, single mother, and Catholic leftist, was to have a definitive and lifelong effect on Berrigan's thought and writing.

Toward the end of high school Berrigan applied to enter the Society of Jesus, having formed an impression of the Jesuits as steeped in heroic and revolutionary traditions. The meaning of his decision to become a priest came home to him in a theater where, with his consciousness relaxed as the film rolled, it seemed as though the "eye of the universe blinked, and darkness fell" so that he felt himself "tumbled out of the world."[5] The training to become a Jesuit would last thirteen years. St. Andrew-on-Hudson, a Jesuit novitiate near Poughkeepsie, N.Y., was to be Berrigan's home for the period between 1939 and 1941. In spite of the isolation of St. Andrew's, Berrigan received during his years in the seminary fragmentary news from all parts of the world.

Furthermore, missionaries from abroad came to speak about their work and inevitably inspired the students to want to give themselves to the poor, the illiterate, and the oppressed of other nations. These visits became a paradigm of Jesuit life for Berrigan, and would help to instill an international consciousness in him from an early age.

Some years later, while studying theology from 1949-53 at Weston College in Massachusetts, Berrigan first came across the writings of the revolutionary French and German theologians who were to have an impact not only on himself but more importantly on the Second Vatican Council: "We passed their articles and books to one another," he has recalled, "convinced the Europeans were putting in cold print truths that lay at the back of our minds, forbidden, disapproved, but breaking new ground."[6] He would address a number of these innovative theological ideas in essays and books written in the late fifties and early sixties.

On the recommendation of one of his professors at Weston Berrigan spent the year 1953-54 in France during which time, among other things, he was expected to develop his command of French in order to read in the vernacular the theologians who had led him at Weston to do some original student writing on the nature of the church. Based at a Jesuit house of studies in Paray le Monial near Lyon, Berrigan came into contact with the controversial French worker priests. The worker priests, many of whom had been in the resistance during the Second World War, lived in small communities, and worked, often in ordinary clothes, alongside the people they served, having dedicated themselves to helping with the vast problem of providing housing for the thousands of people who had been made homeless by the war. Abbé Pierre, the best known of the worker priests, insisted that priests could only properly assess the needs of the poor by living among them, a view which Berrigan took to heart. These priests also helped workers to

form trade unions and to struggle for better conditions of
employment, which inevitably created controversy. Pope Pius XII
suppressed the movement in 1954 while Berrigan was in France.
Stung by what seemed to him to be Rome's heavy-handedness,
Berrigan vowed to continue the ideal of the worker priests in his
own way.[7]

He wrote to his family in December of 1953 that the
French church seemed to be divided between an elite with a gift for
intellectual analysis at the expense of the needs of the average
person - and the worker priests, who were a "marvelous exception
to this."[8]   Nevertheless, the new French theologians had also
created a state of ferment which Berrigan was delighted to
experience after the staid spirituality which he had felt permeated
American Catholicism. He was struck by the irony that, while
French churches were emptying and the French population was
becoming more and more secular, a new generation of brilliant
theologians had arisen on French soil.   He perceived these
theologians as returning to the origins of Christianity, much as the
Protestant reformers had done in earlier centuries, in order to
discover the direction which had been immanent in the church at its
outset and to apply thereby any necessary corrective headings to
the church's course in the modern world.

The three most influential French theologians as far as
Berrigan was concerned were: Yves Congar, who emphasized the
scripturally-based, priestly role of the laity, a conception which the
Protestant Reformation had caused Catholic theology to eschew;
Henri de Lubac, who stressed the communal nature of Christian
culture; and Teilhard de Chardin, the Jesuit paleontologist who
portrayed Christianity as in a state of continuing evolution
regarding its understanding of itself and its relationship to the
world.

De Chardin's was a triumphal view of the church, an attempt to bridge the theories of scientific evolutionists like T.H. Huxley and those of Christian theology. While de Chardin conceded the presence of evil in human history, he did so in a manner reminiscent of writers like Emerson and Whitman, seeing it as a precarious stepping stone in the perfecting of human consciousness. De Chardin's views would pervade Berrigan's theological writings from the mid-1950s to the mid-1960s. From many points of view Berrigan was transformed during the year in France, not only by de Chardin and other intellectual innovators, but in even more fundamental ways: "What I discovered in France for the first time in my long experience of Catholic community," he wrote some years later, "was so simple a thing as personal freedom."[9]

Berrigan's return to the U.S. in the summer of 1954 was by way of Spain, where he visited the birthplace of Ignatius of Loyola, who founded the Society of Jesus in the sixteenth century. Crossing the frontier south of Bordeaux, he had his first, close-up view of a modern police state, an experience which he described in a note to his family as a "revelation." At the border station at Irien he encountered Franco's soldiers, who were as "thick as flies armored with guns and night sticks" merely to conduct a "poor flock of harmless people through customs."[10]

Following the excitement of his year in France Berrigan found himself appalled at the apparent lethargy of the Catholic church in New York: "How could a Church so well established," he wondered, "be at the same time so unproductive, so debilitated by all the illnesses of man's spirit? Where," he continued, "were the imaginative apostolates in Harlem, the friendship and discussions with Jews? Where were intellectual and cultural exchanges with the universities?"[11]

Apart from teaching, Berrigan became the chaplain of a group of Young Christian Workers who were involved in issues of social justice. In a pattern which he was to follow throughout the 1950s and early 1960s, he brought together students from middle-class, suburban backgrounds and those who subsisted in inner-city poverty, in this case Puerto Ricans living on the lower east side of Manhattan. Inevitably in this location, he came into contact with Dorothy Day and the Catholic Worker community. As well as addressing herself to the needs of the poor and the homeless, Dorothy Day espoused an uncompromising pacifism, which she drew from early Christianity but which ironically brought her into conflict with one of the moral traditions of her church, the just war theory originally developed by Augustine in the fourth century. There is no indication that Berrigan adopted a pacifistic stance during the 1950s, but he was influenced by the position taken by Dorothy Day, and her general attitude towards war underlay in part the vehemence with which he denounced the Vietnam War in the 1960s.

In 1957 Berrigan was appointed Associate Professor of Dogmatic Theology at Le Moyne College in Syracuse, N.Y. At Le Moyne, a red-brick, liberal arts college in a comfortable part of the city, Berrigan spent six, relatively happy years - especially since his parents and brother, Jerome, were still living in Syracuse. He brought to his classes in New Testament theology all of the reading and experience which had been part of his contact with the new French theologians, the worker priests, and the Catholic Worker movement, and this in time created a perceptible tension between himself and some of the Jesuit faculty members at Le Moyne. In more practical terms he and a handful of students began an investigation of slum housing conditions in Syracuse that revealed some of the culpable landlords to be benefactors of Le Moyne, and, while the faculty came to his defense on that occasion, the administration became increasingly edgy about his presence there.

During his tenure at Le Moyne he also introduced what were then unauthorized innovations into liturgical practice, such as the saying of part of the mass in English and having the altar face the people. Theologically, Berrigan thought of himself as seeking the pure springs of Christianity fresh from the pages of the New Testament. He did not oppose tradition as such, as can be seen in his respectful assessment of Peter Maurin, co-founder of the Catholic Worker movement: "Tradition," Berrigan insisted, had "made him an innovator."[12] Nevertheless, even in the Le Moyne years Berrigan's reliance upon his own views of how the liturgy should be handled as well as of what the church's pastoral priorities should be left him somewhat estranged from mainstream American Catholicism.

In addition to his rather full life as a priest and lecturer Berrigan did a good deal of writing in the Le Moyne years, squeezing in the writing at night after other duties and activities had been attended to. During the years at Le Moyne he wrote a number of essays and books in addition to publishing three volumes of poetry. Furthermore, he wrote a few religious plays, which were televised in the early 1960s, including one on Edith Stein, the German nun who because of her Jewish blood had become a victim of the Nazis during World War II.

The Bride: Essays in the Church (1959) was Berrigan's first significant religious prose and introduced readers to some of what would become his major themes. The book reflects Berrigan's indebtedness to both Teilhard de Chardin and Henri de Lubac; especially visible is de Lubac's conception of the church moving through history as a unifier of all of mankind.[13] Though conciliatory toward philosophers of history like Hegel and Marx, Berrigan put forward a synthesis based upon the meaning of history from a distinctively Christian standpoint, drawing a picture of human history that was linear and, in accord with Teilhard de Chardin's analysis, progressive.[14]

In particular Berrigan stressed the significance of time as a hidden and unexpected treasure for the church: "Time is to her a perpetual springtime, with unlimited opportunity for the planting time; time is a perpetual autumn, with labors and harvest to try her energies to the utmost."[15] The lyricism of the passage arose from Berrigan's belief that the intervention of Christ definitively transformed history into a process whereby the mind of God became incrementally revealed within matter and time. Moreover, he argued, in coming to know the mind of God through a protracted study of the life of Christ, human beings would in time come to know *themselves* spiritually. Apart from this religiously idealistic conception, *The Bride* is only marginally memorable. The book's audience is limited to believers, and its language is sometimes encumbered by dated, theological terminology. Except for the stiffening produced by this terminology, however, Berrigan's style is flexible and lucid, and the flow of his argument is aptly, if unexceptionally, illustrated by anecdote and metaphor.

The Bow in the Clouds (1961) is a superior book in both matter and style. As a piece of rhetoric the book was praised by the novelist, Walker Percy, as manifesting a "precision and abstemiousness which is as welcome as it is rare in modern religious literature."[16] The title, drawn from the Book of Genesis, refers to the rainbow that followed the flood and that symbolized God's promise of love. The first half of the book focuses on God's relationship with man in biblical history while the second half deals with Berrigan's vision of Christian humanism in the modern world. The connection between the two halves would seem to lie in the emphasis placed upon man's imagination - a rainbow of sorts - in connecting man with God and God with the world.

As in *The Bride*, although Berrigan is deferential toward
the institutional church, his attention is primarily centered on the
archetypal figure of Christ, who is described as "universal man."[17]
Once again, the perspective is historical - with the impingement of
genuine Christianity on history being seen as a "controlled release
of the energies of the risen Christ."[18] Time is once again seen as a
spiral through which humanity ascends as consciousness enlarges;
not only was the past, in Berrigan's view, harvested into the
present, but even man's subconscious - indeed, even the Jungian
unconscious of the race - fold fruitfully into the present through the
modeling of human nature achieved by Christ and made accessible
thereby, though in a more limited form, to others.

The Bow in the Clouds sets forth a Teilhardian gnosticism.
The salient emphasis upon enlightenment is reinforced by
Berrigan's view that in moving forward through time Christianity
had mortised to itself what was finest in man's intellectual
discoveries, rejecting only what was deemed incompatible with
human dignity. In a similar vein Berrigan's perception of man's
relationship to the rest of nature is magisterial in an almost
Shakespearean sense in that the "dominion" man exercises over
"outward reality" is seen as having "no greater marvel to show him
than the order he has established within himself."[19]   Man
epitomizes nature in such a manner that when he "witnesses the
constancy and infinite variety of the nonhuman world," he is
"stirred to his depths - not by a mere extrinsic beauty, but by
something that is rather in the nature of a recognition. What man
sees is, in a true sense, what he is."[20]

Looking, however, at the disarray in the actual order of
things, Berrigan stressed the importance of asceticism and suffering
in restoring the world to its pristine unity and harmony -
particularly through the work of the prophets, both past and
present.   In Berrigan's view the prophets, like the saints,

approached the beautiful things of the world with a penetrating sense of their underlying, spiritual reality, and thus escaped being subdued by them. Berrigan attempts to make clear that he does not advocate an asceticism that disparages the material universe, but rather envisages a "love of God which is nourished by a love of creation."[21]   One is impressed by the exquisite balance of Berrigan's thought in this matter. The world within and without, he observes, will be restored when we are able to see the things of this world transparently - with a full, even sensuous, appreciation of their value and yet also with a sense of their significance as emblems of the divine and of our own spiritualness:

> This is the first task of an adult - to wish simply to know his world. He will see there a poverty which is the cause and symptom of the most terrible spiritual impoverishment. He will see groupings of men standing about like broken images, the caricatures of a community. The rich prey upon the poor, the poor prey upon one another. Men are despoiled in body and soul. . . . He will see men progressively wrung dry of the religious spirit, by a scientific enclave that preaches a corrupt and cheapened messianism.[22]

The passage reveals a development in Berrigan's thought away from the élan vital of Teilhardian cosmology with its serene vision of the essential unity of all of human culture to the social criticism which would mark his writings after the mid-1960s.

In many respects *The Bow in the Clouds* is a transitional work - as in the attitude Berrigan takes toward the church. On the one hand Christianity is affirmed for its commitment to the world: "At no time in her history would she have part in the idea that the world is closed off from her; that she has nothing to offer man's thought or that the genius of man brings no gift to her."[23] On the other hand Berrigan conceded that the church in the modern world had been reduced to a more or less ineffectual status, a process which he dates from the time of the Reformation, a time when, he argues candidly, the heretofore indivisible Catholic church was "unable to put to good use the reforming zeal of some of her own members."[24]

Increasingly, Berrigan was shifting his attention away from the triumphal procession of divinity through time to the view that if "God is the victory of man," nevertheless in this world divine love wears a "face of suffering."[25] He came to see the path of spiritual evolution as inherent in the defeated and victimized, contending that this is one of the ways in which Christianity should be distinguished from other great myths, both ancient and modern. In these other myths, he contended, the heroic demigod is inevitably larger than life, escaping the humiliating limits of the human condition, whereas the experience of Christ was one of abasement, a sinking into the human plight, a death of the spirit that must precede its rising.

In such a context does Berrigan draw in the otherwise savage rituals of animal sacrifice in the Old Testament, which he interprets as historically and spiritually continuous with the agony and crucifixion of the New Testament: "The stench of blood outpoured, the formal gesture, the hieratic rite - all express the urge of men to attain life through death."[26] The significance of sacrifice in bonding humanity historically, not only to God, but to the fulfillment of human nature is one of the major themes of *The Bow in the Clouds*. Through sacrifice, Berrigan contends, humanity can achieve a spiritual poise that fosters both freedom and personal creativity while at the same time aligning the mind with the divine will in an attitude of both creatureliness and hope.

If the central figure in *The Bride* had been the church, the central figure in *The Bow in the Clouds* is certainly that of Christ, the personification of the bow in the clouds whose hybrid nature sewed God into man. The image of Christ is explored from many angles. In one of Berrigan's most distinctive ruminations on the subject he points out that through the figure of Christ there was brought about a "new limiting mode to the omnipresence of God," a divine union with time extending itself through history by means of mankind's emulation of the life of Christ.[27] The idea of God limiting and submerging himself in this manner would preoccupy Berrigan for many years. Increasingly, the figures of God, the transcendent creator of life, and of Christ, the God-man, would not always smoothly overlap, and in the writings that lay ahead Berrigan would frequently limit the compass of his exploration of divinity to the figure of Christ.

While Berrigan's observations in *The Bow in the Clouds* are clearly those of a churchman, there is apparent a fresh openness in his thought. For example, the development of man's knowledge of himself, he observed, though guided by the example of Christ, tended to become stunted or even petrified unless renewed by his social experiences, which had the capacity to refine spiritual self-awareness, correcting insights obtained solely through reading and reflection. While still rooted in the institutional church in *The Bow in the Clouds*, Berrigan would go on in the 1960s to emphasize the social dimension of religious knowledge, maintaining eventually that if it was true that humanity required the truths of Christianity in order to fulfill itself, it was equally true that God worked in the world well beyond the boundaries of the formal church.

Being a poet as well as a theologian, it was natural that Berrigan should place a good deal of emphasis on the role of the imagination in the history of religious experience. Recalling that pre-Christian religions had grounded substantive matters of belief in resonant images and motifs, Berrigan argued that Christianity's understanding of itself had drifted in later centuries in the direction of an overly rational, desiccated tendency toward verbal formulation. In this way it had often ignored and thereby failed to awaken the imaginative and subconscious riches of the souls of its adherents.

In an effort to offset this tendency in theological discourse, Berrigan explores in *The Bow in the Clouds* three symbols which he believes to have been central to the Judaic/Christian tradition: the sacrificial lamb; the suffering servant; and the passage through death and rebirth. For Berrigan, these archetypal images should have nourished the imaginations of succeeding generations, with each generation deepening its understanding of the sacred symbols until they became actualized in experience. In this way the Christian's inventive response to these scriptural motifs would make of the world a laboratory wherein the imagination of the believer experimented with ideas of change stimulated by the ancient scriptural symbols. Following such a course and adhering to central symbolic archetypes rather than to abstract formulations of doctrine, man's spiritual history would avoid being slavishly and literally traditional and yet, because of the concreteness of symbolism, be actual enough to inspire novel and apt courses of action.

Here as elsewhere in *The Bow in the Clouds* one is struck by the balance of Berrigan's thinking - although balance is not a quality that many observers have attributed to him. The principle of balance is reflected stylistically in the antithetical naming of the various chapters, many of them involving pairs of things - as in "Imagination and Covenant," "The Christian and Creation," "Catholicism and the Intelligence," and "Prophecy and Society." These pairings reveal a latent desire on Berrigan's part to move outward from the relatively narrow base of Catholic culture to the larger society that surrounded him but which he had been isolated from during his long period of apprenticeship in the seminary. One notices in addition that the diction and phrasing in *The Bow in the Clouds* are somewhat freer of the sectarian theological jargon that marked *The Bride* and more in harmony with a generalized religious conception in which all human beings ponder their place in the scheme of things.

Between the publication of *The Bow in the Clouds* in 1961 and *They Call us Dead Men* in 1966 Berrigan's situation and outlook altered appreciably. Although he valued his teaching position at Le Moyne, he had written to his superior in 1961, asking to be sent as a teaching missionary to Nigeria.[28] The request, which was denied, arose in part from Berrigan's sense of frustration in being prevented from acting more freely in his own country. For example, in August, 1961, both Daniel and Philip Berrigan had gone to their respective superiors, asking to be permitted to join other American clergy on the freedom rides, as they were called, which were designed to protest racial segregation on public transportation in the South. While Philip was given permission, Daniel was told by his superiors that he could not, even as part of an ecumenical demonstration, enter the territory of other bishops for such a purpose without their permission and that in any case "there would be no question" of his "going on such a project."[29]

Stymied by such refusals, Berrigan found that his sabbatical year in Europe in 1963-64 provided him with another order of experience. In Paris, in order to supplement his meager allowance, he obtained a position as chaplain in a university students' residence situated on the left bank near the Luxembourg Gardens. In this situation he found that he had a good deal of time for reading, reflection, and writing, and he also renewed his contact with a group of worker priests, who had been dealt with more leniently by Pope John XXIII than by his predecessor.

Just before Christmas of 1963, Berrigan was invited by John Heidbrink of the American branch of the Fellowship of Reconciliation, a long-established, international, Protestant peace group, to join in a trip to Prague and Budapest for informal conferences put on by Protestants in the peace movements of eastern Europe. Heidbrink was interested in expanding membership in the Fellowship of Reconciliation to include Roman Catholics, and he believed Berrigan could help him in this. For his part, Berrigan was delighted with the opportunity to travel into the eastern bloc. From Budapest he wrote to his brother, Philip, that he felt more clearly than he had in the West the implications of a worldwide "deep, mysterious universal undertow" which had drawn contemporary culture away from Christianity.[30] At the same time, he became impressed with what he saw as a vigorous Christianity that had engaged party officials in dialogue in Hungary and in other eastern European countries. He felt that Marxism challenged Christianity, "probing the Christian body," he wrote back to a correspondent in the U.S. "as the nails once probed the flesh of Christ."[31] As a result of this visit, Berrigan was to feel increasingly that Christianity had not only survived in eastern Europe - contrary to American reporting - but that it benefited from the opposition of the state and was less likely therefore to be taken in by the values of the state.

Returning to Paris by way of Rome, Berrigan met with Vatican officials in an effort to have the Roman Catholic church represented at the international peace conference scheduled for Prague the following summer. Although nothing came of his efforts, he himself went to Prague in the company of John Heidbrink, James Douglass, a layman pursuing theological studies in Rome, James Forest of the Catholic Worker movement,

Hildegard Goss-Mayr, international vice-president of the Fellow-ship of Reconciliation and other ecumenical participants from the West.

At Easter, Berrigan was invited by Archbishop Hurley of Durban and by the Grail movement, an international, Catholic, social action group, to come to South Africa. In addition to preaching to a black congregation, he spoke against apartheid in a comfortable, white parish, declaring some years later that his remarks had not been well received and remembering acidly "those stony faces, above the Easter finery, like drapery on a hecatomb."[32] More heartening was his meeting with three Dutch Reformed churchmen in Johannesburg, who had been rebuked by their church for taking a stand against apartheid. The meeting stirred Berrigan into seeing the kind of role a priest might play in such matters, and he put in a letter to his family his by now pronounced belief that principles become "iniquitous" unless they were "pummelled and refined in the arena of life."[33]

As Berrigan prepared to attend the Prague peace conference, it became apparent to others that he had changed greatly during his year abroad, even in appearance. His friend, James Forest, for example, who met him in Paris before going on to Prague, noted that the tailored, clerical suit had been replaced by a "black cotton turtle neck, trim black chino slacks, a faded green windbreaker jacket, and a share-cropper-made leather tote bag slung over his shoulder."[34] Perceiving himself to be headed in a direction other than that which Catholic officialdom had chosen to pursue, Berrigan's break with the traditional professional and ceremonial aspects of his church was by this time all but complete.

While he was under no illusions about the propaganda value which the Soviet Union through its official Orthodox church representatives hoped to extract from the peace conference, Berrigan was again struck by the virility of the Protestant communities he encountered in eastern Europe. In an unpublished report on the conference, which included participants from forty countries, he wrote that the Protestants in Czechoslovakia were "offering to their rulers the presence of a mystery; how it is that Christianity, whose demise was predicted with such confidence, has not only survived, but is even beginning to contribute to the new societies."[35] While lamenting the fact that the Vatican had, apparently for diplomatic reasons, decided to isolate the Catholics of eastern Europe, Berrigan was pleased that Rome had through John XXIII's encyclical, *Pacem in Terris* (1963) taken a strong stand against the arms race and against the theory of nuclear deterrence. Moreover, the Pope's call for an effective international body to supersede governments in dealing with political disputes between nations appealed to Berrigan, who, especially after his extensive traveling, felt more and more like a citizen of the world.

A trip to Russia following the Prague conference was disappointing after the fruitful relationship Berrigan had observed between church and state in Czechoslovakia. In a brief article describing his visit to Russia he wrote that the government had succeeded in "keeping religion a strictly outside activity - cut off from the more vital currents of society and from outside influence as well."[36] Nevertheless, in the same article he noted the irony of the Communist government erecting a pseudo-religious social structure to replace the earlier religious culture; he was nonetheless moved to consider - as he surveyed the precious religious artifacts housed in the Hermitage Museum in Leningrad - that a new social wave was always forming and that it inevitably swept tangible glories of the past, including the church's, into museums. Chastened by the visit to Russia, Berrigan slowly made his way back to the U.S., stopping in Helsinki, Oslo, Edinburgh, and finally North Africa. Looking back, he was overwhelmed by the poverty he had seen during his year abroad, a sea of human suffering which would remain uppermost in his thoughts in the years ahead.

Of importance in the development of Berrigan's social thought in the early sixties was his renewed contact with the influential monk and author, Thomas Merton. Berrigan had written to Merton in 1948, congratulating him on the publication of Merton's highly praised autobiography, *The Seven Storey Mountain*, but the relationship between the two did not develop at that time. Berrigan had felt Merton to be too exclusively centered on the contemplative life, but was pleased when a new Merton appeared in print in the 1960s, one who was determined to address himself to social issues like racism and war. In particular, Berrigan was impressed by an article which Merton wrote in the October, 1961, issue of the *Catholic Worker* about the roots of war.[37] In this and in subsequent articles in the early 1960s which Berrigan read with growing interest, Merton argued that the traditional theological underpinning for the waging of a just war no longer held since the harm that would result far outweighed even the most closely reasoned moral justifications for taking part in war. Merton's forthrightness, Berrigan later declared, turned him from "damp straw to combustible man."[38]

He wrote to Merton in the fall of 1961 suggesting that they stay in touch, and Merton was happy to oblige, inviting Berrigan to visit him at the monastery of Gethsemani in Kentucky and proposing a small conference on the peace issues for the following year.[39] Throughout the 1960s Berrigan visited Merton at least once a year, and the two became close friends - with Berrigan keeping Merton in touch with the world beyond the cloister and Merton urging that Berrigan not abandon religious contemplation as he became more involved in social activism. Merton's was a steadying influence in a period when Berrigan sometimes felt at odds with his superiors, as when he was denied permission to participate in a civil rights demonstration in Birmingham, Alabama, in 1963. At that time Merton wrote to Berrigan that a break with his superiors over the issue "would tend to cast discredit on *all* the initiatives you have so far taken and render them *all* suspect as part of a dangerous process leading inevitably to radicalism and defection."[40]

In November of 1964 Merton conducted a retreat at the Abbey of Gethsemani for a select group of Christians who were involved in civil rights protests connected with desegregation and with the peace movement. He gave the retreat the provisional title of "The Spiritual Roots of Protest," and asked each of those attending to lead the discussion of particular topics. Some of the participants included Daniel and Philip Berrigan, A.J. Muste, the venerable leader of the Protestant peace movement in the U.S., John Howard Yoder, a Mennonite theologian, and Jim Forest and Tom Cornell of the Catholic Worker community. American Catholics had historically been among the most loyal and support-ive of U.S. citizens when their country had gone to war. While John XXIII had called for the Catholic church to take the lead in bringing about world peace, the tradition among American Catholics had been to assume that fighting for their country had always been undertaken for reasons which were above reproach. In addition, it can be argued that American Catholics had tended historically to demonstrate their patriotism in order to deflect attention away from the fact that their faith differed from that of the majority and in order to downplay the suspicion that their loyalty to the U.S. was in any way compromised by their allegiance to Rome.

Against this historical background, the publication of *They Call Us Dead Men* in 1966 followed a fitful negotiation between Berrigan and the ecclesiastical censors. The book had originally been part of a larger work written by both Daniel and Philip Berrigan which was judged by the Jesuit censors to be too "critical and harsh in tone," Berrigan confided in a letter written to a friend in March of 1963.[41] The affair confirmed Berrigan's intuition that he had been correct to publish some of his more provocative articles in the early sixties under a pseudonym. One of these articles, entitled "The Council and the Priest," was published under the pseudonym of John Winter, and was a thinly veiled attack on the Catholic hierarchy's traditional penchant for clandestine decisions and authoritarianism:

> An open Church can have very few secrets. And if the Church is to be open, the world will be heard from; a world which is a passionate arbiter of freedom. Jung has in fact given us an excellent criterion for legitimate secrecy in a society; it is simply the good of the members. Under such a rule, it is obvious that matters of conscience will always be respected. It is by no means equally true that certain Roman practices, indulged in by men of no particular competence, will remain defensible much longer.[42]

After the joint manuscript of the book written by Daniel and Philip Berrigan had been turned down by the censors a second time, Berrigan complained both to his superior and to Merton, who as usual sent a message of encouragement and patience. The manuscript was accepted on the third try, and by then had been divided into two books, *They Call Us Dead Men* by Daniel Berrigan and *No More Strangers* by Philip Berrigan.

The title of *They Call Us Dead Men* came from Paul's second letter to the Corinthians (6:8-9) - "They call us dead men, but we are alive." The quoting of the Pauline text was both a refutation of the "God is Dead" slogan widely circulated in the

1960s and a sign of a shift on Berrigan's part toward the writings of early Christianity rather than toward the texts of contemporary theologians. The change came about partly because of Berrigan's feeling that theology was becoming increasingly isolated from the rest of culture, as he indicated in a significant essay entitled "Man's Spirit and Technology" in *They Call Us Dead Men*:

> Theology, as someone has said, has been robbed of its capital letter, and science has had one conferred on it. The ideal of a transcendent unity in which human knowledge was suspended, illumined, and directed has all but vanished. Philosophies of life and theories of knowledge have proliferated until their common sources are uncovered only with extreme difficulty. Again, no theologian with his eye to his world will claim to speak for any but a very small number; beyond his own community, his words are weighed, debated, or ignored with quite the same sangfroid as greets any enthusiast or theorist whose credentials have not passed muster.[43]

Berrigan's enlarging of the boundaries of his theological discussion had the effect of widening his audience. From a similar vantage point he had announced in an essay on modern sacred art, which was published in 1962, that humanity should be regarded by the religious artist as "one in origin and destiny."[44] One of the prominent themes in *They Call Us Dead Men* is that the church must be open to the world. Repeatedly, Berrigan alludes to the social nature of religious activity and to the "supreme value of relationships" in discovering one's own direction and in extending religious consciousness into the world at large.[45] This involved a willingness, Berrigan observed, to "incarnate relationships, to ground ourselves firmly in other lives, to give visible form to the mystery of Christ's brotherhood and, in the process, to extend the mystery itself, to make it apparent, palatable, attractive."[46]

Increasingly, Berrigan came to believe that due to the intervention of God in time through Christ, human history had become a fertile, divinized mystery which was as likely as the church itself to reveal the divine signature and will. Berrigan's personalism had widened to the point where his cosmology resembled at times that of American transcendentalists like Emerson and Thoreau, who were very much part of the Protestant tradition. Berrigan's description of the universe as an order in which all things were joined, "lowest to highest element, in a dense, carefully wrought web of analogy and serviceability" is particularly reminiscent of Emerson.[47] Furthermore, as was true of Emerson, though not of Thoreau, Berrigan tended in *They Call Us Dead Men* to overlook those Darwinian strictures which inevitably cast an ironic shadow over a universe seen to be benignly governed by analogy and serviceability.

His view of contemporary culture in *They Call Us Dead Men* was not so ingenuous, however, and he portrayed contemporary society as a moral vacuum pervaded by a technology that could potentially provide food and health care for all but that instead had been devoted largely to the arms race. In Berrigan's view the linking of war and technology was inevitable in a world in which the imagination and the human spirit were assumed to be impotent in addressing human conflict and in which governments relied on technology to solve non-technological problems in human relations. In an essay entitled "Man's Spirit and Technology" Berrigan wondered whether war was an "embolism in a healthy body" that could eventually "heal its own disease and restore itself" or whether society had become a "technological body, no more

than an organized pandemic illness?"[48] Looking ahead with a
somberness reminiscent of Hobbes, he could see in the blueprints
of the social architects only dispassionate sketches for the technical
management of human life with little research in place into the
causes of humanity's underlying penchant for violence.

In an essay entitled "Poverty and the Life of the Church"
Berrigan portrayed the existing church as feebly equipped to deal
with the sort of challenge which he felt faced contemporary
religion. He depicted the Christian church as suffering from a
spiritual arteriosclerosis which made it more and more preoccupied
with its own survival and less and less preoccupied with the world
beyond its gates. Against this background Berrigan found himself
attracted by the paradox of the courageous, yet non-violent,
qualities of the early Christians, recalling that neophytes were
admitted to the Christian community by way of a "ceremony of
stripping and combat. It was the Church's way," he continued, "of
dramatizing a struggle that was implicit in her view of life."[49]

In addition, Berrigan came in *They Call Us Dead Men* to
advocate a greater personalism in religion as opposed to relying on
ecclesiastical legislation, and he again looked to early Christianity
for a pattern. He found the pattern he was seeking in the life of
Paul, who as a Hellenistic Jew seemed to Berrigan to epitomize the
kind of intellectual passion that balanced contemplative and active
elements:

> In Paul himself, the forces of pagan and Jewish
> history had met like genetic cells. In their joining,
> they took the shape of historical crisis. Indeed,
> such a man could not have been converted to
> Christianity in a corner. The turbulent force of his
> temperament had to be matched by a like violence
> of grace. . . . He did not become less a man in

becoming Christ's man. His view of life remained
full-blooded, critical, and humane.[50]

While Berrigan's choice of the word "pagan" indicates that
he had not entirely weaned himself from clerical linguistic habits,
his attraction to the high energy level of the early church and his
fixing upon the theme of crisis signaled a new direction in his
thought. Moreover, his depiction of Paul as a spiritual innovator
who embodied the sort of experimental creativity and daring that
he believed were needed in contemporary Christianity provided a
way around the inertia created by the historical dominance of
passive Christian symbols like that of the good shepherd:

> This Christian consciousness is not a sheep-fold.
> Nor is it ruled over by an owner of sheep. The
> point is perhaps worth stressing, if only because
> the temptation of massive "doing good," of sheep
> dipping, inoculating, and shearing, can diminish
> our understanding of others, their freedom in
> approaching us, and our freedom in welcoming
> them.[51]

Balanced symbolically with the active, confrontational
figure of Paul in Berrigan's pantheon was the figure of the
suffering servant, typified first in Isaiah and later in Christ. The
icon of suffering, if not that of the servant, would remain a seminal
one in Berrigan's thinking, and would underlie his growing belief
that the decline of Christianity in contemporary society was
fortuitous since it enforced the abased status which Christianity
ought to have adopted for itself all along but which had been
neglected since the fourth century when the Roman emperor,

Constantine, had proclaimed Christianity the official religion of the Roman Empire.

Berrigan's yoking of the images of the activist, Paul, and the biblical figure of the suffering servant resulted in a taut, dialectical spirituality, which he felt to be a more balanced and authentic picture of the Christian mind than was generally available in the heady theological discussions of the 1960s. The two symbols would give rise to distinct, paradoxical behavior patterns in Berrigan's life and writing in the years ahead. Alternately aggressive and resigned, he would confront and provoke, awaiting the rebuff that he felt would inevitably follow anyone's serious attempt to follow Christ, "who cannot be finally exiled from this world, since He claims nothing from it except the privilege of being the last and the least of all."[52]

Although fresher and more vigorous in thought, imagery, and phrasing than *The Bow in the Clouds*, the style and organization of *They Call Us Dead Men* recall the earlier work in that pairs of things - society and technology, poverty and the church, contemplation and action - are antithetically linked in an attempt to explore the meaning that seeps across the membrane when such juxtapositions are created. The effect is enhanced by the addition of new motifs in the Berrigan canon, such as that of the 'irony of God,' which will be discussed in connection with Berrigan's later writings where it plays a major role. In these early prose writings Berrigan's style at its best exhibits a pleasing, symmetrical beauty, clarity, and balance. The corresponding limitation of this style is an inevitable, even if modest, tendency toward reductionism whereby the multifarious complexities of experience and thought are fitted into preordained, symmetrical categories. Later in the 1960s Berrigan would become warier of this sort of symmetrical analysis, and would increasingly anchor his writings in first-hand experience with its attendant irregularity and unforeseen structure.

Notes: Chapter One

1. *Portraits: Of Those I Love* (New York: Crossroad, 1982) 106.
2. *To Dwell in Peace* (San Francisco: Harper & Row, 1986) 44.
3. *Portraits* 109.
4. "The Push of Conscience," *Sojourners* 10 (June, 1981) 20.
5. *To Dwell in Peace* 83-84.
6. "The Seventh Sign," *Catholic New Times*, Sept. 30, 1984, 20.
7. See John Deedy, *'Apologies, Good Friends': An Interim Biography of Daniel Berrigan, S.J.* (Chicago: Fides/Claretian, 1981) 32.
8. Letter from Daniel Berrigan to his family, Dec. 3, 1953.
9. *No Bars to Manhood* (Garden City, N.Y.: Doubleday, 1970) 13.
10. Letter from Daniel Berrigan to his family, Aug. 5, 1954.
11. *The World Showed Me Its Heart* (St. Louis: National Sodality Service Center, 1966) 11.
12. *Portraits* 64.
13. See Henri de Lubac, *Catholicism: A Study of Dogma in Relation to the Corporate Destiny of Mankind*, trans. Lancelot C. Sheppard (London: Burns, Oates, & Washbourne, 1950). Originally published in French in 1947.
14. *The Bride: Essays in the Church* (New York: Macmillan, 1959) 1.
15. *Bride* 142.
16. Walker Percy, *"The Bow in the Clouds,"* *America* 106 (March 10, 1962) 72.
17. *The Bow in the Clouds: Man's Covenant With God*, (New York: Coward-McCann, 1961) 167.
18. *Bow* 168.
19. *Bow* 147.
20. *Bow* 137.
21. *Bow* 128.
22. *Bow* 141.

23. *Bow* 195.
24. *Bow* 198.
25. *Bow* 39.
26. *Bow* 54.
27. *Bow* 155.
28. Letter from Daniel Berrigan to John B. Janssens, S.J., Nov. 16, 1961.
29. Deedy 54.
30. Letter from Daniel Berrigan to Philip Berrigan, Dec. 24, 1963.
31. Letter from Daniel Berrigan to Brewster Kneen, Jan. 6, 1964.
32. *To Dwell in Peace* 159.
33. Letter from Daniel Berrigan to his family, April 7, 1964.
34. James Forest, "Daniel Berrigan," *Witness of the Berrigans*, ed. Stephen Halpert and Tom Murray (Garden City, N.Y.: Doubleday, 1972) 87.
35. "The Prague All-Christian Peace Conference: A Summary Report." [1964] Unpublished manuscript.
36. "Russian Journey," *Critic* 23 (June/July, 1965) 56.
37. "The Root of War," *Catholic Worker* 28 (Oct., 1961) 1, 7, 8.
38. Letter to Congressman William Anderson, quoted in *The FBI and the Berrigans: The Making of a Conspiracy* (New York: Coward, McCann, Geohegan, 1972) 35.
39. Letter from Thomas Merton to Daniel Berrigan, Nov. 10, 1961. Published in *The Hidden Ground of Love: The Letters of Thomas Merton on Religious Experience and Social Concerns*, ed. William Shannon (New York: Farrar, Straus, Giroux, 1985) 70-71.
40. Letter from Thomas Merton to Daniel Berrigan, June 14, 1963. Published in *The Hidden Ground of Love* 77.
41. Letter from Daniel Berrigan to Karl Meyer, March 8, 1963.
42. "The Council and the Priest," *Perspectives* 9 (March/April, 1964) 55.
43. *They Call Us Dead Men: Reflections on Life and Conscience* (New York: Macmillan, 1966) 156-157.

44. "The New Spirit of Modern Sacred Art," *Critic* 20 (July, 1962) 32.

45. *Dead Men* 103.

46. *Dead Men* 113-114.

47. *Dead Men* 19.

48. *Dead Men* 171.

49. *Dead Men* 22.

50. *Dead Men* 125-126.

51. *Dead Men* 104.

52. *Dead Men* 192.

Chapter Two

EARLY POETRY

From the beginning of his life as a priest Daniel Berrigan wrote and published poetry, and from the beginning there existed a potential tension between his priestly vocation and his calling as an artist. The dilemma was not a philosophical one, but rather a conflict about which career had a greater claim on his time and energy. In *The Bow in the Clouds* he addressed the issue in a general manner, and appeared there to have come down firmly on the side of the priestly role:

> The apostle will come to know in the course of his work that the natural values which he had justly considered so precious - values like good taste, love of refinement, the cultivation of music and art - these have ceased to be important or to the point. There is simply no time for these things, in certain crucial lives. In giving himself to men, a man may even be forced. . .into a mode of life which is relatively crude and primitive.[1]

In retrospect, the passage seems prophetic since Berrigan's life, including the serial ordeal of various imprisonments, would indeed draw him into a mode of life which was crude and primitive. While, in one sense, the matter of Berrigan's dual calling

31

is not extraordinary, since most poets give a good deal of time to other occupations and to their families, nevertheless, increasingly, Berrigan would devote himself to causes which would impede the sort of intellectual concentration required for the craft of poetry. There is no doubt that some of the poetry written by Berrigan at the height of his life as a priest/activist suffered from a lack of creative time, some of it having been written when he was literally on the run. On the other hand, what is remarkable is the overall quality of the poetic canon, which includes some ten volumes in addition to a number of separately published poems.

While Berrigan has attached a priority to his roles as priest and social activist, he has not viewed his poetry as wholly distinct from these other roles. For one thing, as he indicated in an essay on religious art in 1961, he has perceived art not only as a mirror of experience but as a shaper of the reader's sense of reality. When an observer looks at religious art, for example, he wrote in "The Catholic Dream World and the Sacred Image," he is invited to become what he has contemplated with "mind and heart and imagination" in order to bring about the "assimilation of the ikon to human life."[2]

In Berrigan's view all art merges at its deepest levels with religion. Like the priest, the artist could "untangle the raveled skein of cause and effect that wound all men into its inescapable circle" - not by means of metaphysical analysis - but by "main force of creation; he made events into something."[3] Similarly, when commenting on the effect of African art on modern aesthetics, Berrigan emphasized not merely the stylistic influence of this type of art but its ineluctable spiritual dimension. The stark, African mask reminds the viewer, he noted, "that his life is an arena of powers and dominations, that his choices are constantly creating his soul."[4]

In July of 1964, when he was on his way home from eastern Europe, Berrigan visited the Scandinavian countries, and while in Oslo he was especially impressed with the monumental sculptures by Gustav Vigeland in Frogner Park, numerous groups of granite and bronze sculptures designed to illustrate the development of man. In a lengthy and illuminating letter to his family Berrigan praised Vigeland's skill and compassion, but felt that the sculpted figures were too immersed in nature to be able to mirror the full range of human experience, and he found himself on reflection preferring the figures of Henry Moore, which seemed to capture through their abstractness some of the mysterious distinctness of the human spirit. Vigeland's figures, on the other hand, struck Berrigan as like "rejects from a forge of the gods," potentially heroic but lacking any clear sense that mankind has ever been able to transcend the organic cycles of birth, death, and evolution.[5] In contrast, throughout his writings Berrigan has, in the tradition of the Romantics, linked mystery and transcendental meaning - as in the recurring use in his poetry of the image of the penumbra.[6]

Whereas Berrigan has always insisted on the spiritual and religious significance of art, he has expressed some misgivings about the effectiveness of religious poetry in contemporary culture. The religious poem, he came to feel, was becoming more and more removed from the experience of most readers, and while he has admired the work of poets like T.S. Eliot, he wondered in an early essay entitled "Faith and Poetry" whether or not a poem devoted to religious experience might not be more exposed than other poetry to aesthetic "blighting."[7] He felt that much inferior religious art resulted from the artist's clinging nostalgically to faded religious symbolism, resulting in "gravures of old ikons," as he put it in a letter to his family.[8] In the same letter he remarked that the religious artist must ground his art in experience even when his subject involved the supernatural.

Furthermore, Berrigan has contended that whether or not the religious artist found his culture spiritually congenial, he would fail to produce significant work unless he somehow rooted himself in his time. For this reason Berrigan has been acutely aware of the effect which science in the twentieth century has had both upon art and religion, acknowledging that the authority of both art and religion with respect to knowledge has all but vanished. Among other things, this has left the poet, he observed in an essay entitled "The New Poetry," with an unprecedented burden and problem, a need to find the answers to questions that "tradition had always answered for him - a tradition that had surrounded the working artist like an atmosphere from his first infant impressions."[9] While Berrigan has probably simplified the position of past artists with respect to the role of tradition, twentieth-century artists do appear to have borne out his view that the artist must create a model of reality in addition to giving that model an appropriate symbolic form. Ironically, though, the best poems written in this century, Berrigan believes, while anchored in their time, are those "whose highest love is hatred of their local scene and time."[10] In this connection one of the salient themes of the modern age, Berrigan has noted, is that of the distance of God, a theme that emerges conspicuously even in his own later poetry.

In spite of the disdain which his father, an ardent but unpublished poet of the old school, had shown toward contemporary verse, Berrigan recognized the value of those who had formed the sensibility of his century. In his years in the seminary he had become acquainted with a number of modern poets including Robinson, Frost, Auden, Pound, and Eliot. While admitting to certain reservations, Berrigan has felt stimulated by the experimentalism of twentieth-century poetry, having been initially

impressed by the symbolist and surrealist art of Eliot, which he felt
made accessible within the poem the subconscious pools of the
mind. The use of surrealistic techniques with their visual and
syntactic transpositions, he has observed, "constituted a return, in
so far as it was possible, to the exact context of the original experience, and the presenting of that material in the frame that first held
it," rather than attempting, as most nineteenth-century writers had
done, to present the subconscious within the structure of the
conscious.[11] Berrigan was to remain wary of the risks of symbolist
and surrealistic poetry and of the collage technique, however,
arguing that there was a danger that the symbols would not be
universal enough, remaining instead the "property of a few
initiates."[12]

Berrigan has also shown an interest in the syntactical
experiments undertaken by a number of twentieth-century poets,
from Eliot to Cummings. He was especially interested in the use of
ellipsis, as is evident in his own poetry, and, once again, he related
the value of this technique to a greater sophistication in portraying
discrete strata of awareness:

> Subject, verb, object - the traditional backbone of
> meaning, can lie implicitly in the thought-group,
> and all of them need not be stated, because the
> mind often operates that way, even in forming
> judgments; operates that way most often. . .when
> the judgment does not express action, but the ego,
> a highly personal coloring, a state of being.[13]

Also attractive to Berrigan was the new poetry's use of
broken lines. This technique, he has commented, impedes the
progress of the reader through the poem, allowing the poet to elicit
unusual attention for isolated words. In terms of cadence he was

especially influenced by Hopkins, whose poems generate, Berrigan
has observed, a "series of minor shocks, peculiar, exciting, slightly
'off center,' every phrase heavily weighted and contributory."[14]
Both fastidious and sensuous in Berrigan's view, Hopkins'
language gave rise to:

> a plenary use of figures of speech, especially of
> inner rhyme, assonance and alliteration - such a
> full use, in fact, that the whole effect is deliberately
> toward the outrageous, the immediate, the exciting.
> In this technique the most pale or neutral objects
> are not allowed to keep their original context; they
> are all subjected to a speed-up, a breathless
> necessity.[15]

Particularly in his early poetry Berrigan emulated nearly all of the
above aspects of Hopkins' style - although without demonstrating
Hopkins' exuberance. Berrigan welcomed the experimentalism of
contemporary poets in trying to reproduce the original ambience of
consciousness, and like Hopkins he also tended to favor the short
lyric, a form that accents immediacy and verbal play rather than
development.

Another influence on Berrigan's poetry was Thomas
Merton, whose religious lyrics in the 1940s and 1950s attracted a
good deal of critical attention and who seemed therefore to have
created a place for contemporary religious poetry in spite of
Berrigan's own misgivings about this sort of verse. In a recent
letter to the author Berrigan confided that Merton's *Thirty Poems*
(1944) "helped keep me going at the time."[16] In the same letter he
expressed coolness toward the work of the academic poets as
contrasted with his appreciation for some of the Beat poets,
especially Allen Ginsberg, who has joined Berrigan in poetry

readings from time to time and who has also been an ally in the peace movement.

Although Berrigan has shied away from discussing his poetry, describing himself as "quite unconscious of the penumbra, hypotheses surrounding this or that writing," nonetheless it is possible to make certain fundamental observations about his approach to poetry.[17] First of all, his reticence in general about discussing critical theory stems from his distaste for discussing aesthetics in a moral void. His essays on aesthetics, for example, tend to relate discussions of art to those of life, invariably in a moral context. Furthermore, unlike many poets in academia, who have tended to be reflexive and hermetic in recent years, Berrigan assumes that the poet can know reality and that this knowledge of reality should play a significant role in the poetry. While he is interested in the drama of perception and has praised the work of poets like Wallace Stevens for whom perception is the primary subject of poetry, he is equally interested in the effect - particularly the social effect - of the thing perceived. In this sense, although Berrigan has been attracted by many aspects of the contemporary sensibility, he believes, with a conviction rare among twentieth-century poets, that poetry should shed fresh light on the ethical dimensions of experience.

On the other hand, as is indicated in the poem "This Word of Gentle Lineage" in *Time Without Number* (1957), his first volume of poems, Berrigan wanted to avoid a crude moral didacticism:

This word of gentle lineage
        has no charge
laid on it: to oppose, convince, elevate
is foreign to its blood.[18]

Time Without Number was a formidable success for Berrigan, winning the Academy of American Poets' Lamont Prize and receiving a National Book Award nomination. The book, which went into three printings, had been recommended for publication by Marianne Moore, whose praise for it was unreserved. The book was also well received by critics, attracting qualified praise, for example, from respected poets like Galway Kinnell.[19]

Broadly speaking, the poems are compact meditations on a few central themes, which are in turn clustered about the motif of time. Correlative symbols - notably that of trees - reinforce the focal subject of time in a series of variations. The perspective is distant and the tone somber, as is reflected in archetypal titles like "The Crucifix," "The Moon," "The Workmen," and "The Men on the Hill." It is as if Berrigan were searching the world of beings for their hidden and final significance.

The two motifs of time and nature are frequently interwoven and layered. The earliest manifestation of nature in *Time Without Number* is a remembered tree, which as a youth Berrigan had thought of as "Some Young God." The Wordsworthian illusion gradually gives way, and as the tree is cut down some years later the older Berrigan feels the "ache" of its passing and the loss of "that total childhood, burning at roadside."[20] The poem locates Berrigan near the beginning of his spiritual journey, where he is evocatively sensitive to the child's passionate sense of the immanence of God - though there is also a foreshadowing of a more conceptual belief in a transcendent deity.

The child's intimation of divine immanence is also echoed in *Time Without Number* in Teilhardian images of the mind's graceful ascent through matter - as in "Lightning Struck Here":

If stones can dream, after some hundred years
shouldering weight, making a wall inch onward
heaving it up a hill, braking its roll,
being only half above ground, taking the crack

of frost, the infernal sun, the insinuating sleepy moss: -
if stones can still long to stand up naked, a new creation
with horizon to see what they do, where the wall goes
                    what shires, forests, it holds -

                            I suppose the dream
might rise, might arc, take color and stance of these
birches that fan out suddenly, bursting the wall
with powerful feet.[21]

The imagery of natural metamorphosis recalls Robert Frost, whose
poetry Berrigan admired, and the deft use of sound, evident in the
alternating sibilant and sharp consonants, is also reminiscent of
Frost. Nonetheless, the hallowed mood and contemplative serenity
of the poem are distinctively Berrigan's.

   With a similar trust and serenity does Berrigan view the
migration of the heron in another of the poems in *Time Without
Number*, depicting the bird as "powerfully steered by its lodestone,
its perfect heart."[22] One of the most beautiful instances in these
poems of the immanence of mind within the natural world occurs
in "Our Very Heart" where, following the shedding of its leaves, a
naked tree is "clothed" by the first snow, a "luminous cloud of
thought."[23]

   Nature in these poems longs to partake of human
experience, like the tree in "Dusk," which envies the children who
pirouette about it. Moreover, nature completes itself only in
interaction with man, requiring in its "stubborn, masked, stillborn"

waywardness, as Berrigan put it in "This Word of Gentle Lineage,"
a "searching imagination laid to it, a deliberate self-imposed
stillness."[24] While nature is depicted as having been launched on
the sea of time by God and while it is thus perfect in certain
respects - as the poem about the heron suggests - nevertheless
man's role is to draw both it and himself upward through time.

In certain of the poems in *Time Without Number* time itself
is golden, a medium in which the most ephemeral of beings can
flower and have its value recognized, like the sumac in "Exultavit
Humiles" (The Humble Shall be Exalted). The sumac plant,
"jostled/by shouldering oaks to the forest edge," nonetheless raises
itself to burn "clearer than they," trembling at dawn like "new-
hammered silver."[25] While the biblical title casts a pale light over
the poem's contents, the strength of the poem lies in Berrigan's
delicacy of observation and exquisite modulation of rhythm and
sound.

In a few of the poems the mood is leaner, as in "The Castle
(Heidelberg)," where time is viewed in its other manifestation, that
of attrition: "Even the elegant monuments have stopped
breathing,/their buttons and swords dropped, their suave/features
blank.[26] The best executed poem about attrition in *Time Without
Number* is "The Crucifix," which recalls a roadside crucifix
Berrigan saw when traveling through Quebec. Time and weather
have eroded the already agonized features of the figure on the cross
so that it seems an emblem of defeat:

> What time had done, breaking the bones at knee and wrist,
> washing the features blank as quarry stone,
> turning the legs to spindles, stealing the eyes
> was only to plant forever its one great gesture
> deeper in furrow.[27]

Lashed by the elements, the figure on the cross is nonetheless a paradoxical symbol of survival. The poem concludes with the statement that the weathered body on the cross "took punishment like a mainsail/bearing the heaving world onward to the Father" so that the villagers in the pious Quebec countryside went to sleep at night knowing that "in the clear lovely morning/he will be there."[28] The poem's success arises from Berrigan's grounding of his theme in a compatible locale and from the skillful placing of his central image against the background ebbing of the years.

If time takes away, it also provides an opportunity not only for resilience, which is a conventional enough theme in poetry, but for an unexpected spiritual rejuvenation. In "The Aunt," which is about the nun Berrigan used to visit in New York when he was a seminarian, the crippling effect of time is palpably rendered. He pictures her in one of the few poems in which he uses end-stopped rhyme as sitting at her "high window" - a phrase that recalls John Crowe Ransom - counting the seasons by "bird-wedges or air of snow/or red leaves of a leaning sky." The image of the leaning sky freshly and succinctly conveys both the shrunken light and the aunt's bent figure. At the same time, we are told that Christ had "fountained in her eyes/and crumpled her face to drought."[29] The poem exemplifies the paradox that if Berrigan visualized God as drawing man and creation triumphantly through a process of material and spiritual evolution, the steps taken by individuals on this journey nevertheless involved suffering and even the outward appearance of defeat. This is a paradox whose truth Berrigan would reaffirm in his own life beginning in the late 1960s.

The ironic overriding of the entropy of time, a theme that occupies Berrigan in a number of the poems in *Time Without Number*, takes a form reminiscent of the metaphysical poets in "In Memoriam (E.M.)," an elegy for a priest whom Berrigan had known. In a manner that recalls Donne's "Valediction Forbidding

Mourning" Berrigan writes that death, which often comes dramatically and violently, here comes "quiet as a winter sun" in deference to the stature of the dying priest. All night long as the dying lengthened, Berrigan recalls, "we remembered invisible Jerusalem/and the king's temple that went up, stone on stone/with no sound of hammers breaking the holy hours."[30] The analogy between the dying man and the silent building of the temple is unexpectedly apt and profound since the reader is then forced to see the death not only as dignified in its spiritual tranquility but as a potentially fruitful process.

Because Berrigan's Teilhardian consciousness of the divine energy latent in the world was so pronounced at this time, his reading of some biblical events became modified. In the poetic monologue, "Loneliness," for example, Joseph draws an analogy between his nominal role in the miraculous birth of Jesus and his everyday experience with nature:

> Every spring I dunged and pruned the peach row
> on south hillside: every autumn, like a stranger
> took down the fruit whose face met my surprise
> with its odor and wet, only half remembered or
> deserved.[31]

Similarly, human imagination and skill are described as sharing in - indeed epitomizing - the divine creativity in the world, so that Joseph is struck by how an artisan can summon "out of a dumb stick some form of beauty,/the fine grain emerging along hand or arm like a pulse," hearing every "sigh of the blade saying, *I did not do that.*"[32]

In the delicate lyric, "Stars Almost Escape Us," starlight is seen as "blossoming/momentarily in hedges" and yet as depending on a man's "stillness: let him come near, and the doe's eye

leaps,/the fireflies leap into a thicket or heaven."[33]   The stars,
though less perceptible than the trees, which mime "man's
destiny," nonetheless represent more fully, if less noticeably, an
ontological drama in which the "true, the beautiful, struggles/in
winds and spaces, and scarcely, perilously wins."[34] Trees are a
more pervasive symbol in Berrigan's poetry, not only as bridges
between earth and heaven, fact and imagination, as in Robert Frost,
but also as emblems of the cross and thus as symbolic of the
victory of the spirit over death - the "tremendous drowning/world
of trees, that first drank from his infinite/roots: and now runs far
ahead, as far as years/arriving on my morning, with my unhurried
tree."[35]

　　　　One of the things that sets Berrigan's early poems apart
from the later poetry is the use of theology and metaphysics in the
early poetry to create paradox and irony in the tradition of Donne,
Herbert, and Hopkins. For example, in the poem, "The Men on the
Hill," which depicts the crucifixion of Christ in Jerusalem, we are
left with the bitter theological paradox that death is "less than
nothing," literally less than the inert or the uncreated: "Nothing
were yet something/if stones would rise and grate/a syllable of
God."[36]   As with the metaphysical poets, Berrigan in his early
poetry was fond of extended metaphors, as can be seen in "The
Coat" in which both the mother of Jesus and Berrigan's mother are
pictured as having given birth to sons who are intimately bound to
one another through the sacrifices of the two women. The central
conceit of the cloth shows Berrigan's mother as having stolen him
from the "bolt Christ" so that he became "more kin of Him than
hers/who cut and seamed me till her body bled." In this poem
Berrigan demonstrates a sophisticated elaboration of his principal
images, as in the scene in which Mary in the depths of her winter
completes the garment of her son's life, stitching him "in and out
by the nodding fire."[37] The image is complex, capturing both the

sharp suffering which unites mother and son while also depicting the atmosphere of loving endurance which envelops both of them. Another example of theological paradox, in this case that of the incarnation, occurs in "In the Grave Lenten Time" where the ascetical discomfort of the fasting believer is ironically matched by the abject dependency of God on the believer so that the voice of Christ whispers pleadingly in the poem: "I am nailed fast to you: I cannot move."[38]

Characteristically, the images in *Time Without Number* are both nimble and evocative, as in the image of the "dark wingbeat of time" in "Each Day Writes."[39] Equally impressive is Berrigan's describing of a maple tree in autumn in "As Rational as Human," where the wind combines with the apron of red and yellow leaves both on the branches and at the base of the tree to create a Yeatsian dancer, a "cloak of flame" surrounded by the coniferous pines which complacently regard the shedding maple tree with complacent detachment:

[the] attentive little dancer, shod in cursed slippers,
cloaked in absolute fire, dancing his careful ruinous
geometrics about them."[40]

Not all of the poems are about religious themes, and among those that are not, "Haydn: The Horn," is particularly accomplished. Picturing the instrument alternately as a "silver throat" and a "green vase," Berrigan weaves these two motifs in an impressionistic account of a Haydn horn concerto. Rooted in its Marvellian motif of a "green world all renewed" the poem builds towards a paradisiacal vision of art as both man's consolation after the fall and his evanescent remembrance of the untainted world that preceded it.[41]

All things considered, *Time Without Number* represents a high level of achievement for a first volume of poetry. On a purely technical level it was as admirable a collection as Berrigan would ever produce. If in retrospect one is aware of both its youthfulness and of the fixed theological origins of some of its themes, the fruit of long hours in the seminary, nevertheless the poems are of a freshly visionary sort, and Berrigan's evocative apprehension of his religious subjects gave rise to some finely-wrought poetry.

With the publication of *Encounters* (1960) Berrigan was characterized by Robert Hillyer in the *New York Times Book Review* as a "powerful poet in small space."[42] The description fit. As in *Time Without Number* most of the poems are formal in tone, syntax, and diction, and few could be described as personal. The book was divided into two sections: a series of dramatic monologues involving biblical figures and a second group of poems on a variety of themes.

In the first part of the collection Berrigan portrays a series of encounters with biblical personages, generally presenting them in chronological order and infusing the characterizations with a modern understanding of their significance. Although these poems and their subjects are formally dealt with in comparison with his later work, they acquire immediacy and drama due to Berrigan's supple use of the dramatic monologue. Figures like Eve, Job, and Abraham are given archetypal and mythic roles which relate them to universal and therefore to contemporary psychological themes. Abel, for instance, sees himself as having inherited a tendency towards perversity from his mother, surpassing her, nonetheless, in his knowledge of evil so that she seems in retrospect more naive and tragic than he:

My mother, the worm that raveled Eden
tents in the parent tree.

New lambs
sniff and shy at my blood: go red fleece
teach death to my mother.[43]

The motifs of raveling and unraveling are used alternately in
Encounters to symbolize the divine design of biblical history -
even when that design is a troubling one, as in the above excerpt.
Similarly, belief in the existence of such a design is tested by Job's
suffering, which crushes him, the just man, and "unravels/fine
clothing, bodies, to a spool of stuff."[44]

What Berrigan gains from his biblical portrait gallery is a
desired perspective on human existence without which what "we
name permanent, tinkering with true order/is a smoke."[45] A similar
perspective is provided in *Encounters* by "Saint Magdalen," whose
encounter with Christ changes not only her view of her own sordid
past but of the lives of other, more conventional women. In a
chillingly synoptic meditation that recalls Blake, she traverses two
scales of time:

I have sought the outlasting essence to give:
since joined hands join but skeletons, and I see
two skulls shed irony on each other's smiles
and diggers arrange the marriage bed.[46]

Berrigan's poetic powers are at their acutest in tracing the
intersection of the eternal and finite, as in the scene in which Mary
accepts the invitation to become the earthly mother of a divine
being - with the words that summon her, "infolding/like a kerchief,
odor and form of him who lay there."[47] Berrigan's sensitive
mingling of an infused immaterial essence with subtle erotic
overtness is typical of the fastidiousness in phrasing realized in this
volume.

In an effort to offset the limitation of presenting a succession of short lyrics, Berrigan included some innovative poems which are arranged in tandem with each other. In "Abraham" and "Isaac," for example, which offer two views of a father and son relationship, there is a sharing of some of the same images, the "stile" and "ditch" for example. In "Saint Joseph" and "Saint John Baptist", two more poems in tandem, each of which in turn is a poetic diptych, the two figures have in common their playing of secondary but essential roles in salvation history. There is also overlapping in imagery, with the sword cutting "time like a parasite from eternity" in the poem about John the Baptist, while in Joseph's poem the "plow blade" which he follows draws him mysteriously closer to the pregnant Mary and thereby to the center of his and of all human existence. Rather than permitting the phallic connotations of the plow image to predominate, Berrigan skillfully manipulates the imagery so that Joseph's masculine role is seen to be merely protective, as he weaves a "furrow about the still tree/and stiller Mary."[48]

A ubiquitous symbol in *Encounters*, one related to the intersection of time and eternity, is that of the stone. Generally in this collection stones embody the intransigence of death and time, as in "Lazarus" and "Saint Ann," as well as referring to the power of God in being able to unlock energy from something as inert as stone. Berrigan uses the symbol with considerable freshness and skill in the self-portrait of Stephen, the first martyr, who was stoned to death and about whom little else is known: "I stood them to a cairn and died/unknowable."[49] The image of the cairn is a brilliant touch since the stones which pile up around Stephen in killing him also make him a sign or marker, a guide for Christian pilgrims.

The life of Stephen is one of many heroic lives recalled by Berrigan in *Encounters*, a rare choice of subject among modern writers. Unlike his contemporaries, Berrigan has shown little

interest in the unheroic or the anti-heroic, being absorbed instead
by the potentiality for courage in the most ordinary lives. In
"Reaching to Quench a Light at Midnight," for example, while
noting the darkness that in general surrounds mankind ("holding
puffs of flame before /old runes") and conceding that only death, if
anything, will unseal the "stern profiles of stone," he nevertheless
calls that "courage transfiguring, that moves forward under no
torch's numen, to the dread presence/whose hand one's hand must
grasp."[50]

Similarly, in "More Like the Sea," Berrigan again hoists
the flag of courage - with the cross as the poem's fulcrum:

(A man is more than two sticks crossed.
He is more like the sea, bringing up God knows what
at any moment: Conrad.)

Nail him to sticks
he stands free and makes sense
even of agony.[51]

The use of internal rhyming in the final two lines accents a
fundamental equation in Berrigan's thinking, that of suffering and
freedom.

For Berrigan, Christ represents the epitome of the heroic,
an expression of a subtle and unexpected potency in suffering that
contrasts with the simplicity of earlier heroic archetypes. In the
poem "Tasks," for example, Orpheus is enjoined to "remember
Christ," while Hercules is pitied for having experienced nothing but
a hopeless sorrow for the "dolorous dead."[52] In another poem Atlas
is urged to "take up the cross."[53] The tone behind the classical
allusions is not condescending but rather sympathetic as Berrigan
attempts to represent Christ as a quantum leap in human

consciousness, transcending and completing earlier human greatness.

In *Encounters* Berrigan focuses not only on human heroism but on the higher purpose for which this reserve of strength exists, as in the poem, "Radical Strength," where the flautist's playing serves a higher beauty in the muscular flexure that issues at its apex in "one crucial delicate finger at the flute stop."[54] Even nature, driven by a mysterious, divine intention, is seen to press its strength upward toward the higher values of beauty and endurance, symbolized in the felled oak which, the following spring, has one "heartbeat unspent: one /handful of leaves in a dead hand" - and in the hill which "eases itself" around a tuft of violets.[55] Heartened by such external signs, man is shown conspiring with nature to proclaim the vital message inherent in his being. An example noted by Berrigan in the poem "But" is the custom of burying and burning old trees in India:

> Old trees too, hidebound, embalmed, holy
> India buries standing, kindles them round
> to a pyre, till flames explode
> last tear from eye or heart.[56]

As in the poems of the great Romantics, memory aids in the resistance to attrition. In "Recollection," Berrigan writes: "I love aftermath of action: the mind's/courteous attendance on memory of sound."[57] In another lyric he celebrates the memory "that clothes/air with trees, trees with dawn, birds with/no net or death plummeting down."[58] Just as Berrigan's emphasis on memory as a rescuer of experience from the erasure of time is indebted to the Romantic tradition, so is his view of art :

Man is more than day denies him:
all things of stone or music, setting against time
a living shoulder, a flower's stubborn
delicacy.[59]

Art's transformation of inert materials to pulsing life, a mirror of the divine creation of nature, is memorialized in a number of poems in *Encounters*, but nowhere more originally and strikingly than in "Chartres," where the flying buttresses of the medieval cathedral are portrayed as wings of a "blackened stone giant" chained to the earth and waiting to rise at evening - "bearing in talons an uprooted planet."[60] Economically capturing the capacity of great religious art to transcend the limitations of time and space, the passage also reveals that the church which lifts the world is nevertheless firmly part of it. In a number of the poems in *Encounters* Berrigan created symbolic alloys that interfused themes of religion and art. While art is seen as preserving some of the features of life from the ravages of time, however, Berrigan draws back from a Keatsian neoplatonism. In the poem "Two Images in a Room," for example, the ancient sculpted characters of Christ and his mother are perceived as irrevocably hammered into the artist's age: "Time gently composes/Christ, mother, artist, into this death."[61]

By 1963, Berrigan's reputation as a poet had grown, and he was included that year in Conrad Aiken's revised edition of the Modern Library *Twentieth-Century American Poetry* anthology. In the same year he brought out *The World for Wedding Ring*, his third collection. In the new poems he showed a greater interest in immediate experience and paid somewhat less attention to biblical archetypes than in the earlier poetry. Reflecting the dualism of its title, *The World for Wedding Ring* is divided into two groups of poems, the first concerned with the world and the second with religious themes. The poems in the first group are clearly the stronger and more distinctive of the two.

The book's title reflected Berrigan's shift away from a preoccupation with the church and toward the world as the spouse of the celibate priest - following the example of Christ, who in the poem "Events" is described as having worn the "world for wedding band."[62] In "The Poet as Observer," where Berrigan reveals his pleasure at being out and about in the world, following tensions in the early 1960s between himself and various ecclesiastical authorities, he visualizes himself as a "liberated blind man/whose eyes bear him like wings/out of night's stinking nest, into this world."[63] In the same poem Berrigan renounces what he calls "reality by definition," and the shape of the poems in *The World for Wedding Ring* relaxes under the new dispensation with the lines tending more toward colloquial phrasing in the fashion of William Carlos Williams, whose poetry Berrigan admired.

Another poet whose influence is apparent in *The World for Wedding Ring* is Wallace Stevens, whose sadly beautiful impressions of the "marriage of light and flesh," as Berrigan put it, had paradoxically made the divinity of the world more visible than ever in spite of Stevens' ingrained skepticism.[64] Nevertheless, if Stevens, who considered himself to be living in the twilight of Christianity, had embraced the notion of the poet as successor to the priest, Berrigan found himself wanting to demonstrate the contemporary validity and significance of the priest as poet.

As Berrigan, the priest, was wedded to the world created by God, so was Berrigan, the poet, who was now prepared to wait on "experience."[65] One of the better poems reflecting Berrigan's new approach of waiting on experience grew out of his looking at a photograph of his dead grandmother. The poem, a compressed and sharply apprehended moment of consciousness, gets underway with a melancholy sense of his grandmother's diminished presence:

My grandmother by time diminished
to a grandson's eye, has no word
that lights the living face to oracle.
She sits and gazes -
stillness were task enough
for a ghost's afternoon.[66]

The pale softness of Berrigan's recollection is surmounted by a concluding contrast as he looks at the "gardens" of her ninetieth summer in the photo, but also notices the window of her bedroom, the scene of her "actual death, a January ruin."[67] The poem brings out one of the pervasive themes of *The World for Wedding Ring*, the fact that the world Berrigan had committed himself to contained not only observable actualities but precious subsurface fragments, some of which were recoverable.

His new approach to experience as the bedrock of spiritual understanding, however, precluded the certitude of rounded, formulated truths and olympian perspectives:

To claim the air as that hawk does -
even as image, fatuous.
At such height, earth is poor
glomerate of no smells, no elbows. I had rather
here.[68]

The syntactic isolation of the word "here" reveals that for Berrigan knowledge would henceforth either arise from the loam of the daily struggle or it would not be taken seriously. His seminary days were over.

Supplanting the certitudes of dogma were "ironies" that drew the mind "free of habitual/animal ease."[69] The realities that Berrigan heeds in *World for Wedding Ring* are tenuous and

ambivalent, sometimes marginally expressible as in his response to
a landscape of "formal will and silken atmosphere," a response that
he can only call a "heart's errand, a bough in one direc-
tion/running."[70] A triumph of judicious phrasing, the lines mark a
shift away from an imaginative pondering of metaphysical and
religious truths to a focusing on emotional nuances and the interpretation of experience. Under these circumstances, the landscapes
presented in *The World for Wedding Ring*, while mirroring the
beauty of their divine origins, are nevertheless valued in and for
themselves. Such is the case, for example, in the opening lines of
"Midwinter:"

> Unmoving light,
> plowed fields, contours under snow
> lightly scarred over, an arrested use -
>
> time unleafed, time fruitless
> black pigment on white, a skeleton
> future will flesh out - [71]

Balanced against the leanness of winter is Berrigan's evident
pleasure in its austere beauty, an appreciation which is not
dependent upon, though also not ignorant of, the knowledge that
spring will follow.

The most noteworthy change in direction in *The World for
Wedding Ring* is Berrigan's support for the life of action. In a poem
about the life of Christ appear the lines "Truest credo is event" and
"Events are orthodoxy."[72] In turn, as Berrigan became more and
more committed to social activism, the poems became more direct
in phrasing. In addition, the poems in *The World for Wedding Ring*
tend to be more autobiographical than in previous collections.
There is a poem about his brother, Philip, and himself, for example,

in which he considers wryly the usefulness of their inherited Irish irascibility: "But who will wear His wounds unhealed, their shirt of fire? - Say it. A priest."[73]

In the autobiographical poem, "A Fortieth Year," Berrigan turns from an assessment of his own life to review parallel developments in American society over the four decades of his life, and what he saw was a river of blood released by a series of wars largely sanctioned by his own church:

> Doctrinaire, red with zeal
> men drown the human in a sacred stream
> and generate, row on row, eyeless faces
> out of this world.[74]

The war dead are viewed as doubly dead because they died in the act of killing their fellow human beings so that from the point of view of eternity they "rot, not rise."

The tone of the poems in *The World for Wedding Ring* is heavy with concern. While there are some poems in which Berrigan delights in the play of language - as in "Sun" with its bold puns - on the whole there appears little time for such verbal playfulness. Even the usually innocuous subject of style is given unexpected portentousness when its tragic side is depicted in the image of the "long shadow" a man's style casts "at evening," isolating "all he is not."[75]

Living in New York during the 1960s, Berrigan gave poetry readings at the Guggenheim Museum and at the New York Poetry Center, and although he did not associate himself with any particular group of poets, his poetry, reflecting the mood of the 1960s, became increasingly informal and irreverent - as had his attitude toward both ecclesiastical and secular authority. Moreover, his tone, which began to modulate more and more toward moral urgency, gave him a distinct poetic voice.

While still wedded to the world and to time in his next volume of poems, *No One Walks Waters* (1966), Berrigan was determined to resist a subservience to either. There would be no

> totems, weights, measures,
> woodbins, diets,
> midnight arrogance of clocks,
> the cat's somnolent metaphysic - [76]

Nominated for the National Book Award in 1967, the poems in *No One Walks Waters* are generally of high quality, and range over a diversity of subjects. While the title refers to the incident in the gospels (John, 6, 16-21) where Christ is seen to walk on water, Berrigan wonders aloud in a poem entitled "Astonishment" about a God who appears to regard history impassively while human beings are repeatedly broken "in the kiln, on the wheel"[77]. Against such misery and such divine aloofness, Berrigan questions the value of a traditional piety of patience:

> What use
> the tarrying savior, the gentle breath of time
> that in beggars is contentious and unruly,
> that in dumb minds comes and chimes and goes
> that in veins and caves of earth
> sleeps like a tranced corpse, the abandoned body
> of violated hope?[78]

Inevitably, Berrigan's thematic focus on this world led to a growing naturalism - even in his treatment of religious themes. In "Last Day" the speaker undercuts the general Christian expectation about the end of the world so that, instead of a cosmic conflagration, he laconically forecasts an ordinariness that will cause "preachers" to cry like "frogs:"

Not a sleeper's hair turned, not one.
Where the living dwelt, He took breath; where the dead
lay cold as stones, or stood, long stones on end,
He troubled none alive. They were safe from Him.
                    . . . Not one
dull standing autumn weed denied
its windless hour, warmth and seed.[79]

What gives these poems their dramatic energy is the tension between Berrigan's growing belief in the customary non-interference of God in human affairs, a departure from his earlier prose writings, and his emphasis on the divine intervention of Christ in human history. A similar tension surfaces in the poem, "Holy Communion," in the unresolved contrast between a spider in a squalid room, a symbol of death, and the "grail cup" which Berrigan as priest had brought to console a dying man.[80] While Berrigan in these poems continued to be interested in the incarnation, it is as if, having emphasized the buoyant aspects of that doctrine in his earlier writings, he came to dwell on its darker aspects in the poetry and prose of the middle period. Indeed, it can be said that if God can be seen to have gathered up human history in Berrigan's early work, it seems in the later phase as if history had come perilously close to swallowing God.

Similarly, the new emphasis on contemporary actualities tested Berrigan's belief in Teilhard de Chardin's spiritual evolutionism, and he came to regard modern man as all but collectively unredeemable in his intellectual pride and moral indifference. Moreover, in a departure from the iconography of volumes like

Encounters, he rejected in *No One Walks Waters* the sort of historic biblical saga painted by Michelangelo as a way out of the contemporary malaise:

> I would whitewash the whole.
> Then, in favor of religion,
> place there for a poverello's sake
> for his gospel's eye, Cézanne's *Card Players*, say.
> . . .Divine things
> need only look human. The cards deal and fall
> fair as leaves or creation; we are in good hands.[81]

The necessity for divine things to "look human" sprang from Berrigan's sense that man would only follow divine mandates if these were within the capacity of ordinary human beings - hence his choice of Cézanne rather than Michelangelo. The poem thus implicitly turns the theme of defeat in the Christ story into one of modest, or perhaps minimal, hope - with Christ as the new and not altogether welcome template of human nature. In another poem Berrigan savors the irony that human beings will instinctively reach out for a more "burly" god than the apparently ineffectual one they received.[82]

Thus, through a serious of permutations Berrigan's title theme modulates to become: no one should *try* to walk waters, and this would include the ethereally minded clergy satirized in "We Are in Love, the Celibates Gravely Say." In an elegiac and yet not uncritical poem about a Jesuit professor of philosophy at Fordham who had died at forty, Berrigan contrasts the man's remoteness with the teeming scene in the Bronx, "hemmed in by trucks and tumbrels," which lay just beyond the university gates. Berrigan wishes for the dead priest in the hereafter the palpable experience of humanity that he so sadly lacked on earth:

I wish you, priest, for herald angel,
a phthistic old man . . .

For savior,
all unsavory men
jostling for a wino's dime
a Coxey's army, a Bowery 2 A.M.
For beatific vision
an end to books, book ends, unbending minds,
tasteless fodder, restrictive order.[83]

Technically, the poem exhibits Berrigan's familiar fondness for
consonance and internal rhyme in order to yoke otherwise disparate
items - as in the case of "savior"/"unsavory" and "beatific"/
"books"/ and "unbending." Sharply etched by means of these
devices, though softened by an overtone of compassion, is the
underlying image of the self-imposed aridity of the priest's
religious vision.

For those in the religious life who plunged into the
problems of their society, on the other hand, there was   another
kind of danger - not that of imposing an a priori order on existence
- as was the case with the dead Jesuit professor - but rather the
danger of losing all sense of direction:

Life; a vast knot of stinking
wet net, and no nimble fingers to undo it,
no chanty to sing why, no fish
headlong, bullheaded to jump in and be

my congregation, my fish course - [84]

What the contemporary priest can strive for is illustrated in the carefully-worked poem, "Talisman." In that poem the silver scapular medal worn by the priest exhibits the face of Christ, "incised/in the year's acid." Replete with puns, the poem balances the monetary against the spiritual value of the silver medal, but, more importantly, through the image of acid indicates that the life of suffering will make of the priest's life a likeness of Christ.

In the 1960s Berrigan began to see his poetry as the shadow cast by his life. This intimacy between life and art was sketched in the envoi to *No One Walks Waters*, a poem entitled "This Book." The speaker begins by noting that, as his life goes by, "poems follow close," the "mind's dark overflow, the spill of vein/we thought red once, but know now, no."[85] The internal rhyming skillfully captures the transmutation of the blood of life into the blood of poetry. Eventually, the poem goes through a series of analogies in which the pattern is reversed and in which the life of Berrigan is perceived as a book of verse composed by a divine hand which some day will show

the last, first line,
the shadow rise,
a bird of omen

snatch me for its ghost

and a hand somewhere, purposeful as God's
close like two eyes, this book."[86]

In *No One Walks Waters* all of creation looks toward humanity to provide the sort of paradigm for itself which Christ is seen to provide for man. Searching the night sky in May, for example, Berrigan perceives a "blind moon in search of intellect," and hears the importunate cry of a kildeer, repeating "*man, man, is my passion.*"[87] The thought consoles him, and lifts the depression which had hung over the opening of the poem. On the other hand, even while looking toward man, nature, although unconscious, is seen to possess an innate wisdom that is indispensable for the survival of all life. "Nothing blind," Berrigan writes; even the "mole sees" in spite of the fact that "hard clay is his crystal."[88] The sharp consonants reflect both the impenetrability of the clay and the marvel of the mole's purposeful progress through it by means of its instinctual lens. Using a similar paradox, Berrigan portrays the sexual act as "Blood and flesh" uniting to become a "seer."[89]

A number of the poems in *No One Walks Waters* grew out of Berrigan's sojourn in Paris in 1963-64. For Berrigan, Paris was a spiritual home and a place where everything presented itself under the aspect of beauty. Indeed, he manages to evoke a trace of dusky beauty even from urban shabbiness, as in the image of the dark, narrow streets with "windows like blank eyes/starved/for one burning realizing blue."[90] As was the case earlier for E. E. Cummings, Paris for Berrigan was a city made to human measure - unlike New York, whose concrete towers dwarfed humanity and engendered alienation. It seemed to Berrigan that the Parisian ambience embellished the ordinary and redeemed the ugly, as is evident in "Paris, You Could Press Wine from Thistles" in which the city is seen to be capable of making:

> . . . easter eggs of gutter stones.
> Your metaphysical butchers chop and chop,
> time's neat headsmen. Irony and grace
> hold like a lifted shrug, all life in fee.
>
> What unlikely thing is not your poem?
> one leaf in Luxembourg Gardens

trodden, dried, a Simian brown
But hold it up; a fan, a lover's lattice.[91]

The filigreed refinement of these lines would never be surpassed in
Berrigan's later work.

In *No One Walks Water*, even when the harshness of the
external world seeps into the poems, it usually does so in a way
that is primarily aesthetic. An example is "The News Stand":

In cold November
the old man stood
like a stone man, all day
in a flimsy canvas box
of struts and patches; a lung, a world
billowing with . . .
wars, death, time's bloodletting and getting.[92]

Elevated by the serene procession of the images, the
poem's emphasis is primarily pictorial, a matter of colors, shapes,
and composition. Nevertheless, the lines are given a moral twist
toward the conclusion:

At sundown the world came apart,
a shack of cloth and board, roped, hefted.

Last, rolled up his pages; the leonine faces
snuffed without a cry, dead as all day.[93]

Drawing a parallel between the temporary and portable aspects of
the news stand and the ephemeral nature of those who dominate the
political stage, Berrigan generates some perceptible moral
overtones in his otherwise painterly subject.

A similar sort of complexity is achieved in "A Beggar, First" in which he observes a sleeping vagabond who has fashioned a pillow out of a newspaper in which President De Gaulle's

> disgruntled snowman face
> crumpled under head, made a pillow
> like ambergris
> floating the brain gently nightlong
>
> in a grand savory sauce
> of power and rhetoric.[94]

The beggar picks up a scrap of newspaper containing the face of Molière to cover his head with. Although the image of the great French satirist morally redresses the poem's dominant polarities of wealth and powerlessness - paying tribute thereby to the ethical leverage of art - Berrigan's vantage point is once again essentially contemplative and ironic.

In "Dachau is Now Open for Visitors" one notices the same sort of restrained emotion, which contributes successfully to the poem's dramatic tension:

> The arabesque scrawled by the dead
> in their laborious passage,
> leaf and flower mould of their spent bodies,
> faces frost touches gently and coldly
> to time's geometric - [95]

The elegiac interfusion of aesthetic detail and the moral reverberations of the death camp gives the poem a carved intensity that is reminiscent of Allen Tate's "Ode to the Confederate Dead."

Berrigan came closest to social comment in the poem, "Year of Our Lord (Algeria, 1961)," in which the war between Algeria and France became the occasion for a surrealistic vision of human violence whose blunt intensity would prefigure Berrigan's later poems: "World spins like a headless top,/butchers put up their shutters,/Caesar in dreams sucks red thumbs clean."[96] The image of the "headless top" is disturbingly ambiguous; rather than being a sign of an incipient belief in deism, though, it is simply Berrigan's rendering of the viewpoint of a world that shows little regard for God.

The accent in this collection, though, is on beauty, and one of the most successful poems on this theme is "Henry Moore in the Garden." Observing one of the sculptor's primitive, rounded, stone figures, Berrigan was struck by the perfection with which Moore's art disappeared into the created form, the mystery of whose "hard wrought face/of time and human life" yielded nothing to a "poking eye." Awed by the greatness of Moore's elemental work, which caught the shape of the life process without opening itself to analysis, Berrigan concluded pithily: "The egg of the universe/bakes here."[97]

In theme and form *No One Walks Waters* is a transitional work, bringing to a poetic ripeness the musings of a scholarly Berrigan who was nevertheless on the threshold of his most demanding years as a social activist. With a few exceptions, the poems advanced from the metaphysical intricacy of *Time Without Number* - with the imagery drawn from moments of experience rather than from biblical and theological contexts. Some of the diction remained bookish, as in phrases like "climacteric of anguish" in the poem, "Darkness," but on the whole the language is exact, natural sounding, and convincing in comparison with the earlier verse.

The poems in *No One Walks Waters* are generally succinct, having been composed when Berrigan was at the end of a working day or in transit. At the same time he leaned towards brevity as a matter of artistic principle, noting in an essay in 1964 that in matters of form the "old irony rings true: to add is to subtract."[98] Although Berrigan would take up the long poem briefly in the early 1970s and experiment with poetic sequences in the 1980s, he was never to feel comfortable with the extended poem. The question of length is more than a superficial one in Berrigan's case. It wasn't simply that the demands of life took him away from writing but that increasingly as both priest and writer he became attracted in the 1960s to a lifestyle built around movement and innovation. His gravitation toward brevity and improvisation in both poetry and prose would inevitably involve both stylistic advantages and limitations.

Looked at in retrospect, the first four volumes of poetry form a limpid surface of relatively formal work that conveys a distinctive poetic voice infused with moral and religious values that had become exceedingly rare in recent poetry. In the early and middle poems he explored with sensitivity and originality what being a Christian poet meant, demonstrating in time that that role was not irrelevant in modern culture even if it might seem anomalous to some. Furthermore, while he gradually departed from the practice of grounding his poems in biblical and theological motifs, he has continually believed that one of the major purposes of poetry is the conveying of moral truths. In subsequent volumes he would scrutinize American society with a moral forthrightness unusual among contemporary poets, illuminating from yet another angle the cultural wasteland portrayed by many twentieth-century writers. In doing so, however, he was distinctive in not failing to depict in both the early and later poetry those individual examples of sacrifice and compassion which justified humanity's journey through that wasteland.

Notes: Chapter Two

1. *The Bow in the Clouds* (New York: Coward-McCann, 1961) 165.
2. "The Catholic Dream World and the Sacred Image," *Worship* 35 (Sept., 1961) 550.
3. *The Bride: Essays in the Church* (New York: Macmillan, 1959) 6-7.
4. "Africa: A People's Art," *Jesuit Missions* 41 (Jan./Feb., 1967) 22.
5. Unpublished letter by Daniel Berrigan to his family, July 24, 1964.
6. See *To Dwell in Peace* (San Francisco: Harper & Row, 1987) 323.
7. "Faith and Poetry," *America* 70 (1944) 354.
8. Unpublished letter by Daniel Berrigan to his family, undated but probably sent in 1952.
9. "The New Poetry," *Modern Humanist* 8 (Autumn, 1951) 7.
10. Ibid. 8.
11. "New Poetry" 9.
12. Ibid. 10.
13. Ibid. 8.
14. Ibid. 3.
15. Ibid. 3.
16. Unpublished letter from Daniel Berrigan to the author, Feb. 11, 1986.
17. Ibid.
18. "This Word of Gentle Lineage," *Time Without Number* (New York: Macmillan, 1957) 53.
19. Galway Kinnell, "Four First Volumes," *Poetry* 92 (1958) 183.
20. "Some Young God," *Time Without Number* 21.
21. "Lightning Struck Here," *Time* 28.
22. "Its Perfect Heart," *Time* 8.
23. "Our Very Heart," *Time* 22.
24. "This Word of Gentle Lineage," *Time* 53.
25. "Exultavit Humiles," *Time* 26.

26. "The Castle (Heidelberg)," *Time* 51.
27. "The Crucifix," *Time* 2.
28. Ibid. 3.
29. "The Aunt," *Time* 6.
30. "In Memoriam (E.M.)," *Time* 41.
31. "Loneliness," *Time* 46.
32. Ibid. 46.
33. "Stars Almost Escape Us,", *Time* 1.
34. Ibid. 1.
35. "Resurrexit," *Time* 50.
36. "The Men on the Hill," *Time* 18.
37. "The Coat," *Time* 7.
38. "In the Grave Lenten Time," *Time* 16.
39. "Each Day Writes," *Time* 52.
40. "As Rational as Human,"*Time* 25.
41. "Haydn: The Horn," *Time* 39.
42. Robert Hillyer, "Selected Poems, Each Voice His Own," *NYTBR*, 109 (April 10, 1960) 40.
43. "Abel" *Encounters* (Cleveland: World, 1960) 14.
44. "Job," *Encounters* 18.
45. "What We Name Permanent," *Encounters* 37.
46. "Saint Magdalen," *Encounters* 28.
47. "Christ," *Encounters* 21.
48. "Saint Joseph" and "Saint John Baptist", *Encounters* 24-27.
49. "Saint Stephen," *Encounters* 32.
50. "Reaching to Quench a Light at Midnight," *Encounters* 38.
51. "More Like the Sea," *Encounters* 63.
52. "Tasks," *Encounters* 67.
53. "Atlas," *Encounters* 59.
54. "Radical Strength," *Encounters* 64.
55. Ibid. 64.
56. "But," *Encounters* 44.

57. "Recollection," *Encounters* 50.
58. "I Sing Memory," *Encounters* 53.
59. "Man is More," *Encounters* 54.
60. "Chartres," *Encounters* 70.
61. "Two Images in a Room," *Encounters* 42.
62. "Events," *The World for Wedding Ring* (New York: Macmillan, 1962) 5.
63. "The Poet as Observer," *World* 28.
64. "To Wallace Stevens," *World* 34.
65. "The Poem Waits on Experience," *World* 19.
66. "Photo," *World* 62.
67. Ibid.
68. "The Effort of Understanding,"*World* 11.
69. "Ironies," *World* 52.
70. "Landscapes There Are," *World* 4.
71. "Midwinter," *World* 17.
72. "Events," *World* 5
73. "The Spirits That Speak in Us," *World* 75.
74. "A Fortieth Year," *World* 9.
75. "Style," *World* 20.
76. "The Writing of a Poem," *No One Walks Waters* (New York: Macmillan, 1966) 2.
77. "Astonishment," *Waters* 30.
78. Ibid. 31.
79. "Last Day," *Waters* 45.
80. "Holy Communion," *Waters* 32.
81. "The Sistine Chapel," *Waters* 42.
82. "Astonishment," *Waters* 31.
83. "In Memoriam," *Waters* 29.
84. "You, too, by the Sea," *Waters* 38.
85. "This Book," *Waters* 78.
86. Ibid.

87. "Keep the Hour," *Waters* 3.
88. "Come and See," *Waters* 22.
89. "The Act of Love," *Waters* 24.
90. "A View from a Side Street," *Waters* 66.
91. "Paris, You Could Press Wine from Thistles," *Waters* 68.
92. "The News Stand," *Waters* 69.
93. Ibid.
94. "A Beggar, First," *Waters* 61.
95. "Dachau is Now Open for Visitors," *Waters* 55.
96. "Year of Our Lord (Algeria, 1961)," *Waters* 41.
97. "Henry Moore in the Garden," *Waters* 8.
98. "The Eight Hundred Years of Notre Dame," *Critic* 22 (June/July, 1964) 35.

Chapter Three

WRITER/ACTIVIST

The prose and poetry written by Berrigan from the mid-1960s to the early 1970s was intellectually and artistically rich, no small feat given his intense involvement in social activism at the time. One of the reasons the period was fruitful from a literary point of view is that Berrigan's intellectual composure remained intact during these years of social turmoil, something that would be less true in the mid-1970s when the grinding effects of a life of activism and a term in prison began to take their toll.

Before leaving for his sabbatical in Europe in 1963, Berrigan had been led to believe that he would be returning to teach at Le Moyne College. In the summer of 1962 the head of the New York province of the Jesuits wrote to Berrigan suggesting that he take his study leave in 1963-64, adding that a "year away should do you much good."[1] Instead of being assigned to teach theology at Le Moyne upon his return, however, Berrigan was made associate editor of *Jesuit Missions* magazine in New York City. Although the appointment was unexpected - and probably resulted from the liturgical innovations and confrontational social programs that had ruffled some of the Le Moyne administration and faculty - nevertheless Berrigan wrote to Thomas Merton that he looked forward to being close to those involved in the civil rights and peace groups in the more liberal climate of Manhattan. He looked forward as well to being near his brother, Philip, who was already involved in the civil rights movement and who was teaching in a Josephite seminary in Newburgh, N.Y., just up the Hudson.

Berrigan further confided to Merton that the "dim kind of existence I lead, somewhere in the twilight zone of the official church, is likely to continue."[2] He took his new position on the Jesuit missionary magazine seriously, having become acutely conscious through his travels of the economic gulf that divided both America from most of the rest of the world and Americans from each other. Early in 1965, he wrote an article entitled "The Other America and the Other World," which was published in a bulletin put out by the Agency for International Development and which attracted the attention of the Kennedy and Shriver clans.[3] Sargent Shriver, who was then head of the Peace Corps, was particularly interested, and invited Berrigan to meet with him. Berrigan argued that economic issues and those of social justice were connected, adding that if American Christianity failed to act it would simply be left behind. "With or without the Church," he cautioned, "men will endure the journey which leads from slavery to freedom."[4]

As well as writing for *Jesuit Missions*, Berrigan administered from his editorial office the newly formed Catholic Peace Fellowship, and found himself more and more in sympathy with Thomas Merton's conviction that social activism ought to have a contemplative root.[5] In this connection he wrote to Merton about the liability to the peace movement of "those who want change, without having submitted themselves to change."[6] Though they were in agreement about the need for a balance of contemplation and action, Berrigan was aware that Merton had not left his monastery to support the causes that they had both written about so vigorously in the 1960s and that he himself would inevitably be more tangibly and vulnerably involved in public protest than his cenobitic friend was to be.

By early 1965, American bombers were flying sorties over North Vietnam, and Daniel and Philip Berrigan responded by signing a "Declaration of Conscience" in the February, 1965, issue of the *Catholic Worker* in which they pledged to obstruct the war. The statement, which advocated draft resistance, was also signed by Dr. Martin Luther King and Dr. Benjamin Spock. Some months later, in front of the American Delegation at the United Nations building in New York, Berrigan felt himself drawn to protest the war from the streets for the first time. Looking at some young war protestors who were being intimidated by the police, he suddenly crossed the line that separated the demonstrators from the onlookers, an act that had an immediate and salutary effect. Because he and a companion were in clerical garb, he has recalled in an unpublished interview, the police suddenly "stopped the arrests and stopped the brutalizing."[7]

The scene at the U.N. building would smolder in his memory, including the gratuitous brutality of a policeman who stood on the hands of a protestor while another was "grinding the wrist of a young girl with his heel."[8] Berrigan observed that a third policeman had a woman pinned between the uprights of a barricade and that "he had her blocked there through her neck with his leg" so that she was almost choking.[9] The incident helped to convince Berrigan that violence, as he had perceived in the South as well, could be legitimized in an otherwise lawful society and that therefore civil law itself was not above reproof.

On October 15, 1965, David Miller, a young member of the Catholic Worker movement and a former student of Berrigan's at Le Moyne, burned his draft card in New York in the presence of the media and F.B.I. agents. Miller's action was given wide publicity, and he was quickly arrested and sentenced to a five-year prison term. The incident piqued Berrigan's sense of guilt over his own inaction, and he joined with others in forming the interdenominational group, Clergy (later Clergy and Laity) Concerned About Vietnam, in the fall of 1965 - co-chairing the group with Rabbi Abraham Heschel of the Jewish Theological Seminary and Rev. Richard Neuhaus of the Lutheran Church of St. John the Evangelist. Among those who agreed to support the new group were Martin Luther King, Reinhold Niebuhr, William Sloane Coffin, Robert McAfee Brown, and Harvey Cox. Under the aegis of Clergy Concerned About Vietnam some three hundred clergymen signed a letter of protest in the *New York Times* on October 23, 1965.

Few in American Catholicism were sympathetic to the anti-war protestors at this time, particularly in the New York area where the high-profile prelate, Cardinal Spellman, was still making his annual Christmas visits to American troops serving abroad. Moreover, in November, 1966, the American bishops issued their first statement on the Vietnam War, saying fundamentally that, in the light of the principles of Vatican II and of the traditional morality of the just war, American involvement in the Vietnam conflict was justified. The differences between Berrigan and Cardinal Spellman came to a head in November, 1965, when a young Catholic pacifist named Roger Laporte, known to be an admirer of Berrigan's, immolated himself in front of the U.N. building in protest against the war, and died shortly afterwards. Cardinal Spellman treated Laporte's death as a suicide, and reiterated the Catholic church's opposition to suicide. Berrigan was told by his superiors to avoid making any public statement about the matter. Nonetheless, in a memorial service at the Catholic Worker building, Berrigan declined to call Laporte's action a suicide, characterizing it instead as a religiously inspired, sacrificial act. Reflecting on the matter some years later, Berrigan recalled: "We had never known an occasion where a person freely offered his life, except on the field of battle or to save another person. But the deliberate self-giving, a choice which didn't depend upon some immediate crisis but upon thoughtful revaluation of life - this was very new to us and was, indeed, an unprecedented gift."[10]

Though Berrigan hadn't regarded the homily at the Catholic Worker as constituting a public statement, his remarks about Laporte were reported in the press, and an immediate, though temporary, effect was a telegram from Thomas Merton, asking that his name be removed from the list of sponsors of the Catholic Peace Fellowship. It seemed to Merton that Berrigan and others had given approval to violence as a means of pursuing peace. Berrigan did not, in fact, deal squarely with the issue of the violence of Laporte's act; nor did he, in comparing Laporte's action to Christ's, point out that Christ was slain by the violence of others. Furthermore, the whole matter of Laporte's mental stability at the time, a question mark for those who knew him, was not addressed by Berrigan.

Merton eventually withdrew his objections, placing his trust in those, who, unlike himself, were on the scene, but Cardinal Spellman did not. Though he was attending the Vatican Council in Rome at the time, Spellman dispatched the chancellor of the New York archdiocese to evict Berrigan from the diocese. Berrigan's Jesuit superiors cooperated, and within two weeks of the Laporte affair Berrigan was on his way to Central and South America on an indeterminate assignment for *Jesuit Missions* in the company of a fellow Jesuit. Angered over what had happened, Berrigan wrote to Merton, telling the latter he was tempted to leave his order, to which Merton replied that Berrigan should regard the posting as a splendid opportunity since it was in Latin America where valuable innovations in the church would likely occur.[11] Echoing Merton, Dorothy Day, who also knew the inside story behind Berrigan's new assignment, nevertheless rejoiced in that assignment.[12]

Included in Berrigan's itinerary were Caribbean islands like Trinidad as well as larger destinations like Mexico, Venezuela, Brazil, Argentina, and Chile. Berrigan was curious to see how the church and the people of these nations were surviving in a part of the world not known for democratic practices. He confided in a letter to his family from Caracas that he was not reassured by what appeared to be the indifference of the church in Latin America to the plight of the *campesinos* in the face of both poverty and social injustice: "I do not see the church here as particularly *with* the revolution of hopes. I suspect the opinion will remain with me. Too much money, too much foreign interference, too little native explosion."[13] In Brazil he met with the dynamic church leader, Dom Helder Camara, who assured him that his misgivings about foreign domination were well founded and that he should work to see that U.S. anti-trust laws were applied to American companies doing business abroad.[14] In Berrigan's absence from the United States a well-organized protest over his exile had been mounted. On December 12, 1965, an advertisement appeared in the *New York Times*, signed by hundreds of supporters, demanding an end to Berrigan's exile, and the pressure kept up until the authorities relented and Berrigan found himself back at *Jesuit Missions* in New York after a hiatus of three months. Under the circumstances he had every reason to feel confident, and he wrote to Merton in March, 1966, that he was "now operating with a full mandate of freedom in peace work."[15]

During Berrigan's trip to Central and South America he kept a journal, which was published, along with two earlier journals, under the title *Consequences: Truth and...* The journal begins with entries of a general nature in a section called "Journey Toward Fidelity" - followed by a brief section entitled "Journey from Sharpeville to Selma" - and it concludes with a section on Berrigan's exile in Latin America. As the subtitles indicate, the central motif of the book is that of a series of journeys, both literal and spiritual, undertaken in the period from 1964-66. Berrigan's exploration of social justice was more than a metaphysical inquiry since he was attempting to narrow the customary gap that exists between thought and action. At the same time, he was resolved not to be precipitous, noting that a "tentative mind requires a long life to embody and express its view of life. Realities recede as they are approached; they must be surrounded and penetrated slowly."[16] The tenuous mood and aphoristic style of *Consequences: Truth and...* marked a new stage in Berrigan's writing, one in which the fluctuations in his experience would give rise to writing characterized by shorter rhythms and a scattering of subjects. With its tolerance for brevity, diversity, and inconclusiveness the journal would serve as a usable literary medium for years to come.

The "Journey to Fidelity" bristles with searching questions, many of them close to the marrow of Berrigan's faith. Did Christianity "awaken questions at all, in the sense that the universe always awakens man to a living interrogation point, and thence to wisdom? Or is the faith a kind of drugged seedcake tossed out to seduce Cerberus?"[17] Looking out at the intellectual world beyond the church, Berrigan saw, as did Teilhard de Chardin, that the twentieth century was characterized by a passion for consciousness: "Today a passionate self-consciousness, and the ironic simultaneity of achievement and of desperate insecurity, make man and his universe into one erect 'I,' make man a kind of universal exposed nerve and root. You cannot touch creation anywhere without touching him."[18]

At this point in his life Berrigan's thinking about the relationship between consciousness and nature was ambivalent. On the one hand he perceived consciousness as epitomizing, even surpassing, nature, and he was therefore unwilling to allow the "creeping tyranny of the unconscious or of history to assume control over conscious life - a life which in principle cannot bear with the prospect of shrinking alternatives."[19] If Berrigan appears sanguine about the supremacy of consciousness over matter in this excerpt, he also found himself puzzled by the parables of Christ, which frequently drew analogies between external nature and man. Did Christ really mean, he wondered aloud, that we are to "learn from the lilies and ravens the complexities of a providence which He connects with the cycles of lower nature?"[20] These conflicting views of consciousness and nature would perplex Berrigan for years as he attempted to penetrate the enigma of the mind of God, which appeared elusive and subtle, if not impervious, certainly not readily reducible to a pastorale like that of the gospel story of the lilies of the field.

Berrigan's preoccupation with consciousness and with potentiality is evident everywhere in *Consequences: Truth and...* Only when imagination and freedom reveal alternatives to our actual lives, he argued, has one truly seen one's life. Imagination, rather than analytical thought, is emphasized in this journal, as Berrigan's confidence in the usefulness of the sort of analytical essay writing he had been doing came more and more into question. Experience, including its mysterious, religious dimension, was simply too complex for even the most abstruse formulations, Berrigan came to believe, as he turned away from theological inquiry toward symbolic readings of culture and history. The knowledge he would gain, he felt, would have the "imprecision of involvement, rather than the 'clarity and distinctness' of logic."[21]

With the artist's respect for concreteness, Berrigan came to feel in *Consequences: Truth...* that the web of the configuration of experience was too subtle for the sort of a priori thought he had given himself to, and he called on religious and other intellectuals to become more closely involved in the social phenomena they attempted to describe: "Logically, the first man to the block, or on the picket line, or to prison in social crisis," he wrote, "ought to be the intellectual."[22] Furthermore, intellectuals whose social consciences had awakened had a responsibility to articulate their awareness to others:

> Fidelity to a vision carries some far ahead of others along the same road. So a man of vision may become a mere ghost or mirage to his friends - too great a distance for communion. One's responsibility, consequently, on any point of the road, is to close or at least lessen the distance between man and man, by a passion for sacrifice and communion. To be near, to intersect, to converge. A star stands, not light-years distant, but in the very eye of him who regards it.[23]

Berrigan's shift toward action in the mid-1960s was not only based upon moral considerations but upon an empirical sense that truth would likely emerge existentially from the ground up: "Truth that descends only from the top eventually ceases to flow at all. It becomes glacial or sterile, or both."[24] The direction in which Berrigan moved would henceforth be dictated not only by his understanding of Christian thought and tradition but also by a cumulative, existential consciousness issuing from reflexive insights into his own experience as a moral activist.

In *Consequences: Truth and...* Berrigan described historical reality as harboring in any one period a series of crises that should awaken individuals to alternatives which paralleled the present course of their lives. Moreover, the search for these moral crises beneath the skin of normalcy was identified as the *sine qua non* of religious faith. Without this search, faith became mere intellectual assent flanked by formal ritual, as exemplified by the good churchgoers in Francois Mauriac's novels who in Berrigan's words took their religion as they took their "vitamins."[25] Berrigan's new vantage point involved living patiently and apprehensively at the "edge," paradoxically the only place from which he could reach the "true center."[26]

Living at the edge, a central metaphor in the "Journey to Fidelity" and in Berrigan's writings throughout the 1960s, implied a degree of asceticism that he had associated with early Christianity and that appeared to be on the wane in contemporary American culture with its anti-Puritan backlash. A proximate purpose of asceticism in Berrigan's view was to trim the ego and thus to create the sort of flexibility that would allow one to respond rapidly and effectively to a perceived social need. On the other hand he perceived mortification in a deeper sense as distinct from altruism, its essential function being to drain the subject of a personal volitional life and to replace the ego with the mind of Christ. Indeed, the ascetic was not meant to suffer so that the "world may be one" or even that the "will of God may be accomplished" since the ascetic is during the deepest suffering "evacuated" of any real purpose at all.[27] Berrigan's observation here reveals the contemplative springs whose blue depths lay far below a surface self that pressed for social justice.

Such asceticism amounted to a walk in the dark, unrelieved by a distant promise of reward which, Berrigan argued, belonged to superstition and magic rather than to Christianity. What hope there was, issued from one's having journeyed to the outer limits of hopelessness - through which one discovered that despair had a "limit," and went beyond it.[28] The Christian, Berrigan wrote provocatively, should adjust to the thought of being victimized as a matter of course for the reason that only through the sign created by such suffering could many otherwise successful and respectable evils be illuminated for what they were. For this reason he defined the "historic sin of Christians" as "overcontrol of others," the remedy for this being "modesty, anonymity, service."[29] The Christian, moving sensitively between contemplation and action, would make of his or her life a symbol that was explicable and attractive to others only in religious terms: "The attitude of faith is no more easily described than a glass of water: colorless, tasteless, odorless; but still, mysteriously refreshing. And when held to the light of day, a prism that captures all the delight and mystery of the world."[30]

In the second, extremely brief section of *Consequences: Truth and...* Berrigan compared his memories of being in the hostile, racial atmosphere of Selma, Alabama, in the spring of 1965 to his earlier visit to Sharpeville, South Africa, in 1964, a few years after South African troops had massacred blacks protesting the apartheid laws. The narration shuttles symmetrically between the two locales, accompanied by an overlapping atmosphere of *déjà vu*:

> One had the sense, rightly or no, of having landed here before. It was not merely the red ground underfoot, swirling in the hot wind, kicking up a red cloud around cattle and men and cars. Nor the earth coming to life again, after winter in July, or winter in January. Nor the plain that ran flat to the horizon in both places, far as the eye could reach. . . . It was in the air. It held the eyes of people to a stranger's eye - too long or too briefly for comfort. It was in the air; it was in the shuffle of the Negroes, it clung to the unpaved streets, the open garbage, the children playing in the dirt. It could

almost be touched; it was pervasive as memory; something terrifying and obscene.[31]

The Latin American journal, which comprises the third section of *Consequences*: *Truth and...* is shot through with the poignancy of Berrigan's awareness of being an exile, which he refers to at one point as a "terrible burden."[32] Many years later, reflecting on the experience of exile, he confided that he found it impossible to describe, even to himself, those "sulphurous hours, hours like weeks, weeks like years" during which the "heavens remained closed, turned to adamant; no rain fell."[33] On the other hand the traveling was filled with picturesque incident and the stimulation of new experience - as the following description of an unnerving landing in Mendoza, Argentina, illustrates:

> This evening we came in by plane in choppy, vicious weather, all the more deceptive and dangerous because the winds fought us in a clear and brilliant air whose eye seemed to disclaim any double-dealing. And midway in, one (of only two extant) motor failed us. The plane dipped and swam sidelong, like a whale with a stricken fluke. And I was too sick to look up, and took the whole thing for another jolt in the storm. And so we landed, green as whey and ignorant as a stone.[34]

The passage, flecked with humorous detail and inventive metaphor, reminds one of St. Exupéry, and reveals Berrigan's fine descriptive power.

Overshadowing these descriptive impressions, however, is a social landscape that Berrigan found overwhelming. Across centuries of neglect, he wrote, stood the "undeclared violence of underdevelopment - the thorn in the luxurious flesh, the dream of retribution long nursed, soon to be launched."[35] From his perspective in the mid-1960s Berrigan saw the looming clouds of revolution, which he anticipated in spite of his pacifism with an emotion that can only be called cathartic. Against the centuries-old exploitation of the poor Berrigan viewed the Latin American church of the 1960s as of little assistance, and even the missionaries from Europe and North America seemed to him not to understand the structural causes of the bottomless poverty they walked through daily.

A group of worker priests in Sao Paulo, Brazil, constituted an exception, and their example revived Berrigan at a time when he had begun to conclude that the church in Latin America was spiritually entombed:

> How is it that these men awaken in my heart a relish for the Church which springs up again despite all that seems at the moment most destructive and devouring. . . suddenly - in no more space than a step from a fouled street into a garden - one knows: The Gospel works; one is again at the center of things."[36]

A meeting with the saintly bishop of Recife, Brazil, Dom Helder Camara, also heartened him, and offset the tales of prelates living in sumptuous surroundings while thousands within their flocks lived on "ten or five cents a day," chewing coco leaves to "immunize themselves from cold and hunger."[37] As a priest who was also a poet, Berrigan believed that the time was ripe for a new "myth" of the priesthood, and he called in *Consequences: Truth and* ... for an urban priesthood far removed from the outdated figure of the village curate. The new archetype of the priesthood would be based on the experiences and reflections of the worker priests in teeming cities like Sao Paulo and their like.

Almost everything Berrigan saw in Latin America seemed a presage of revolutionary change: "Events are like a wave of fire unfurling along a wild, rank growth of forest. The real growth has a chance to start only when the parasites are burned and toppled." Even good things, he added with a Leninist calm, "become parasitic when life is struggling for new forms."[38] The note of violence here, paradoxically cradled within a philosophy of pacifism, became more pronounced in Berrigan's writing in the late 1960s and early 1970s, generating a tense and complex emotional torque that would become the hallmark of his writing style.

If society could be altered by intelligence and zeal, the same could not be said for nature, which in *Consequences*: *Truth and...* remained a disquieting mystery to Berrigan. While he was in Rio in January, 1966, he visited the *favellas*, the sprawling, squalid outskirts that contained thousands of homeless persons following recent flooding in which scores of people had died. "One has so little to say," he noted blankly, "before the spectacle of death. So little to write; one's reflections seem empty and pointless." One reason for this, he speculated, might have been the "stasis that always accompanies tragedy. The window dressing seems to have been stripped away. Very little of life remains subject to doubt or debate before the faces of the dead."[39] The quotations point up the value of the journal form in showing the writer in an unguarded though heightened moment of experience. Helplessly mute about the relationship between the death floods and divine providence, Berrigan could not and would not pretend to justify the ways of God to man.

A pivotal image in this section of *Consequences*: *Truth and...* is that of the withdrawal of God. The image is pivotal in the sense that it is both a source of spiritual loneliness and of moral opportunity. "The great contemporary signs of God," Berrigan argued, were the "lives of men."[40] Conceding that his thinking might appear anthropomorphic, he contended that the mystery of the incarnation, of the God-man, had shifted the weight of divine activity in human history onto human shoulders. Taking the point a step further, he wrote that it was "not so much the presence of a world of sin that renders Christ inadequate or utopian in history" but rather the "presence of sin, concretely and historically, in Christians themselves."[41]

Inching ever closer to social activism, Berrigan determined to strive for balance and thereby for resiliency: "A refusal of extravagant inner gestures of elation or of discouragement. The false fruits of a false paradise which the rigorous Gospel neither promises nor confers. Not stoicism, either, as alternative, but a modest Christianity."[42] As part of this preparation he chose to jettison anxieties about the past and future which would drain him of energy and resolve, noting that faith, properly understood, substituted "space for time."[43] By this he meant that an attentiveness to the present, freed from future and past detail, permitted one to consider aspects of the terrain of the present that would otherwise be overlooked. Although his immediate prospects during his Latin American journey were nebulous, Berrigan appeared to be on his way to defining the myth that would at least underlie *his* priesthood. The artist in him was harnessed to the task as well. There could be no more "armchair artists," he declared, while others were being "broken on the wheel of life."[44]

Judging by *Consequences: Truth and...*, Berrigan found the journal form's mixture of extemporaneous autobiography and reflection to be a comfortable medium. Moreover, with his life suspended in Latin America during the winter of 1965-66, he took stock of the sanction that had been meted out to him, and decided that it had been fortuitous. His life *should* be lived close to the edge, where the air was thin and the wind strong. *Consequences: Truth and...*, especially in its final section, vividly captures this development in Berrigan's thinking on a day-by-day basis with the suppleness and immediacy of the writing allowing the reader to experience the sprouting thoughts and impressions in all of their green uncertainty.

Upon his return from Latin America, Berrigan, working with his brother, Philip, plunged into the anti-war effort. In the spring of 1966 he met at the home of Sargent Shriver with Robert Kennedy and Robert McNamara, the Secretary of Defense, and his notes of the meeting were not encouraging. Among other particulars he recalled McNamara comparing the U.S. action in Vietnam to the occupation of parts of Mississippi by federal troops in the 1960s in connection with court-ordered racial integration; in both cases, McNamara argued, the intent had been to restore legitimate order.[45] Later in the year Berrigan went to Europe to attend the Pax Christi Conference in Italy. His notes reveal dissatisfaction with this international Catholic peace group, which appeared staid, hierarchical, and too narrowly Catholic. Incongruously present at the meetings as well were Catholic chaplains from the European armed forces, some of whom carried messages from their ministers of defense.

Nevertheless, Berrigan felt at the time that the group, due to its opposition to the Vietnam War, might be of use to the Catholic Peace Fellowship in the U.S. He had written in June to the head of the Jesuits in Rome complaining that the American bishops had "given virtually no leadership to Catholics on the moral import of the war. They have remained silent," he continued, "in the face of the repeated appeals of Pope Paul for a cessation of bombings and a determined effort to bring the war to negotiations."[46] He was also preoccupied with the reaction of Catholics within Vietnam, especially with the combative attitude of the many thousands who had fled the North, resettled in the South, and who were in Berrigan's view opposed to a political solution.[47]

The cooperation that Berrigan perceived between the hierarchy of his church and the political establishment in both the United States and South Vietnam seemed in the mid-1960s to be symptomatic of a longer and more intractable historical pattern. Practically all states, he observed in an essay entitled "Reflections on the Priest as Peacemaker," had come into being through some form of war so that "it should not be thought strange that we will accept only with the greatest difficulty the idea that war itself is obsolete."[48] In the same paper, however, he argued that this historical inertia could be mitigated through "personal and spiritual change," a reflection of Berrigan's billowy faith, in 1966, in the power of an inspired individual to shape history:

> By individual passion, and by communities which
> extend his reach farther than his own resources or
> lifetime, he can create the world, and he can make
> it habitable, spiritually and artistically. The world
> is his, not merely in the sense that he has a lien on
> its resources, but in the far more mysterious and
> powerful sense that he is the shaper of its con-
> science, the maker of its spiritual forms, the creator
> of its moral atmosphere.[49]

During the summer of 1967 Berrigan was invited to become associate director of Cornell University's United Religious Work, and he accepted. He was the first Catholic clergyman to have been offered a position in the interdenominational, university-sponsored organization. During his tenure, from 1967 to 1970, he established outreach programs involving student volunteers in Ithaca, N.Y., and in other American cities. United Religious Work offered non-credit courses, and Berrigan gave well-attended lectures on such diverse topics as the plays of Pirandello, the history and practice of nonviolence, and the symbolism used in John's gospel. His correspondence mushroomed at this time as his leadership of the anti-war movement at Cornell became more widely known. Often he would accept speaking engagements that allowed him to link his literary interests with those of social action, as when he joined writers like Robert Lowell, Richard Wilbur, Arthur Miller, Paul Goodman, and Louise Bogan in a poetry reading sponsored by the Fellowship of Reconciliation in New York on November 12, 1967.

Before long he was accompanying conscientious objectors to draft board meetings and courtroom appearances all over the northeastern states as well as counseling students on campus about how to resist induction. On October 22, 1967, he was arrested in front of the Pentagon with a group of Cornell students for refusing to move on when so instructed by a policeman. In *To Dwell in Peace* he recalls that nothing had prepared him for the spectacle of the Pentagon - that "awesome pile of utterly characterless masonry, pretentious as a pharaoh's tomb and as morally void."[50] Upon being released from jail a week later, he heard with pleasure that his brother Philip and three others had been arrested in Baltimore for pouring human blood on military draft files.   On campus Berrigan helped to coordinate a protest against the university's financial support, through holdings in the Chase Manhattan Bank, of the South African government. He also put pressure on the university to construct low-income housing, and supported the desire for greater recognition on the part of the many black students from American urban ghettos who had been admitted to Cornell during the 1960s. While Berrigan was pleased at the liberalism of many of the faculty members at Cornell, he characterized the approach which he encountered among many academics as "platonic almost beyond cure."[51] That some of the faculty resented the agitation by the many of the new black students and by other student radicals has been confirmed by Allan Bloom, who was teaching in the Philosophy Department at Cornell in the late sixties and who has characterized the effect of these students as a dismantling of the "structure of rational enquiry:"

> The professors, the repositories of our best traditions and highest intellectual aspirations, were fawning over what was nothing better than a rabble, publicly confessing their guilt and apologizing for not having understood the most important moral issues. . . expressing their willingness to change the university's goals and the content of what they taught.[52]

In response to what he regarded as a narrowness in the outlook of certain members of the faculty and student body, Berrigan and some of the members of the Students for a Democratic Society founded the magazine, *Year One*, in September, 1969, pledging among other things to examine the university's relationship to the defense industry and to corporate America.

In 1968 some of the black students at Cornell took over the student union building, demanding a greater input into the curriculum. They had called attention to racist elements that had been perceived in some of their courses, and the university administration had been slow to respond. Faculty members were divided over the issue, but voted initially to discipline the students for various violations of campus regulations, later changing their minds, according to Berrigan, as they scented a change in the wind. Berrigan and the S.D.S. had supported the black students all along, and the campus reeled as the issue swelled, with the affair eventually leading to the resignation of the president of the university.

The building in which Berrigan worked became such a hotbed during his years at Cornell that the chapel which it contained was gutted following the assassination of Martin Luther King in the spring of 1968. Although the arsonists were never conclusively identified, Berrigan described the incident as a "strange kind of inverted compliment" in which he and his clerical colleagues were seen to be at the center of the emotional vortex that gripped the university in the late 1960s.[53] Twenty years later, however, writing in *To Dwell in Peace*, his assessment was more sober, and he conceded that, if he and others had taught the students to oppose the war, they had nevertheless failed to teach some of them how to "make peace."[54]

Not all of Berrigan's writing at Cornell reflected the pressures of the times. *Love, Love at the End* (1968), a small collection of allegorical tales and meditations, may be regarded as an exception among the writings of the late sixties. Berrigan became attracted to allegory, he confided to a correspondent, as a fresh way of writing theology.[55] Although a few of the pieces allude to topical themes, the mood of the collection is fanciful and whimsical. Typical of the collection is "Alleluia!," which centers on an affluent white man who dies and is reborn as a black woman. Another tale, "No Humans on Friday," takes a sardonic look at religious rituals and regulations.

A more significant tale is "No Cutting Loose," an allegory about the relationship between body and soul involving a surreal incident in which a man finds himself bound by his feet to a shadow that rebukes him. The layering of narrative and allegorical meaning is handled dexterously and imaginatively:

> He had never cast himself as a protagonist, but his
> shadow forced the issue, giving his colorless and
> self-condemned existence a kind of neutral
> radiance. Its glory was neither great nor evil nor
> seductive, but it isolated him and rendered him, by
> the dark presence of an opposite number,
> incandescent, solitary, a sour spontaneous bloom
> in a desert.[56]

In a nocturnal apotheosis the protagonist is granted a
dreamlike respite from his constraining body/soul relationship:

> It seemed that hands, his own hands, the hands of
> his shadow, removed the foul burden of his
> clothing, lifted his skull like a steel casque and put
> it on, dismembered his bones and stepped into
> them. He was left insubstantial and airy and
> weightless, free alike of impure joy and false hope,
> the dark lees of his blood drained away, his spirit
> dry and resonant as a bleached shell.[57]

At dawn the cycle is completed and there are only the protagonist's
clothing, bones, skull, and shadow "hung on a nail on the wall,
awaiting morning."[58] The sketch, barely a story, is woven out of an
intricate metaphysics and psychology and yet is as light in texture
as a soufflé.

"The Single Rose" is equally memorable. In this parable
the speaker encounters an old, poor woman in an etching who
materializes accusingly in the speaker's consciousness:

> Her face was dark as blood in moonlight. So the
> artist had seen her, and so she approved what he

saw, and triumphed for him, lending her dark life
to his eyes and hands. She sat there, his skill and
her reality. Dark, dark, her eyes lowered, her skin
blackened in time's acid, her look turned inward.
She wore an old shirt, open at the throat, a bandana
was folded about her forehead, tied at back. She
was ugly and serene, a dense clarity enveloped her;
age, attrition, silence.[59]

Of particular merit is Berrigan's modulating of physical detail with
impressionistic shading - as in "dense clarity" - a suggestive phrase,
whose complex resonances take us far below the narrative surface.
Although the speaker concludes that an impending death ("time's
acid") is etched on the woman's face, he concludes that she is
perfect as she is, that his task is not to lament the passage of time
but to create "a measure of harmony in which she might dwell."[60]
Berrigan's theme is thus not a plea for the removal of human
suffering but for the creation of an environment that values and
honors the suffering that is an inevitable part of life.

Berrigan would continue to write allegories like those in
Love, Love at the End throughout the 1970s - although rarely as
successfully. The form provided something of a release for the
latent didacticism in his writing. On the other hand, as he entered
the vortex of social activism, he turned to allegory in order to put
an aesthetic distance between the chafing of immediate experience
and the mind's response to that experience. Thus, even amid the
passion, urgency, and volatility of life at Cornell in the late 1960s,
the artist in Berrigan had his uses; as the public world demanded
more and more of his time, it was the artist in him who helped to
nourish the contemplative side of his nature.

More representative of Berrigan's writing than *Love, Love
at the End* during the Cornell years was *Night Flight to Hanoi*, a

diary of his trip to North Vietnam in early February of 1968. He
made the trip in the company of Howard Zinn, a political scientist
from Boston University who, like Berrigan, had been invited to
make the trip by David Dellinger, the editor of *Liberation*, a
magazine opposed to the Vietnam War. Dellinger had in turn been
approached by peace groups in North Vietnam, who had asked for
representatives of the American peace movement to take custody of
three captive U.S. fliers. The occasion was the New Year Tet
holiday, traditionally a time of reconciliation for the Vietnamese
people.

The flight to Hanoi came on the heels of an earlier,
projected trip to Vietnam that had produced a crisis in Berrigan's
relationship with the head of the New York province of the Jesuits.
Berrigan's superior had refused to allow him to join a small group
put together by the Fellowship of Reconciliation to carry medical
supplies to North Vietnam as a non-political gesture designed to
open the way for such responses in future. Although Berrigan
demanded and received an arbitration on the matter from a group of
his fellow Jesuits, an appeal that was successful, the exchange led
him to write to Merton that he might have to provoke expulsion
from his order. Merton's earlier response to Berrigan about the
same sort of tension when Berrigan was exiled to South America
had been sage and balanced. Without advising Berrigan whether or
not to leave his order, Merton observed that the moment of truth
would arrive when Berrigan found himself having to "resist the
arbitrary and reactionary use of authority in order to save the real
concept of authority and obedience."[61] On the occasion of the
medical mission to North Vietnam Merton offered similar advice,
and Berrigan was careful not to provoke a dismissal.

Berrigan's overall view of the Vietnam War was that it did
not conform to the classical description of the just war articulated
by Augustine and Aquinas, let alone conforming to the refined

form of that doctrine which he felt must apply in a nuclear age. In the first place, he argued, the U.S. had not explored every other means for a settlement. Secondly, the U.S. military exceeded the justifiable employment of force in ignoring the distinction between combatants and non-combatants in allowing the torture of prisoners, permitting executions without trial, and defoliating large areas of the countryside. Thirdly, the U.S. had not recognized the right to self-determination of the Vietnamese people.[62] In this connection, Berrigan observed, the U.S. had never implemented the 1954 Geneva agreement because the American administration knew that if an election were held in Vietnam the Communists would probably win 80% of the popular vote.[63]

Berrigan's attack on U.S. policy in Vietnam in *Night Flight to Hanoi* drew fire from Jesuit censors, and he replied with a letter justifying the strong language he had chosen to use. In addition to citing evidence against the war from the Stockholm War Crimes Commission, he explained that the purpose of the book was not to mount an academic study but rather to tell what he himself had seen in Vietnam. In the same letter he objected to what seemed to him to be the partiality of the censors, who appeared to have no objections to books written by Jesuits offering moral support for the war.[64] In the end the book was published according to Berrigan's wishes.

The central, dualistic motifs in *Night Flight to Hanoi* are those of imprisonment and release, the images in the title being variations on these motifs. The brief opening section, the "Letter from Three Jails," which was based on Berrigan's experience following an anti-war protest at the Pentagon in the autumn of 1967, recounts his movement from jail to jail following his initial refusal to obtain bail. For one week he fasted, and shared experiences with a tiny community of peace activists that developed behind bars. From his new vantage point of theological

existentialism, it was a time, he announced, when theology was
being written "on the run."[65]

Before departing for North Vietnam, Berrigan and Zinn
were given letters to deliver from the wives of American fliers and
servicemen who were believed to be imprisoned in North Vietnam;
the two peace emissaries also carried with them a much longer list
of prisoners who had been designated by the U.S. military as
missing in action. As well, there was last minute pressure by the
State Department, which insisted on issuing passports authorizing
the trip to North Vietnam, a directive resisted by both Berrigan and
Zinn. There was also pressure to have the released fliers return on
U.S. military transport rather than on civilian aircraft. On the latter
point Berrigan and Zinn agreed that they would leave the choice up
to the airmen themselves - though both wanted the trip not to
appear to be related to either the U.S. government or to the
military. Finally, there was the melancholy realization that the
mission undertaken by peace activists would be frowned upon by
both supporters and opponents of the war in Vietnam. Traveling
by way of Rome, Tehran, Calcutta, and Bangkok, Berrigan and
Zinn touched down in Vientiane, Laos, after a grueling, thirty-hour
flight, only to be told that because the Saigon airport had been
under attack by the Viet Cong they would have to wait a week
before catching the Hanoi International Control Commission flight,
which originated in Saigon. They would spend a week languishing
in Laos and a hectic week in North Vietnam before returning home.

Although some of the entries in *Night Flight to Hanoi* are
set down verbatim - as when Berrigan reproduces interviews with
government officials - the bulk of the journal is set in the recent
past. Eleven poems were included as well, which were
subsequently published as a unit in *False Gods, Real Men*. The
week of waiting in Vientiane was a desultory experience during
which the two Westerners spent their time visiting embassies,

strolling through Buddhist temples, and chatting with Laotian villagers and representatives of the Pathet Lao, all the time wondering whether or not the I.C.C. plane would arrive and allow them to complete their mission. Touring the embassies was a particularly deadening experience; Berrigan described them as a "guarded playground," where the real world flowed around like "calliope figures around the filthy turbulent machinery at the center."[66]

At last they flew out, and in spite of the aging aircraft and the precarious corridor through which it had to fly, they landed in Hanoi where they were greeted with flowers. First impressions were good; in spite of the technologically underdeveloped nature of North Vietnam Berrigan liked the fact that "everything we have seen seems to respond to the consciousness of the people."[67] Although the remark is not an isolated example of ingenuousness, it was offset to some extent by Berrigan's subsequent meetings with party officials, who subjected their American visitors to numbing political monologues. Listening to one of these, Berrigan commented that it was "only now and again, like landmarks of hope on a painted ocean, that a bit of humanity would force its way through, and the officer would strip the epaulets from his mind."[68]

In spite of the fact that he knew he was being subjected to a form of indoctrination, Berrigan was greatly disturbed by the photographs of bombed hospitals and churches shown to him, just as he was moved by the pictures of medical and other professionals sharing the food, housing, and terror experienced by ordinary villagers. Most painful of all were the images of those Vietnamese people who had been seared by napalm with its adhesive fire - as in the photograph of the "pitiful, crisped remains of a woman, burned to a twisted black remnant in the midst of which there remained only a patch of flesh as evidence of her unborn child."[69]

In spite of its title, *Night Flight to Hanoi* is in part a book about America, as indeed are nearly all of Berrigan's writings. In particular, it was America's betrayal of its own revolutionary history in becoming a predatory superpower that preoccupied Berrigan. Thus, the emotional and dramatic center of *Night Flight to Hanoi* is his meeting with the three American fliers. He was struck by their freshness and apparent health in spite of the public humiliation and, in some cases, the beatings to which they had been subjected:

> These were the faces that had launched a thousand newsmen - from Tokyo, from Korea, from Bangkok. The airmen entered in single file, dressed in black pajamas, two-piece outfits, no socks, sandals. They marched in, stood in a row before their table, and bowed to the waist in the direction of their military captors. I was struck by the thought, How well they look, how ruddy, how clean cut, how unkillably American. They looked better than their pictures, better than us, better than the hundreds of thousands of people we have seen laboring and cycling through the streets.[70]

The scene bristles with ironies, not the least of which is an underlying tone of disappointment, mingled with awe, that the prisoners were not a little more reduced and abject than they appeared to be. The senior officer, a major, Berrigan found particularly astonishing and depressing:

> When crisis came he walked out of the rags and sewers of his experience like a kind of secular Lazarus. He was restored in every limb, in every

muscle and reaction, to his pristine literal vigor, the
strength of the war-maker. I know no way to
account for such a fact, except to appeal in a
general way to the enormous deformative power of
militarism and nationalism. . . . The major
responded at Vientiane, on Friday night, as a
spotless knight.[71]

The psychological drama of the three pilots, which
Berrigan deftly describes, involved a conflict between the
moralities of honor and obedience, a drama that Berrigan centers in
the young ensign, Methany, who had not only been punished
physically by the North Vietnamese but who had also had to endure
104 days in solitary confinement where his only reading was
material put out by the American anti-war movement. Although the
young officer had been the least militarized of the group, he
acceded after some hesitation to the decision made by his superior
officer not to return to the U.S. in a civilian aircraft. Methany,
Berrigan observed wryly in *Night Flight to Hanoi*, was "an
obedient man. And that is nearly everything there remains to be
said about him. It is his obituary. . . . there are thousands of
Methanys; they crowd the womb of the Air Academy, clamoring
for birth, clamoring for wings."[72]

While the episode of the fliers marks the dark denouement
of the book, the narrative owes much of its overall vitality to
Berrigan's patient recording of his contact with his new
surroundings. Much of his skill as a writer derives from his ability
to enter an unfamiliar place and to present the face of that place
with heightened awareness and sharpened sensations. An example
is his visit to a North Vietnamese farm cooperative about thirty
miles outside of Hanoi:

> We had traveled the bitter cold along dark roads
> passing the multitudes of people, the camouflaged
> convoys that bumped along the narrow road like
> elephants in procession. We arrived like visitors of
> the Emperor, between the flooded fields, at the
> edge of a long dike that led through a noble
> perspective, to the reflected image of a large villa
> in the French style. We exchanged greetings and
> entered and were seated by smiling invitation. The
> windows were still closed and the lanterns lit; then,
> within fifteen minutes of our arrival, after servings
> of the first inevitable cups of scalding tea, the
> shutters were thrown open. The dawn flooded in
> upon us like the first assailed day of creation.[73]

The final phrase is the capstone for an orderly series of impressions in which exoticism and danger are intermingled. In some ways the scene is a microcosm of *Night Flight to Hanoi* since it captures both Berrigan's openness to the features, rhythms, and culture of Southeast Asia along with his ironic consciousness that his mission of peace was endangered daily, as was his very person, by the raining down on him of bombs from his own countrymen.

Like the Buddhists in South Vietnam with whom he identified, Berrigan wanted to establish a place for non-governmental action that might help to resolve conflicts when governments were either unable or unwilling to do so, and while the mission itself amounts in hindsight to no more than a historical footnote, Berrigan's published recollections were influential in helping to recast American thought about the war. Widely circulated reviews of *Night Flight to Hanoi* praised the book for cutting through the abstractionism that had surrounded debate about the war and giving readers a palpable sense of the American decision to bomb the North.[74] Berrigan had helped to shift the American perspective of the war from the bombsights of the B-52 to a ground-level walk through the ruins. What he found was not just the human misery he had anticipated, but a resilience, even a cheerfulness, among the survivors that he had not anticipated. The experience was a seminal one, which both deepened his opposition to war in the years to come and toughened his respect for the human spirit.

In May, 1968, Philip Berrigan travelled from Baltimore to visit his brother at Cornell in order to propose that Daniel join him and others in a public burning of draft files as a way of forcing the issue of the legality of the Vietnam War into the courts. Daniel was taken aback, having felt that in marshalling student resistance at Cornell, he was doing his piece. Philip convinced him, however, that the years of lawful protest had been ineffective in altering the government's course. The example of Gandhi, who had used civil disobedience to bring about change, had shaped the thinking of both brothers - although Philip, more than Daniel, seemed ready to accept violence - if only violence against property - as an instrument of social change, a view expressed in his subsequently published *Prison Journals of a Priest Revolutionary.*[75]

The proposal to commit an unlawful act of civil disobedience was spurred by the conviction that the American government had been waging an undeclared and therefore illegal war. Congress had not voted for the war, and the courts had been silent as the executive branch of government expanded the military effort. In Berrigan's view the separation of powers, which had been designed by the framers of the Constitution to prevent any one part of government from proceeding unchecked, was proving a fiction; "ball and joint," he wrote scathingly, "were fusing like the bones of an aged body."[76]

On May 17, 1968, Daniel and Philip Berrigan, along with five other men and two women, all Catholic activists, entered a draft board office in a Knights of Columbus Hall in Catonsville, Maryland, where they seized 378 A-1 draft files. They then proceeded to a nearby parking lot where they poured homemade napalm on the files, and burned them while media representatives, who had been invited, took notes and photographed the event. The technical guilt of the Catonsville Nine, as they were later named, was never to be at issue. In order to drive home the symbolism of what they did, the Berrigans wore clerical suits, which was unusual for both of them.

The trial judge made it clear that the defendants would have had a stronger case if they had destroyed one symbolic file instead of 378. The large number of files taken changed the offense from that of a nominal crime to one that, according to testimony, slowed down the induction of many recruits for a number of months. Berrigan and the others had in fact intended not only a symbolic gesture but a thwarting, even in a small way, of the war machinery. After a brief deliberation the jury found the defendants guilty on all counts, and at subsequent sentencing on November 6, 1968, Daniel Berrigan received a harsh sentence of three years. An appeal was launched immediately, but the decision would eventually be upheld by both the appellate and supreme courts, reinforcing the growing perception in the peace movement that the courts were reluctant to challenge the executive branch of government in a time of war even if they had been willing in the 1950s and early 1960s to overthrow legislation that had impeded the civil rights of black Americans.

The trial was attended by large demonstrations, speeches by high-profile Americans opposed to the war, and a great deal of publicity. In using the courts as a venue for public debate on the legality of the war, the Berrigans developed a social theater that they and others in the peace movement were to exploit in the years to come. Daniel Berrigan dealt with the theatrical possibilities in a more conventional manner, however, in writing the play, *The Trial of the Catonsville Nine*, which he hoped would offset the inevitably ephemeral effect of the actual trial. Working in the mode of what he called factual theater, he composed the play through a selective editing of the court transcript, which amounted to some 1200 pages. In a letter he explained that his intention was to "convey some sense of that moment of history."[77]

The play, which appeared in print before it was staged, attracted the attention of the producer, Leland Hayward, who gave it a successful tryout in Los Angeles in the summer of 1970 before putting it on in New York. Berrigan wanted the actors to be able to improvise, and he also wanted the audience to participate in a discussion of the issues raised by the play, but he was turned down on both requests. Nevertheless, although at the time when the play opened on the west coast Berrigan was a fugitive from the law, he taped a message to the actors, which was played to the audience on opening night. Portraying the theater as a "circle of imaginative protection" through which the audience's emotions were heated by the dramatist, he described the actors' function as a temporary, artistic "tightening" of the mood of crisis which existed in American society during the Vietnam War.[78] Following its New York run, which was generally praised by reviewers, the play opened in a number of American cities. Among other honors it won the Los Angeles Drama Critics Circle award for 1971. A film, using the New York cast, continues to be screened both in the U.S. and abroad.

Following the sequence of events in the actual trial, the play focuses on the background and lives of the nine male and female defendants and on their struggle, in the name of a higher moral authority, against the law of the land. In this sense the play's theme is of universal significance, and respected commentators, like John Wain in the *New Republic*, had no hesitation in calling *The Trial of the Catonsville Nine* a "moving and important" work.[79] Adding weight to Wain's judgment is the fact that the play has been staged in many countries in recent years in addition to being published in a number of different languages.

Selecting the most significant and eloquent pieces of testimony, Berrigan embellished the speeches by presenting them in stanzaic form. Because the defendants were all essentially relating the histories of their lives and of what led them to Catonsville, they can be said to have roles in a dramatic sense. At the same time, in spite of the elevated mood engendered by all nine defendants, the dramatic center of the play is ironically the judge. While the men and women facing him are single-mindedly admirable in purpose, this very simplicity militates against successful drama. The judge, on the other hand, is a complex figure, intelligently loyal to the laws he has sworn to uphold, and yet sympathetic to the moral persuasiveness of the defendants' lives - if not of their claims before the law. Indeed, the liveliest moments in the play occur when the judge engages one or other of the defendants in discussion; unfortunately, Berrigan cut out much of this part of the transcript.[80]

Thus, while the play has a certain understated power as a written text, it lacks the flame of conflict that creates successful courtroom drama. Nevertheless, many of the speeches cling to memory, as in the case of Daniel Berrigan's own haunting concluding statement:

Our apologies   good friends
for the fracture of good order the burning of paper
instead of children the angering of the orderlies

in the front parlor of the charnel house
We could not so help us God do otherwise.[81]

The play's importance derives as much from its implicit
themes as from those that are explicitly addressed. Raised
implicitly, for example, is the question of a society's tolerance of
those dissenting individuals within it who, as in Shaw's *Saint Joan*,
may turn out to be its saints and heroes. As in *Saint Joan*, *The Trial
of the Catonsville Nine* derives part of its value from its historical
significance, an evanescent theatrical enhancement that may be
discounted only by the most pedantic critics. Looked at overall,
Berrigan's play has gained an enduring place in the theater as a
documentary play, even if not as a full-blooded and fully rounded
drama.

Berrigan's ideas about art had been evolving through the
late sixties, when he found himself more skeptical than in the
1950s about the relationship between faith and art. In the 1940s,
from the vantage point of youth and of the seminary, he had argued
in an early essay that the Christian poet's faith gave him or her an
advantage over other poets, at least as far as subject matter was
concerned.[82] In later years, having become conscious of the
sublime religious works created by artists like Chagall, Rouault,
Leger, and Matisse, whose faith was either heterodox or non-
existent, Berrigan wrote - in an essay entitled "The Tension
Between Art and Faith" - that any assumed relationship between
faith and art must founder "upon the heavy waters of genius."[83]

More importantly, by the late 1960s, he came to regard the
theoretical problem of the relationship between art and faith as of
little importance:

It is not to be thought strange that in a world so
ruled, in a landscape where the visible figures are

those of death and the dealing of death, that the
symbols of faith should be largely invisible. I am
convinced in fact that ours is not a time for making
art at all. It is a time for the preliminary, rude, even
destructive faith of which the prophet speaks:
"pluck and break down, destroy and overthrow."[84]

The allusion to Jeremiah in the final, fiery lines of this
passage is a sign of the ferment that had overtaken Berrigan's ideas
regarding both faith and art. The membrane between the artist and
priest was dissolving rapidly as he came to feel that his poetry
would overflow naturally from a "life offered for others" instead of
centering himself on art and thereby inhibiting his connection with
social activism.[85] In an interview given in 1974 he went further in
suggesting that the tendency of many contemporary American
poets to write hermetic poetry, which he saw as a failure to set up
"contrary rhythms in their lives," led to the impoverishment not
only of their lives but of their poetry.[86]

False Gods, Real Men (1969), a collection of poems that
came out as Berrigan awaited at Cornell the outcome of his judicial
appeal, is experimental and diverse in form compared to his earlier
verse. The collection, which is Berrigan's strongest and which
included a number of poems previously published in prestigious
publications like *Poetry* and the *New Yorker*, traced the outline of
his life through the late sixties, including his exile to Latin
America, his trip to Hanoi, and his life in New York as a partially
de-institutionalized urban priest. The poems tend to be both candid
and provocative - as in "I must Pour Life," which focuses on
contrary images of the contemporary priest. The first is that of the
cleric who is detached from the life stream and who is described in
some of Berrigan's most trenchant language:

Bronze celibates
thread space like spiders. Hands
inoffensive as lizard's
wave effete farewell
to arms, to full-blooded
speech, to country matters.[87]

Also unsatisfactory, though, is the priest who so immerses himself
in the problems of his flock that he ceases to have a distinct identity
and function:

I saw a priest once
mired in his people's lives
hunching a hundred-pound sack
up four flights of stairs
pulling for breath on the top landing.[88]

Apart from anything else, the phrasing marks a departure from the
bookishness of some of the earlier poetry. Moreover, as can be seen
in this extract, much of the power of the poems in *False Gods, Real
Men* stems from their sharply etched intensity.

The false gods motif refers to the waywardness of the
historical church. In one of the poems composed during his exile to
Latin America, for example, Berrigan ruefully accepts the caustic
vision of the church portrayed in the murals of the Mexican painter,
Diego Rivera. In one of the scenes, following the torture of certain
Indians by the Spanish conquistadors, "monkey-faced monks" are
shown complaisantly holding before the dying Indians "the lying
crucifix." Berrigan paradoxically depicts the Spanish priests
themselves as prisoners within the Roman collar.[89]

Abandoning the typology of his earlier religious poetry, Berrigan offers studies of the ordinary face of nature in these poems - as in "Farm:"

four rotted berry crates
two screen doors
a broken barrow
a compost heap,
weeds springing, bold, ripe
unkillable, voracious for life.[90]

In the manner of William Carlos Williams, Berrigan fragmented his lines into discrete images and phrases so that each object receives maximum attention while the speaker still maintains a natural voice rhythm. Unlike the farms in Williams' poems, though, Berrigan's farm has transcendental overtones:

New heavens and a new earth
begin here, in the last hour
when evening sun
like a compassionate knowing mind
lighting on foulness, lights

the pearl in the world's sty.[91]

Unlike poets such as Williams and Roethke who heighten their depictions of nature by using human metaphors to illustrate the experience of plant and animal, Berrigan describes nature as straining toward higher levels of being - as in the poem "Butterfly:"

My big moment -
lighting on a stallion's shoulder
too feeble to be twitched off, heard

like electric shock, that black
buried engine, that well of oil or blood
struck; mine! mine!"[92]

The butterfly's monologue conveys not only its startling discovery
but also its unexpected ambition and tenacity, which are wittily
juxtaposed with its ostensibly slight and vulnerable appearance.
"Butterfly" is one of Berrigan's most original and well-executed
poems, incisively combining surface detail and symbol with
lurking metaphysical drama.

Perhaps reflecting the fact that he was teaching modern
drama at Cornell at the time, Berrigan created a persona in *False
Gods, Real Men*, named Horatio, whose soliloquies somewhat
resemble those of Henry in John Berryman's *Dream Songs* -
although Berrigan has said that he does not recall having been
influenced by Berryman in these poems.[93] Through Horatio, whose
name was derived in part from Horatio Alger, Berrigan explores in
an off-beat style the failure of religion to challenge the domination
of American culture by the rapacious, real-life descendants of
Alger's entrepreneurial heroes. "Sun" is a representative example
of the Horatio poems:

Sun

always comes on strong
Horatio, the preacher said,
even, preferable, after a bad start
God says so, he thumped, *so do I!*
(In whose interest
the sun damn sight better had!)

But Rev. Potash addressed an audience
in the Poconos; whereas our

Alger, creeping about under Con Edison's
tarry mantle,
and Big Burning Brother
slogging it above,
never quite
actually
       made
          connection.[94]

While the theme is a familiar one in Berrigan's writing - the
bromides offered to contemporary culture by a church that thinks in
terms of verdant surroundings instead of modern urbanization - the
form is startlingly new. The language is hip and irreverent, and the
staccato rhythms exhibit urban speech patterns whose fragmenta-
tion in this case appropriately mirrors the disjunctive relationship in
American society between religion and conduct. Not only is
conventional Christianity satirized, but so is its archaic public
voice, which is satirically echoed in phrases like "tarry mantle," a
variant of "starry mantle."

    "Baby" is another Horatio poem. In this case the reader
witnesses Horatio's birth in which he emerges not trailing clouds of
glory but ejected into the lethally competitive American jungle:

It was uphill all the way
dodging the fish they threw -
the wrong road signs, road blocks,
poltergeists, the midwife's face
red as an elbow. I tell you I just made it.
                . . . *Horatio*
she whispers in my blood, if *I love you*
move it out of here, daddy
death wants you for field hand. No. You go.[95]

The mother's voice, urging the uncertain Horatio out of the secure birth canal into the free-fire zone of society, recalls Randall Jarrell's famous poem about the death of the ball turret gunner. What makes Berrigan's poem different from Jarrell's, though, is that there is no conflict between the mother and the state; Horatio's mother is herself a child of the state. Furthermore, the gravity of Jarrell gives way in Berrigan to a biting humor.

The fractured structuring of the Horatio poems is shared by a number of the poems in *False Gods, Real Men*:

Somewhere the Equation Breaks Down
    between the perfect
        (invisible, Plato said)
and the imperfect
    that comes at you on the street,
    stench and cloth and fried eyes;
between the wired bones of the dead
        stuttering, shamed
and the marvelous lucid spirit
    that moves in the body's spaces
    a rainbow fish behind glass -
decide. O coincide.[96]

The internal consonance and assonance in the last line reveal Berrigan's sense that the open form he was pursuing included the freedom to use traditional devices like rhyme when they were deemed to be suitable. On the other hand the modernistic, asymmetrical arrangement of the lines is effective in showing the disjunction between the lofty Platonic ideals alluded to in the poem and the quagmire of contemporary urban life.

Enhancing the complex ambiguity of the poem is the counterpointing of imagery about the material and immaterial worlds. The physical world, for example, is pictured positively through the glass of the aquarium and negatively through the street addict, while the spiritual world is represented by the positive image of the colored fish and the negative presence of the "shamed" soul or ghost. The polarization reflects the speaker's underlying reluctance to accept Plato's view that perfection and immateriality are synonymous. For Berrigan, who writes in a more Aristotelian tradition, the possibilities of good and evil, beauty and ugliness, permeate both matter and spirit.

Using the collage technique pioneered by Pound and Eliot, Berrigan constructed elliptical and fragmentary lines in a number of the poems in *False Gods, Real Men* which depict modern culture in general and New York in particular as a surrealistic procession of the dead - as in "The Clock in the Square:"

Ineffectuals
chained, reined to time's beaten track -
simulacra all, strangers to action, passion

strike the hour, lurch away
pale as linen
the pharaohs of long refusal.[97]

Subjugated by the deadening habits of their culture, the characters resemble not so much the cosmic orphans of Robert Frost's "Acquainted with the Night" - a poem that is recalled by Berrigan's title - but rather the hollow men of Eliot's poetry. Distinctive in Berrigan's poem, however, is the metaphorical flourish in the final line, the sardonic breaking of the surface of despair by the poet, if not by those he observes.

Other poems about New York recall the poetry of Hart Crane - especially "Subway:"

The worm is full of people, death reversed!
I heard an old man
cry terror
his face covered with mottled hands

A gnat, an apocalypse; the subway
gathering fury as it sped -

he screamed and screamed. We pulled
like a last demented day into the Concourse;

he climbed out, ragged, resigned
the Styx traversed, immediate hell ahead.[98]

Though not as dense in style, the poem captures the sense
of confusion, alienation, and hopelessness that permeate Crane's
depiction of New York. At the same time, while Crane, in *The
Bridge*, borrowed Eliot's theological symbolism in order to create
surrealism - without exhibiting a religious sensibility himself -
Berrigan portrays the city as as authentic a hell in a religious sense
as one could expect to encounter. In spite of its toll of human
suffering, New York as a microcosm in Berrigan's work has its
green retreats, particularly Central Park, which he describes in one
of the poems as descending on Manhattan "like a celestial napkin,
as if heaven/were all of earth, the fusty smell/of animals in arks."[99]
Unlike the debased Thames in Eliot's *Waste Land* Berrigan's city
park is a sufficient world, as is the throbbing life around it - in spite
of its clamor and misery. The city is perceived as sufficient in that
it is real if not beautiful, vulnerable if not spiritual.

Those poems in *False Gods, Real Men* that grew out of
Berrigan's trip to Hanoi in 1968 are terse repositories of

compressed themes. An example is the poem Berrigan composed
while waiting in Vientiane for the shuttle plane to Hanoi:

The birds of dawn are crying, drawing
     the great sun into conflict
a contested light
the bloody challenge taken, the spurred leap, roof
after roof.

. . . SUN
who alone cocks eye (eyeing that cock)
                         and not
   burns his socket blind; from his
intolerable equinox, seeing in the sea
     himself rampant, eye to eye
lives in that cry nor turns to stone
             nor no, shall die [100]

The montage of the fierce cock's eye and the aggressive sun arises
appropriately out of its steamy, war-torn, Asian setting. So does an
unquenchable penchant for survival, which is also symbolized by
both sun and bird. The poem mirrored Berrigan's state of mind as
he prepared to move through the charnel house of war toward the
possibility of a modified human consciousness on the other side.

The air raid shelters in Hanoi figure in a number of the
poems. In "Bombardment," for example, the speaker disappears
into the shelter like a "blown match," lamenting the loss of "sun
and moon/and one other face" - while above the gases of war "flare
on the world's combustible flesh."[101] "Children in the Shelter" was
occasioned by the sight of three children in a bomb shelter who,
Berrigan noted in his journal, appeared like a "frieze against the
wall in the half darkness, come to life." [102] Berrigan picks up a

little boy who was being fed by his sister, reflecting that in his arms was the "messiah of all my tears."[103] While conveying a note of fulfillment, the messiah image unexpectedly and subtly undercuts the mood of pathos with its inevitable trace of condescension.

"The Pilots Released" plays on the classic theme of American innocence. Thinking of the three downed pilots who had been released by the North Vietnamese, Berrigan reflects wryly: "When I think of you it is always (forgive me)/of disposable art; 50 designs drawn from the damp woodcut/of 50 States, the physiognomy of camp."[104] Following the woodcut motif, the speaker provides a portrait of the youngest of the pilots on the journey out of Vietnam in the shuttle aircraft:

> In the old moth-eaten plane (one-eyed - heroic
> as a pirate carp) the youngest pilot
> lived it over and over roped like an animal
> to the water wheel drawing up
> buckets water blood honey spleen
> lug and tug 104 days in solitary
> loneliness near madness interrogations
> brainwashing of that brain already
> hung high and dry as a woodcut
>
> of himself, by himself; *Our Boy; Spit, Polish,*
> *Literal Death.*[105]

Steeped in the die-cast outlook of his military school, the young pilot is helplessly immune to the possibilities of change that are implicit in his suffering at the hands of the outraged Vietnamese. The poem is of interest, stylistically, because it demonstrates Berrigan's increasing reliance upon increased spacing rather than traditional punctuation as a means of separating language.

The title poem in *False Gods, Real Men* is unusually long. Divided into nine parts, the poem begins with a chronology of the Berrigan family in America, including their proud tradition of producing energetic priests and nuns and their honorable participation in previous wars. The rest of the poem considers the ironic spectacle of Daniel and Philip Berrigan as lawbreaking priests, an affront to the family's patriotic service to both country and church. The poem was grounded in real emotion since some of Daniel Berrigan's older brothers, for example, were hostile to the anti-war activities of their younger brothers, especially the draft card burning at Catonsville. Referring to the burning of the draft files in the parking lot at Catonsville, Berrigan writes that the "foul macadam/blossomed like rosemary/in the old tapestry/where unicorns deigned/to weave a fantasy."[106] The allusion is to the sixteenth-century unicorn tapestries housed at the Cloisters museum in New York, tapestries that appear in the final section of William Carlos Williams' long poem *Paterson* as a symbol of the timelessness of art. Here, though, the visionary symbol of the unicorn illuminates the childlike character of the Catonsville incident, which, as the poem brings out, had been preceded by the participants going on a picnic. The symbol goes deeper, however, since the unicorn of the tapestries is also a symbol of the crucified Christ, who, giving himself into captivity for the sake of mankind, became the spiritual well from which the Catonsville Nine drew.

Toward the end of the poem the dreams of peace of the Catonsville protagonists are contrasted with the chimeras of their society:

The cure for foul dreams
is day, dawn. For chimera's claw marks
flesh! For false gods, real men
for Honor Mace, his insect secret, tears

that freshen, springs. For foul, fair
say it, shout it; fair for unfair, in courts of
law-
lessness. For pulpits
                    (rotten as
wormwood, the propped skeleton
his thimble fingers grasping like throats
book and eagle, flag and altar stone)
                    O you
dishonored priest, your retinue
the last, least men of this
                    most sorrowful world![107]

The broken lines mirror the stabs of memory that propel
the poem as Berrigan recounts his drop into the judicial vortex. The
judiciary, accountable only to itself, is insect-like, while the clergy
are described as decayed and ineffectual, with the two locked in an
unholy union that parodies the authentic ideals of both church and
state. The phrasing, here and in many of the poems in *False Gods,
Real Men* is splintered and dissonant, with blunt and raw language
jostling with more formal and restrained speech.   There is also a
new frankness in dealing with topics like sexuality, as can be seen
in the Horatio poem in which the Christian church's traditionally
desiccated approach to sexuality is lampooned. In another poem
there is a metaphorical reference to an "issueless king's/dry stick,
wet dream."[108] The boldness in diction reflected Berrigan's attempt
to move away from the somewhat cloistered tone of his earlier
work.

On the whole, the poems in *False Gods, Real Men* are
vigorously original in both form and theme. The use of the Horatio
persona was especially effective, but a number of other poems
benefited from Berrigan's interest in the drama at this time,

allowing him to project a variety of voices. Even in the autobiographical poems there are strong fluctuations in tone and mood that tend to keep the reader off guard. Furthermore, more than ever, the poems, as in the case of the title poem, involve elements both of form and theme that are held in suspension beyond the end of the reading. By the late sixties, both Berrigan's identity as a priest and his rhetoric as a poet had become far more fluid and experimental than had earlier been the case.

The fall of 1969 was darkened by the passing away of Berrigan's father, just as the previous autumn had brought the disheartening news of the accidental death of Thomas Merton in Thailand. Berrigan had been at his father's bedside for the last eight hours of his suffering during which, as he confided in a letter to friends, "we prayed together the good prayers of his boyhood. When I held his hands, he answered with that workman's grasp I had known so well."[109] While not fully understanding the actions of his younger sons in the late 1960s, Thomas Berrigan, approaching his ninetieth birthday, had supported them in spirit, and this had helped to alleviate some of the residual bitterness from Daniel's boyhood days on the farm. The death of Berrigan's father with its attendant ambivalence would germinate in his mind and writing over the next few years.

In 1970 a book of Berrigan's essays entitled *No Bars to Manhood* was brought out by Doubleday, where his longtime editor and friend, Elizabeth Bartelme, had moved after leaving Macmillan. The collection received a National Book Award nomination for 1970 and won the Frederick Melcher Book Award. *No Bars to Manhood* contains autobiographical sketches, essays on Christianity and culture, and studies of contemporary religious figures like Gandhi and Bonhoeffer.

One of the more stimulating essays in *No Bars to Manhood*, one that grew out of Berrigan's teaching at Cornell, is

"Lear and Apocalypse." In this essay juxtaposing the Book of Job with Shakespeare's play, Berrigan injects provocative moral insights into the discussion of Shakespearean tragedy. He takes exception, for example, to the widely held view that Lear's mistake lay in dividing his kingdom among his daughters, arguing instead that he ought to have offered them more - the "proper disposition of his heart" - a fuller measure of love, a lesser measure of parental and regal condescension.[110] In this way, Berrigan believes, he would have avoided the vain test of his daughters' love, and stirred his one true child to protect him from the schemes of the others.

In comparing Lear to Job, Berrigan notes that Lear's suffering is particularly bleak because he has no God to appeal to and is thus enclosed by his pain. In Berrigan's view this results in a tragic narrowness that contrasts Lear even with his fool: "The fool can be bawdy, even in bad weather," whereas the king, Berrigan adds pithily, "can only be tragic. And this is his tragedy." In discussing the fool, Berrigan again questions conventional interpretation, contending that the fool is indeed foolish in urging the king toward a merely strategic reconciliation with the dark agents about him. Reflecting his own experience in this matter, Berrigan observes coolly that in a world in which "power is exercised in the normal way, it is in the strictest sense a foolish thing to ask that men grant space to one another; to live, to rejoice, to adhere to one another."[111]

Berrigan's remarks about Cordelia are illuminating in the light of his own struggle at this time:

> We are not even sure of Cordelia or of her game;
> we are given evidence only that her soul is well
> knitted, a unity. She appears on stage briefly;
> rumors about her have mainly to do with reverence
> or contempt before her suffering compassion. But

> she remains somewhat abstract and shadowy: She
> does not have the harsh texture, the immediate
> clamorous impact of her two sisters. *Their* projects
> are always clear; there is that to be said for them.
> But Cordelia is a little bloodless, like a Dickens
> heroine. We can only be grateful for her, and
> mourn that we cannot know her better.[112]

In responding in this way to Cordelia's shadowiness, Berrigan was led to contrast her embodiment of goodness with the model that he was attempting to fashion for contemporary man. The customary behavior of virtuous people, he observed, had led to the placing of goodness modestly in the shade, whereas he came increasingly to believe that goodness needed to be full-bloodedly and vividly presented in contemporary culture.

In *No Bars to Manhood* Berrigan argued that a perennial awareness of crisis was a required mode of perception for the Christian. Similarly, a mood of normalcy was described as an obstacle to the Christian sense of identity - a condition that Berrigan describes as a "clouded mirror."[113] As is often the case in Berrigan's writings, the peril of modern society is depicted as arising not from autocrats but from a well-intentioned though marginally conscious majority. He characterized such a majority as supporting the idea of peace, for example, both domestically and abroad, without being willing to bear the cost of making peace. Throughout *No Bars to Manhood* Berrigan contends that many observers, even the more sophisticated, tend to mistake stability for peace, an error in judgment that in his view will prove to be catastrophic. Berrigan further believes that, in confusing a tactical relationship with one based upon trust, governments have the habit of speciously attempting to justify their prohibitively expensive preparations for war while failing to feed and clothe the peoples of the world.

Furthermore, in Berrigan's view, even those who recognize the distinctive moral crises of their age must also come to terms with the social and political responsibilities which society places upon the shoulders of its members. Once the ambience of moral crisis has descended upon the Christian, in particular, he argues, duty, whatever its ethical claims, must be weighed along with other variables which the reformer must take into account. Law, itself, is not immune; indeed, the greater the moral implications of particular laws, the greater the need to test those laws that appear to weaken or dilute the search for social justice.

While Berrigan traces the mood of crisis inherent in Christianity back to the persecution of the early Christians, he came to believe that the imprinting of this sense of crisis on the *subsequent* development of Christianity has been salutary. Thus, in an essay on the Book of Revelations in *No Bars to Manhood* in which he explores the psychological landscape of the Christian consciousness of crisis, he argues that the biblical symbols, while arcane and in need of careful interpretation, illuminate a continuum of history that is "forever beginning anew, forever being crushed by illegitimate power and immoral circumstance." The result is that people find themselves "perpetually torn from the bowels of yesterday, forever threatened by the multiple forms of death that press upon them from this world. They spend their lives in the experience of a deathbed or of a room of birth, they scarcely know which."[114] These words illustrate how far Berrigan had moved from the evolutionary ethos of Teilhard de Chardin; indeed, the historical view taken in *No Bars to Manhood* seems at times rather Spenglerian and fatalistic in comparison with Berrigan's earlier writings.

Citing the "shining case and writings of Thoreau," Berrigan moved ever closer to the case for civil disobedience in *No Bars to Manhood*, especially in the autobiographical essay, "Trial by Fire."[115] In this essay, which drew on a lecture that he gave at the Cornell Law School in December, 1968, he maintained that the law should be "remade in the imagination of those who purvey the law, those who violate the law, and those who suffer under the law, in order that the law itself become what it says it is: *corpus humanum* - a human body."[116] The essay is typical in pointing up the overlapping waves of Berrigan's life and thought at this time as he extruded moral insights out of his confrontations with civil and judicial authorities.

"Exit the King and Crisis of America" explored the specious role played by liberalism in a time of crisis, inhibiting change "at exactly that point where change is needed, which is to say at the depths of man's spirit."[117] The problem with liberalism, Berrigan noted, is that it tends to focus myopically on particular evils rather than on the widespread spiritual malaise that underlies these evils. Moreover, because that malaise goes unrecognized, the connections between various social and political symptoms may escape the liberal's attention. In the essay "Bonhoeffer: God is Neither Here Nor There" Berrigan concluded that the failure of liberalism derived as well from its very reasonableness, in particular its attempt to do justice to all sides. In so doing, according to Berrigan, it absorbed the complexities of an issue to such an extent that it became worn down, with little achieved.

Berrigan echoed Bonhoeffer's view that neither private virtue nor modern humanism were sufficient to extinguish the major dehumanizing influences in contemporary culture. Even the moral heroes of Christianity, he added, had frequently fallen short of castigating major social evils. St. Paul, for example, according to Berrigan, could have been more vehement in dealing with the subject of slavery, and so have inhibited subsequent compromises between Christianity and the institution of slavery.

From a stylistic point of view, some of the essays in *No Bars to Manhood* are continuous with those in *They Call Us Dead Men* in that they explore questions and issues primarily through analogy. There are analogies presented, for example, between figures like St. Paul and Dietrich Bonhoeffer. Similarly, an absurdist play by the French dramatist, Ionesco, is examined in order to throw light on the moral crisis in America in the 1960s. The analogies were not only rhetorically based, but proceeded from Berrigan's prior use of them in trying to determine a spiritual direction for himself:

> Analogies are a little like the toeholds one grasps
> on a steep slope; they enable one to take the next
> step in a dangerous geography. The next step is the
> point in question: is it possible? The question, for a
> climber, cannot be an abstract one; he must create
> as he goes. And he draws breath, when the air is
> very thin indeed, from the example of those who
> went far, who died in the breach, or who made it
> further.[118]

Events in the 1960s had led Berrigan into an activist mode that caused him to reconsider his roles as both priest and writer. Nevertheless, although he had temporarily brought the anti-war protest to a boil at Cornell and elsewhere, he was left at the end of the decade with a bleak outlook regarding the prospects for social change in the 1970s. He wrote to a friend in the summer of 1971 that the "old Newman distinction" was applicable - "minds are 'potentially' rather than 'really' awakened to alternatives. But so remote are the other options and so staked about with OFF signs" that most people end up dabbing their "wrists in sea water" while imagining a life and death immersion.[119]

In spite of Berrigan's feelings of dejection as the 1970s began, he had accomplished much in the preceding half-dozen years. The period from 1965 to 1970 can be seen as his most productive as religious activist and artist. While the life and writing moved closer to each other during these years, the writing retained a poise that prevented it from being swamped by the causes that Berrigan had taken up. The strivings of both artist and activist were held in a vigorous balance, and this gave the writing a high imaginative energy without any attendant loss in the wit and craftsmanship that had characterized the earlier work. In terms of Berrigan's ability to accommodate both the contemplative and active principles, the late sixties appear in retrospect as a snowy summit.

Notes: Chapter Three

1. Letter from James Shanahan, S.J. to Daniel Berrigan, July 18, 1962.
2. Letter from Daniel Berrigan to Thomas Merton, June, 2, 1964.
3. "The Other America and the Other World," originally published in *A.I.D. Dialogue*, Jan./Feb. 1965, was reprinted in *Readings in Social Theology*, ed. Everett J. Morgan, S.J. (Dayton, Ohio: Pflaum, 1969) 321-323.
4. "The Modern Concept of 'Missio,'" in *Jesuit Spirit in a Time of Change*, ed. Raymond Schroth, (Westminster, Md.: Newman Pr., 1968) 212.
5. For a perceptive study of the relationship between the spiritualities of Thomas Merton and Daniel Berrigan see Thomas C. Oddo, "The Monk and the Activist: A Comparative Study of the Spirituality of Thomas Merton and Daniel Berrigan." Ph.D. dissertation, Harvard, 1979.
6. Letter from Daniel Berrigan to Thomas Merton, March 18, 1966.
7. Interview with Rosemary Bannan, Oct. 31, 1968. Manuscript, unpaginated.
8. Ibid.
9. Ibid.
10. Daniel Berrigan and Thich Nhat Hanh, *The Raft is Not the Shore* (Boston: Beacon, 1975) 59.
11. See Deedy 25-26.
12. Dorothy Day, *On Pilgrimage: The Sixties* (New York: Curtis, 1972) 257.
13. Letter from Daniel Berrigan to his family from Caracas, Venezuela, dated January, 1966.
14. Letter from Daniel Berrigan to his family from Recife, Brazil, January 10, 1966.
15. Letter from Daniel Berrigan to Thomas Merton, March 18, 1966.

16. *Consequences: Truth and...* (New York: Macmillan, 1966) 24.

17. *Consequences* 59.

18. *Consequences* 30.

19. *Consequences* 34.

20. *Consequences* 53.

21. *Consequences* 21.

22. *Consequences* 54.

23. *Consequences* 27.

24. *Consequences* 24.

25. *Consequences* 45.

26. *Consequences* 17.

27. *Consequences* 31.

28. *Consequences* 48.

29. *Consequences* 36.

30. *Consequences* 3.

31. *Consequences* 65.

32. *Consequences* 79.

33. *The Mission: A Film Journal* (San Francisco: Harper & Row, 1986) 32.

34. *Consequences* 115.

35. *Consequences* 120.

36. *Consequences* 108.

37. *Consequences* 122.

38. *Consequences* 95.

39. *Consequences* 106.

40. *Consequences* 88.

41. *Consequences* 86.

42. *Consequences* 110-111.

43. *Consequences* 106.

44. *Consequences* 88.

45. Berrigan's notes of the meeting are dated April 25, 1966.

46. Letter from Daniel Berrigan to Fr. General, S.J., June 4, 1966.

47. See "Father Daniel Berrigan: Interview with a Dissenter on Vietnam," *National Catholic Reporter* 8 (Sept. 8, 1965) 2.
48. "Reflections on the Priest as Peacemaker," *Jubilee* 13 (Feb., 1966) 29.
49. Ibid. 23.
50. *To Dwell in Peace* (San Francisco: Harper & Row, 1987) 206.
51. *No Bars to Manhood* (Garden City, N.Y.: Doubleday, 1970) 190.
52. Allan Bloom, *The Closing of the American Mind* (New York: Simon and Schuster, 1987) 313.
53. "The Path of Greatest Resistance," *U.S. Catholic* 35 (Jan. 1970) 9. Interview with Daniel Berrigan by Harry Cargas.
54. *To Dwell in Peace* 245.
55. Letter from Daniel Berrigan to Sister William Anne Ryan, April 3, 1968.
56. "No Cutting Loose," *Love, Love at the End* (New York: Macmillan, 1968) 3.
57. Ibid. 4.
58. Ibid, 4.
59. "The Single Rose," *Love, Love* 25.
60. Ibid. 25-26.
61. Letter from Thomas Merton to Daniel Berrigan, February 14, 1966, *The Hidden Ground of Love: The Letters of Thomas Merton on Religious Experience and Social Concerns*, ed. William Shannon (New York: Farrar, Straus, Giroux, 1985) 91.
62. See a summary of Berrigan's position in James Finn, *Protest: Pacifism and Politics* (New York: Random House, 1967) 142.
63. Berrigan's remarks were quoted in William Pierce, "Father Daniel Berrigan: Interview with a Dissenter on Vietnam," *National Catholic Reporter*, Sept. 8, 1965, 2.
64. Letter from Daniel Berrigan to Rev. James Somerville, S.J., Aug. 20, 1968.
65. *Night Flight to Hanoi* (New York: Macmillan, 1968) 4.

66. *Night Flight* 27.
67. *Night Flight* 106.
68. *Night Flight* 50-51.
69. *Night Flight* 67.
70. *Night Flight* 85-86.
71. *Night Flight* 90-91.
72. *Night Flight* 93.
73. *Night Flight* 98.
74. See, for example, Saul Maloff, "Jailbird," *Newsweek*, Oct. 14, 1968, 74D-75D.
75. Philip Berrigan, *Prison Journals of a Priest Revolutionary* (New York: Holt, Rinehart and Winston, 1970) 98.
76. "Introduction," *The Trial of the Catonsville Nine* (Boston: Beacon, 1970) x.
77. Letter from Daniel Berrigan to Justus Lawlor, Sept. 5, 1969.
78. "Father Berrigan Speaks to the Actors from Underground," *America Is Hard to Find* (Garden City, N.Y.: Doubleday, 1972) 90.
79. John Wain, "Art, Play, and Protest," *New Republic* 162 (June 20, 1970) 24.
80. For a good discussion of Berrigan's editing of the transcript, see Friday, pp. 214-215.
81. *Trial of the Catonsville Nine* 93.
82. See Daniel Berrigan, "Faith and Poetry," *America* 70 (1944) 353-354.
83. "The Tension Between Art and Faith," *Critic* 26 (Aug./Sept., 1967) 35.
84. Ibid. 36.
85. "Path of Greatest Resistance" 10.
86. Harriet Shapiro, "Berrigan in Crisis," *Intellectual Digest* 4 (May, 1974) 6.
87. "I Must Pour Life," *False Gods, Real Men* (New York: Macmillan, 1969) 63.

88. Ibid.
89. "To the Prisoners," *False Gods* 72.
90. "Farm," *False Gods* 93.
91. Ibid.
92. "Butterfly," *False Gods* 96.
93. Letter from Daniel Berrigan to the author, June 7, 1986.
94. "Sun," *False Gods* 104.
95. "Baby," *False Gods* 101.
96. "Somewhere the Equation Breaks Down," *False Gods* 34.
97. "The Clock in the Square," *False Gods* 29.
98. "Subway," *False Gods* 97.
99. "Diary (Easter, 1966)", *False Gods* 60.
100. "Waiting Vientiane," *False Gods* 11.
101. "Bombardment," *False Gods* 15.
102. *Night Flight* 56.
103. "Children in the Shelter," *False Gods* 16.
104. "The Pilots Released," *False Gods* 21.
105. Ibid. 22.
106. "False Gods, Real Men," *False Gods* 5.
107. Ibid. 7.
108. "I Wonder, Do You," *False Gods* 36.
109. Letter to Friends, October 3, 1969. Mimeograph.
110. "Lear and Apocalypse," *No Bars to Manhood* (Garden City, N.Y.: Doubleday, 1970) 87.
111. Ibid. 87.
112. Ibid. 85.
113. "Trial by Fire," Ibid. 39.
114. "The Book of Revelations," *No Bars* 91.
115. "Trial by Fire," *No Bars* 39.
116. Ibid. 41.
117. "Exit the King and Crisis of America," *No Bars* 76.

118. "Notes from the Underground," *New Blackfriars* 51 (Oct., 1970)
     454.
119. Letter from Daniel Berrigan to Daniel and Linda Finlay, July 15,
     1971.

Chapter Four

UNDERGROUND AND PRISON WRITINGS

After receiving word that the U.S. Supreme Court had refused to hear the appeal of the Catonsville Nine, Berrigan was instructed to begin serving his three-year sentence on April 9, 1970. In consultation with others in the peace movement he delayed turning himself over to the authorities, choosing instead to attend a large anti-war festival at Cornell from April 17-19. The event, which was called "America is Hard to Find," involved a weekend of speeches, films, poetry, plays, and music, and included authors Paul Goodman and Leslie Fiedler, attorney William Kunstler, and theologian Harvey Cox. Over 10,000 people crowded into Barton Hall, including F.B.I. agents, who where there to arrest Berrigan for failing to begin serving his sentence. After his address, which was received enthusiastically, Berrigan decided, following the urging of friends, to make his escape, which he did by concealing himself within a large, papier-mâché puppet, leaving behind incensed F.B.I. officers, who had decided to make their arrest towards the end of his appearance on stage. Fleeing first to a friend's home in New Jersey, Berrigan began an almost four-month odyssey as a fugitive.

Although he expected to be captured in a short time, Berrigan intended his life underground to provide him with the opportunity to enunciate his protest against the Vietnam War under the most favorable media conditions, i.e., when maximum attention would be given to him. Thus, between April and August, 1970, he was interviewed on television, as well as in the *New York Times* and the *Saturday Review*, and delivered a number of lectures and sermons to audiences throughout the northeastern U.S. His activities were not a balm to all observers. William Buckley, Catholic and editor of the *National Review*, asked, for example : "Might one ask, *where* is the FBI? Father Daniel Berrigan, the gifted Jesuit priest, entered a Selective Service office, destroyed and burned its files, was caught and convicted, and it is nowadays much likelier that you will see him on Johnny Carson's show, thumbing his nose at American jurisprudence, than behind the bars he belongs behind."[1]

There were, in fact, many, including a number of Catholics, who felt that Berrigan's evading of his prison sentence had cast a moral shadow over the anti-war protest. While sympathetic to Berrigan's intentions, for example, the well-known Catholic scholar and conscientious objector, Gordon Zahn, doubted whether the American public would perceive him as anything but a fugitive priest.[2] There can be little doubt that Berrigan had undermined his effectiveness by not allowing the state to expose its harshness and injustice by imprisoning a morally sensitive individual for an essentially nominal offense. Berrigan's fellow Jesuits were also divided over his behavior, although he felt that he had acted in the best traditions of his order, whose priests had gone underground in, for example, both Elizabethan England and twentieth-century Russia.

During his time underground Berrigan generally stayed with middle-class, professional people, reading and meditating during the daytime when the houses were quiet, engaging in conversation about the war and his own protest in the evenings.

Part of the purpose of his going underground had been to encourage ordinary people of good will to appreciate their own power against what appeared to be the overwhelming might of their government. While committed in principle to the causes for which Berrigan stood, some of his hosts experienced a certain amount of submerged tension as they came to terms with their own collusion in hiding a lawbreaking priest. In addition, Berrigan became acutely aware at this time of the way in which American children, caught up in consumerism, neutralized the readiness of their parents to commit themselves to public confrontation. For this reason he came to question the uncritical eulogies on the family by his church, later describing the American family in an interview with the psychiatrist, Robert Coles, as offering the "greatest resistance to change."[3]

There were happier moments, though, as in the following vignette provided by one of Berrigan's hosts, who had nervously acceded to his request to go swimming on a public beach:

> Our children raced for the water, trailing sand-pails
> and strainers and inner tubes. My wife and I were
> making cautionary glances left and right, but Dan
> had already stripped down to a baggy borrowed
> bathing suit and chased after the kids, running into
> the cold water without breaking stride. They
> played together in the surf, children and man, and
> we began to get some idea what we were
> celebrating.[4]

On April 21, 1970, Philip Berrigan was arrested for failing to begin serving his sentence as a member of the Catonsville Nine, and he was held in the maximum security prison in Lewisburg, Pennsylvania, an unusually severe punishment, meted out it was thought at the time in order to induce his brother to give himself up. It was ironically through Philip's incarceration at Lewisburg that Daniel was eventually captured by the F.B.I. on August 11, 1970. A prisoner named Boyd Douglas, who was regularly granted day passes and who had befriended Philip Berrigan, carried letters covertly between him and Sister Elizabeth McAlister on the outside. In one of the letters Sister Elizabeth revealed that Daniel was hiding on Block Island in the house of his friend, the lawyer and author, William Stringfellow. The go-between, Boyd Douglas, turned out to be an informer, and it wasn't long before Daniel Berrigan was apprehended by F.B.I. agents.

While living underground, Berrigan had kept a diary of his experiences and reflections, and this was published in 1971 under the title, *The Dark Night of Resistance*. The book, a compendium of prose and poetry and of gradations in between, is enveloped by the voice of the narrator, who appears alternately as picaresque philosopher and disaffected wag. The title was drawn from the contemplative classic, *The Dark Night of the Soul*, by the sixteenth-century, Spanish mystic, St. John of the Cross. Berrigan had re-read the book while staying with one of the families who had given him shelter during the summer of 1970.

St. John of the Cross described the soul's passive and helpless ordeal in awaiting the presence of God without words, thoughts, or mental images. Although, as the title of Berrigan's journal indicated, there had been nothing passive about his life underground, he had felt impelled to enter the sphere of invisibility - though in a quite different sense than his spiritual mentor:

> I start these notes quite literally on the run. In town, the spring is breaking out in a cataclysm - unexpected! as though in midwinter, dark and pandemic, a healing had been found. I walk down

streets like a shadow or cardboard man, invisible
as the mild air.[5]

As Berrigan moved furtively from house to house, the
visible cycling of the seasons refreshed his spirit and anchored him
in the external world:

> I look out on the leaves of a single tree in a
> backyard. It has accompanied my long-distance
> dash of the last weeks; all the frenzy and hilarity
> since Cornell. It was standing dead as a pike staff,
> frozen in one of the gorges when I left that scene. I
> knew it there; it was part of the sublime untouched
> earth art, the enchantment of that place. It raced
> ahead of me to Jersey like a witch's perambulating
> broom; fast, slick as a vapor trail, single-minded,
> even obsessive, like a witch's arrow. It wore no
> disguise; anonymous as a broom, peeled down to
> use, and wearing a wig.[6]

The image of the foliated wig reveals how freely descriptive and
supple Berrigan's imagination was beneath the constraints of his
life as a a fugitive. The seasons formed the ephemerally beautiful
foreground for the darkness in which he lived as a fugitive. Writing
in *To Dwell in Peace* a number of years later, Berrigan recalled his
conflicting consciousness of the beauty and stability of nature on
the one hand and his apprehensive expectation of imminent arrest
on the other. He lived through a "burgeoning" summer, which had
about it a "shadow, a plaint - as of something held, and then let go
before its time. High summer in the air - and yet an autumnal
mood."[7]

The familiar theme of the axis of a life balanced between action and contemplation is the subject of an elegant internal monologue in *The Dark Night of Resistance,* rather wordily titled, "Wherein a Series of Contradictions is Pointed Out in View Perhaps of a Resolution of Truth." In this prose poem Berrigan begins by observing that the complete contemplative tends to adulate the "*tabula rasa*/upon which the divine may trace his austere lines/the mind which is pure lotus before weather,/pure unknowing before knowledge," thereby escaping active engagement with the world.[8] Employing the tone of bemused savoir faire that pervades *The Dark Night of Resistance,* Berrigan reasons that, in an uncompromising world, Zen texts should consist of

> blank sheets of handmade paper
>> page after page fanning out in the hand
> to release like the cards of a prestigitator
>> those numinous presences
>>> alike and most unlike
> birds poets flowers desires light inhibitions
> whose exorcism is the gentle and liberating task
>> of the masters of the soul.[9]

The passage is typical of *The Dark Night of Resistance* in its reflexive portrayal of an exuberant and arching mind at play.

The solution to the polarity of contemplation and action is located finally not in explanation but in art - as is illustrated in a painting by Jean Arp:

> . . . a wooden cutout of a limp disc
>> gray; stuck on a light blue board.
> there are bulges like necks at opposite ends of the jug

areas of white paint issue from these and stream
off
      broadening as they go toward the edge and
         beyond.
      streams of what? we must say simply
         everything anything nothing
      light darkness seed spirit water
      It is a Zen image The jug of the universe
      The stream of creation The life of the mind.[10]

The passage is an example of how Berrigan's thought and practice
as an artist could have profound effects on his thought and life as a
priest. With its ability to silently fuse matter and idea, the work of
art encompasses both contemplation and the world that is
contemplated in a union in which each is so satisfyingly present
that neither strives for a separate existence. Such a reconciliation of
thought and action became a paradigm for Berrigan, who was
feeling his way spiritually during his life underground and in need
of such a beacon:

the dissidence and fury of the human frame
      that the lotus gesture
inwardly composes accepts
      even as it resolutely sets limits
   to what?
to that journey; its mischance its stages

                                          defeats

      the graves that mark its portages
   the skeletons mounded beside camp fires
   the forgiveness also the epiphanies
      the subservient hope that fuels the heart
   piercing the mirages presenting in obscure

> penumbra
> the shape of things to come
>   which
>   it
>   makes
>   come [11]

Within the welter of experience, some of it harsh, as can be seen in the skeleton image, some of it illuminating and tender, the mind perceives reality, but only by experiencing it first. In this poetic braiding of the motifs of contemplation and action Berrigan sustains discursive waves of thought and feeling, using widely flexible lines and rhythms. In the final lines, where a single word fills each line, the halting path to the future and the force needed to bring that future about are graphically pointed up.

In *The Dark Night of Resistance* Berrigan calls for contemplative "masters of the spirit" who are also active "saints," capable of engendering in contemporary culture a "vital embodied memory."[12] Thus, he urges the monks of various religious traditions to become more actively interested in their societies, as the Buddhist monks in Vietnam and as his friend, Thomas Merton, had done. In addition, Berrigan's master of the spirit, John of the Cross, had, like himself, been both contemplative and reformer, and had been imprisoned for his views, just as Berrigan faced imminent imprisonment.

What attracted Berrigan to John of the Cross was not only the saint's balancing of contemplative and active energy but the fact that John was also a poet of stature. As such he necessarily existed, Berrigan believed, between the sublime and the absurd, a true Doctor de la Nada. For Berrigan, both religion and art involved dialectical tensions that John of the Cross both embodied and enunciated, not only a fastidious balance between thought and action, but also between action and passivity, the latter being a form of the soul's dark night, the "shaping of man into a receptacle for the light and rain of heaven." If John was Promethean, Berrigan continued, a "world shaper in the justest sense of that word", he not only "stole fire," but fulfilled as well "that other, less scrutinized episode of the myth: he was chained to rocks, his vitals were eaten by predators."[13]

Following John of the Cross in preparing himself for the ordeal of prison, though moving in a more active and less mystical direction, Berrigan nonetheless depicted his soul as suppressing its intellectual and imaginative flights in order to await the wisdom that was the fruit of contemplation; moreover, he attempted to be open to suffering, whose value lay in its indeterminate absurdity, something that Berrigan had felt acutely at times in his appearances before the courts and in his bizarre flight from justice. Indeed, in the months spent living as a fugitive, he became convinced that, as John of the Cross had done, he too was following a God of the absurd; indeed, the ability to risk absurdity in imagining provisional, alternative models of reality is seen in *The Dark Night of Resistance* as an indispensable state of mind for those who would pry themselves loose from what Berrigan regarded as the hedonistic trance of contemporary culture.

The central symbols in *The Dark Night of Resistance* are light and darkness. As a symbol of contemplation, for example, darkness appears positively as the mystery of God brooding over human history. As a symbol of action, on the other hand, darkness appears positively as the flower of resistance, a "no, spoken with the heart's full energies" in a time for "burning out the accumulated debris of history."[14] That 'no' in turn, delivered in a moment of confrontation with one's society, is perceived as bringing the one who utters it fresh perspectives that are "closer to the dark roots of our existence, to beginnings, to the heart of things."[15]

The traceries of light and darkness provide the book with
both its ornamental and its thematic richness. Images of darkness,
for example, characteristically evoke the loamy womb of creation
either within matter itself or within the mind:

> CONFUSION   In Greek myth, the rich original
> batter and mix of all differentiated creation . . . To
> be born of which is both honorable and inevitable,
> as, e.g., a noble French crêpe.
>   To remain in which is ruinous and indeed
> against the course of nature, as the self-willed,
> unborn drown in their own juice and element.[16]

Darkness here becomes a seal of entombment if the life stirring
within the womb of time fails to move out of that womb in order to
"grow new organs," as Berrigan put it elsewhere in *The Dark Night
of Resistance*.[17]

Extending the womb motif, Berrigan pictures the church as
promoting a "culture of infancy savored and prolonged."[18]
Similarly, a prolonged infancy is associated both with Europe's
excessive attraction to stability and ritual - the tale of the tribe - and
with America's addictive consumerism: "The father as salesman;
and the death thereof. Mama holding the reins of the team, father
and son castrated in service to the goddess and her trivial suburban
vision."[19] A variation on the motif of darkness in connection with
Berrigan's reflections on contemporary America is that of amnesia:
"The amnesiac nation; inability literally, vitally, to grasp the
forward moving implications of its own beginnings."[20] As an
alternative to succumbing to the American dream, Berrigan
advocates choosing the shade, even the shade of a prison - the
"kingdom of bluebottle flies" - with its attendant risk of death.[21]

While forsaking the optimism of Teilhard de Chardin's spiritual evolutionism in the 1970s, Berrigan clung to the conception of time as a continuum whose unfolding was its most precious and paradoxical aspect. In *The Dark Night of Resistance*, for example, the way forward, toward the light, is a passage through darkness, an Orphean underground in which one joined the "vast network of the unborn and the dead" and in which one went beyond America in order to "join the heart of man."[22] From this darkness would emerge the new man, one who is "haunted" - "infested by the spirits" - a "miraculous tropical fish, in motion while we observe him, attempt to get to know him."[23] Contrasted with the new man are the denizens of the contemporary world who "breathe shallowly our slovenly air" while the "fish flip belly up in our murky waters."[24]

For Berrigan, the experimental life lived by the new man depended crucially upon imagination, a reflection in part of Berrigan's own idiosyncratic juggling of religious contemplation, art, and social reform, which was inspired in turn by the imaginative genius of Christ:

> He offers ways, apertures, lights them up, smashes them
> open even to let in air. . . . We must see him in a kind of
> nightmare frenzy, moving like a madman down the dry ar-
> teries of time, tipping over the desiccated properties of the
> dead, invading the coffinmakers' shops, setting Caesar's
> coins spinning into corners to lie among the bat turds,
> ringing the tocsin, crying up the dead under pretext of fire,
> flood, shipwreck, Hamlet's father's murder, the disappear-
> ance of the town children into a mountain in company with
> a ragged flute player.[25]

Christ is presented here as a dynamic figure whose revolutionary features have been concealed for centuries beneath insipid commentaries. Cultivating the art of pentimento, Berrigan reveals the strength and forcefulness of the original. Embedded in the life of Christ, he implies in the above passage, were dynamic moral imperatives that had become blurred at times through habits of, often institutionally condoned, passive piety.

The Dark Night of Resistance contains some of Berrigan's most innovative and stimulating writing. An example is a long poem with a streamer of a title: "*Now If You Please in This Darkness Choose Your Image of the World Inhabit It Walk Within It Peacably or Run Like Hell the Other Way*." Alternating between sinuous prose paragraphs and tighter verse stanzas, Berrigan proposes fifteen dreams and myths for the reader to choose from, beginning with a stoical vision of the earth as a "plague-ridden ship" captained by an "anti-hero," a Job figure who is patient, decent, and brave but uncomprehending. Like Joseph Conrad's secret sharer, the captain is haunted by an alter ego, the spirit of a mysterious dolphin - a Christ figure - who swims along in the ship's wake conveying "greetings from other worlds" but who does not interfere with the ill-fated ship.[26]

A second visionary tableau is of the olive branch "borne in the orange beak/of a dove, over a flood, from a promontory/where by inference, the deluge has/turned back, the olive grows/plentifully. Where?"[27] The images are of reconciliation following the anguish of the voyage in the first canto. The appended question "Where?" causes the Noah incident to flow into the contemporary context where the same question may be put. In the third canto the image of the flower undergoes a metamorphosis where it becomes a lilac blossom, a child's paradisiacal vision of the cosmos.

A more mottled beauty appears in the fourth canto through the image of the swan with "her despised moles, pads and bunions, a creature of three elements."[28] Like a human being the swan moves amphibiously and not always gracefully between discrete worlds. In the fifth canto the reader is presented with a large, prehistoric horn, convoluted like a sea shell, "the sea in motion, the arc of space that dizzies the mind, lying like the breadth of Blake's cosmic giant, between choice and choice. It is the reveille of the tribe, its colors the striations of a complex imperfect quartz, its inner coil, that of ear, earth, or music itself."[29] As with the symbol of the Hesperides in the sixth part, the fifth canto has to do with the freedom of art, in particular with the possibility of creating either noble or ignoble acts of the imagination. Similarly, parts seven and eight briefly touch on the arts of folk cultures, but in acknowledgement of the triumph of technology over such folk traditions the poem soon veers towards the hedonistic dreams of the West and the antiseptic, yet voyeuristic, scientific establishments that support them:

> APES build cages for Rhesus monkeys
> who are (apes say)
> both strange and familiar enough
> to merit the Sunday PM interest
> of urban apes and their spring-offs.
> The RMs hunt for lice
> in surgically clean cages
> and masturbate with ardor
> even in off season.
> They are thus (writes Professor AP)
> an indispensable link
> to recessive practice and malpractice
> long vanished from our people [30]

The laboratory setting and staccato rhythms of the eleventh canto recall Thomas Merton's long poem, *Cables to the Ace*, which was published three years before *The Dark Night of Resistance.*

In the twelfth section a cobra rises as a symbol of the sort of endemic evil overlooked by the academic managers of human behavior, a viper that uncoils in an "insensate leap" of "inflamed intelligence."[31] The final scenario is that of a "madhouse at full moon," the inevitable destination of the American dream. There, the basket that had contained the cobra metamorphoses into the human skull in a dense and complex passage:

> Return again and again
> after favorable prognosis, regrettable alas
> recurrence there amid deviant cries remove
> the trepanned cover from the cranial
>   jar
> dip the vessel deep in the cold moon
>   well
> taste: bile sourest lees the death shriek
>   of Christ's clotted lung
> yes and burgundy there; of the world's hung vine [32]

A procession of psychiatric patients is inexorably woven into Berrigan's tapestry of the American dream so that the demons that are seemingly expunged from the external environment through the efforts of technology return to torment humanity from within the "cranial jar."

Instead of providing relief to the inflamed mind, night merely brings further anxiety, thoughts of death. Suspended like a thread amid these dark musings, though, is the Eliotic image of Christ as the hanged man, a potential brother to those who have also been hung on the world's vine. The images of the vine and of the wine that flows from it combine to offer an alternative to the motifs of suffering and death that attend the hanging symbol. The metamorphoses of the blood that becomes wine and of the cross that becomes a fruitful vine conclude the poem, justifying, from a religious point of view, Berrigan's otherwise depressing journey through the contemporary world. With its unusual and stimulating combinations of images and themes and its archly perceptive narrator *The Dark Night of Resistance* is something of a *tour de force.*

The world to be created out of the modern scene appears in some exuberantly visionary passages in the second half of *The Dark Night of Resistance.* One of the more distinctive and whimsical is about Paradise Park, a pastoral reserve in which those who would live according to ethical norms live a quarantined life, taking as their Edenic emblem a "painting by Blake or Rousseau, of naked lovers."[33] A more complex version of an earthly paradise appears in an absorbing poem with the provisional title: "I Am Not Sure That the Following Is a Visionary Statement: Decide Please for Yourself." Anticipating the work of poets like John Ashbery, Berrigan composed a two-columned poem in which the meaning flows from left to right as well as vertically. Unlike Ashbery's "Litany," however, the two sides of Berrigan's poem are continuous with each other, the result being an interior colloquy in which the speaker engages in a yin/yang dialogue with himself. The yin/yang design is yet another variation on the light/dark motif, in this case a study of the darkness that is said to be a "deliberate blindness" imposed by God.[34] The darkness is test of the disciple's faithfulness, a regime of suffering leading gradually to the light of wisdom.

The poem's primary symbols are the bird and the flower, which are associated with both the Christian and Buddhist traditions, and both are linked to the male/female intertwining that is part of the yin/yang motif in Chinese philosophy. As the poem moves toward its bifurcated conclusion, the figures of Jesus and Buddha slowly emerge and intertwine:

> the hands of Jesus while
> time endures wide apart
> the forced wracking
>   of the cross alienation
>
>   anomie agony
>
> the hands of Buddha
>   more gently disposed
>
>   resting apart
>
> the distance between them
> measuring
>
>   the millennial patience
>   of that lotus
>   bud and bloom [35]

While the images depict the active suffering of Christ in contrast to the contemplative serenity of Buddha, the dominant effect of the passage is to point up the universal character of the spiritual world lying beneath the patchwork of separate cultures and states.

In both conception and execution the poem is a dazzling exhibition of an imagination at the peak of its powers. Moreover, it encapsulates the larger dualism that governs the shape of *The Dark Night of Resistance*, which alternates between commentary and dream. In this respect Berrigan intended to follow the method of St. John of the Cross, which he described as "rational and coherent, but whose content is also, and from another point of view, surreal, nightmarish."[36] Above the surface movement created by this alternation, however, is the lodestar of the book's central theme of darkness, the darkness inhabited by a restless mind at odds with its traditions on the one hand and in sublime possession of those traditions on the other. In the final analysis the religion that had in part contributed to the spiritual impasse faced by modern man would also be, Berrigan believed, the force that would allow that impasse to be overcome.

From August, 1970, to February, 1972, Berrigan was incarcerated in the medium-security federal prison in Danbury, Connecticut, about sixty miles from New York City. The large cement building sat atop a hill surrounded by a hundred acres of treeless expanse, a no-man's land that separated the prison from the rest of society. Although the prison was designated a medium-security institution, it did not house violent offenders. At first Berrigan was put into a windowless room that was part of a long block that opened in front to the noise emanating from the tiers of cells at all hours of the day and night. The lack of privacy and the din were a shock to Berrigan's nervous system, a situation that was only slightly relieved by walks in the enclosed prison yard. Nevertheless, the yard nourished his sensibility, so that he could write to his mother in the spring of 1971 about the "beautiful crocuses in the yard that nod away in the wind," a "kind of beauty that bows before harsh weather and comes up smiling."[37]

Things improved after a few months when he was moved into one of the honor houses equipped with individual cells, which contained windows that overlooked the prison yard where the two Berrigan brothers could meet at the end of the work day. Philip had been assigned to the library while Daniel was made an assistant in the dental clinic, though in the final months of his sentence he too worked in Danbury's sadly neglected library. Prisoners were permitted only five hours of visiting time each month so that they had to endure long periods of blankness. Using carved erasers, Berrigan spent part of his time stencilling what would become water-color designs on letters to his friends - tulips, phoenixes, fish, trees in full foliage, images whose brightness belied the drabness of prison life. Both Daniel and Philip, who lived in different prison houses, began small discussion groups in order to offset the numbing effects of imprisonment. The groups were designed not to offer therapy but rather to enlarge the intellectual and spiritual experience of the prisoners, and Berrigan approached these sessions with the same degree of intellectual seriousness that he had brought to his classes at Cornell. The range of authors studied was considerable, and included Gandhi, Swift, Locke, Socrates, St. Matthew, Pascal, and Rousseau, as well as contemporary writers who analyzed American culture from a non-violent point of view.

During the year and a half he spent in prison, Berrigan kept a remarkable journal, which was subsequently published in 1974 under the title *Lights On in the House of the Dead*. His immediate reason for keeping the journal, he confided, had been to guard his sanity.[38] A further, more problematic motivation lay in his sense that many would ask him what the days of incarceration had been like and that he would be unable to tell them: "It has to be tasted; like aloes, like brimstone, like the taste of the needle of death - loneliness plunged to the hilt, the taste of common desolation, the punishment that seeps about like the smell of a Dickens graveyard."[39]

Beginning his journal with a rumination on Socrates' ill-fated relationship with the state, Berrigan initiates a Socratic dialogue in which he poses the question as to whether or not the just man can survive in the state, concluding blandly: "He ought not to care."[40] Drawing the title of his journal from Dostoevski's account of his life in a penal colony, Berrigan includes reflections about prison life as a house of the dead. Gradually overcome within prison by a feeling of stasis, he pictures himself "like a rat in a drainpipe, unable to go backward or forward."[41] The sensory impact of prison life, particularly in the first few months, was stupefying: "I live twenty-four hours a day, in a cage with rutting jackdaws, all of them pitifully drenched in every avenue, ingress, egress, and dead end of sex."[42]

Within the mausoleum of the prison, which was constantly illuminated by artificial lighting, day became indistinguishable from night, and the most tangible signs of life were those of pain - gout, an ulcer, and a continual state of enervation that left Berrigan feeling like a "shell without its snail."[43] A mood of acedia pervades the journal, varied only by minute, textural variations and fine differences in shading. At times the mind divides from the rest of the self so that Berrigan feels that he is living with a "dying relative or friend."[44] On another occasion he succumbs to the hopelessness induced by the prison routine, a "sort of black necessity whirring away at the edge of consciousness like bat wings" that "seizes the heart like a physician of the dead."[45] The images reveal poignantly that Berrigan's consciousness of the sources of his acedia provided little defense against it.

There are moments, however, when the spirit rallies as can be seen in the undercurrent of black humor that enlivens some otherwise melancholy episodes:

> Life around here is dead as a dog's jawbone, long buried. Officially speaking, that is. That bone may have bayed at the moon, turned up its burning eyes in a seasonal love howl, ground member to member in ecstasy of a small kill, a fight. No matter; you turn it up with a spade in the spring - dead, calcified, grimacing, jeweled like a Neanderthal necklace with its row of rotting studs.[46]

If Berrigan had meditated poetically about the dark night of the soul while he was living underground, the image acquired a painful, literal significance in prison: "I was so shot full of pain, cortisone, weakness, and malaise of spirit that I wept tonight for some fifteen minutes, calling upon an absent one, so near a nobody as to be no relief, no opposite number to the *horror vacui.*"[47] Saying mass in the chaplain's office with his brother, Philip, (they were not permitted by the prison authorities to celebrate mass in public), Berrigan found on one occasion that he could not "scrape together a single thought - whether of acceptance, aversion, hope, response," describing himself as a "vertical corpse," taking the bread and wine, "empty as a plank, dry as a stone."[48]

In January, 1971, J. Edgar Hoover, who had been angered by Berrigan's eluding of the F.B.I. during the preceding spring and summer, moved to indict the Berrigans and five others for conspiring to kidnap a high government official (thought to be Henry Kissinger) and with passing contraband in and out of a federal prison. Absurd as the charges were, they brought Berrigan to the brink of the void. In May, the indictment against himself was stayed while the government proceeded against Philip and Sister Elizabeth McAlister on a lesser charge of moving contraband in and out of the prison. The contraband comprised love letters that the two had ill-fatedly exchanged through the informer, Boyd Douglas.[49]

Some of the darkest patches in *Lights On in the House of the Dead* appear early in the book when Berrigan was most disoriented and bewildered about the direction in which God seemed to be leading him. His anguish arose from a sense that he would "die under the knouts here, with nothing accomplished." [50] The nadir of Berrigan's psychological free fall in the early months of prison life was his recognition that his own ordeal might after all be of little apparent use to others. Major, contrasting, thematic motifs in

Lights On in the House of the Dead are the fading light of hope within Berrigan, which is polarized with the prison glare without, and a mounting anger within, which is set off against the grey weight of institutionalism from without. A focus of this anger is the Catholic chaplain, a priest whose freedom - in contrast to Berrigan's imprisonment - coexists with his inability and apparent unwillingness to perform the spiritual work that Berrigan felt prevented from carrying out. The chaplain, a comfortable, paid employee of the state is dismissed acidly by Berrigan as a "savior gone to seed."[51] Here, as elsewhere, Berrigan's salty depiction of prison life quickens sections of the narrative that are otherwise sunk in oppressiveness.

In reflecting on his experience in prison some years later, Berrigan observed that the society of inmates was as stratified as that beyond the prison walls, a fact of life tacitly recognized by the guards and prison officials. Furthermore, through bribery, those at the top - whom Berrigan dubs "entrepreneurs on ice" - were able to procure illicit goods and pleasures, nourished by money that "purred elegantly into the visitors parking lot" where it "dismounted in furs and furbelows. The molls announced themselves at the gates like silly chatelaines of a castle long gone to ruin."[52] Thus, one of the more ironic motifs in *Lights On in the House of the Dead* is that of the prison as a symbol of the American dream, a novel approach to an old theme.

Berrigan portrays his fellow inmates as devotees who worshipped the American dream too well, even in prison longing to return to the "spoiled playground" of American society.[53] In turn, Danbury is described as a "pop prison" with its hall of mirrors, snack bars, comfort stops, newsstands, and "functionaries who lock and unlock the future, the present, the past, the prestigitators of release, opening again the can of culture for the dislocated."[54] Berrigan's discovery that the inmates were treated to salacious films during recreation hours cemented his belief that the prison, which had initially appeared so distinct from the life he had lived outside, was in fact a microcosm of the larger culture.

Polarized with the thematic filaments of the American dream are the strains of an earlier idealism - as in the case of the ex-seminarian addict whose dream of communal living dimly recalled the experiments in communal living by the American transcendentalists of the nineteenth century, whose writings had stood against the greed of "the gargantuans, the slave traders and robber barons."[55] Berrigan's consciousness of his continuity with the American transcendentalists is ubiquitous in his journal. Scribbling late at night in his cell, for example, he described contemporary America as "becalmed and rotting like a Liberty scow,/lashed to the Hudson pier; rats, rotting, the captain mad/or drunk," imagery that recalls both Thoreau and Melville.[56]

The fulcrum of the various lines of imagery in *Lights On in the House of the Dead* is the motif of absurdity, a motif which is flecked ambiguously with both dark and light elements: "If he is a political prisoner," Berrigan noted, the inmate had to live with a double absurdity, with his "act of criminal virtue," and with the "impossibility of purging himself from virtue as though it were vice."[57] The sense of the absurd reaches its zenith in an incident that occurred in June, 1971, at which time Berrigan nearly lost his life after suffering an allergic reaction to an anesthetic while in the dentist's chair. Describing himself in retrospect as having struggled like a "blue baby" for the better part of an hour, he recalls looking up from where he lay into the "impassive spider face of a crawling wall clock," aware in a passive manner of how long it took his life to "keep unskeining." Even a few hours after resuming breathing, Berrigan thought of the crisis as a "curiously secular event."[58]

Berrigan's absurdist scrape with death forms the dramatic center of *Lights On in the House of the Dead* with the tide of darkness leading up to it and the pale light of equilibrium flowing from it, a light founded upon the "equanimity and surplus with which I was able to face death."[59] Reinforcing the mood of a turning toward life are images of nature's tenacity, as in the two small, barren, December trees that held a "weightless burden of sparrows."[60] In a similar vein, in late February, 1971, Berrigan recorded the following scene:

> I can see from my window, at dawn and dusk, a single struggling maple, taking on its changed form of spring. The sparrows cling to it noisily. Today being Saturday (no work) I was able to stand beneath it; on each bow a tiny hand and fingers were sprouting; the buds had opened, their inhumanly delicate colors, from green to pink and white, were drinking the light. From a distance, the tree seemed to stand in an anchored cloud, somewhere between a gossamer and a sigh of acceptance.[61]

While the "inhumanly delicate colors" pointed to the breathtaking otherness of nature, it was nature's anthropomorphism, captured in the image of the tiny hand and fingers, that rallied Berrigan's spirit. At the same time, the persistent order of nature was reassuring in its very distinctness from man, a parallel ecosystem going about its own affairs that kept alive in Berrigan the reality of alternatives at a time when the weight of enforced uniformity was crushing.

One of the most pronounced symbols in *Lights On in the House of the Dead* is that of the monk. The prisoner, Berrigan observed, was a "monk without portfolio," required to be "patient, chaste, poor, obedient, industrious" in service to the state, which received his vows with "bloody hands."[62] Noting that his fellow inmates wore a common garb, ate the same food, and lived under a common discipline, he added that they were also as isolated as Trappist monks. The branching of this conception can be felt throughout the journal, often in modestly positive contexts: "We have only a few simple obligations here; among which must be counted cheerfulness, tolerance, the will to survive, the *conversio morum* of the monks."[63] Berrigan became conscious of assuming the role that Merton had played in their relationship so that the assuming of the cowl within prison walls, even if only metaphorically and somewhat wryly, had become at some level a source of comfort.

Considering the circumstances surrounding its composition, *Lights On in the House of the Dead* has a remarkable stylistic vitality. Berrigan's forte in his prison journal is his command of irony, the result of a recurring inner collision between a vehement idealism and a tireless skepticism. The following description of the scene outside of his cell in early spring is a representative example: "Snowing rapaciously outside, peaceful as December inside."[64] The initial expectation of a contrast between outer cold and inner warmth is neatly undercut by the lifeless image of an interior December, a sudden revelation of the moment's underlying bitterness. The passage, which again plays on the theme of a disparity between outer and inner worlds, has the sort of cutting irony that marks it as vintage Berrigan.

Aphoristic paradoxes abound. Time, for example, is depicted as at the "mercy of Eternity."[65] God, on the other hand, is portrayed as "at the mercy of men."[66] A more sardonic example is: "Come to prison, nothing less will satisfy the heart of a man who wants winds of surprise blowing into his soul."[67] The disorientation of prison life contributed to the making of aphorisms rather than to the composing of more sustained reflections. Nevertheless, amid the procession of fragmented thoughts and images in *Lights*

On in the House of the Dead, there emerges the powerful, cumulative narrative of a hungry consciousness determined to scour its grey surroundings in search of meaning and, not infrequently, finding it.

A collection of Berrigan's essays and letters entitled *America Is Hard to Find* (1972), which was put together by his brother, Jerome, while Daniel was still in Danbury, is an uneven book. Polemical in tone, the writing tends to be turgid at times. Such lapses are certainly evident in the letters, not only in those sent home, but also in the public letters to the Weathermen, to the judge who presided over the trial of the Catonsville Nine, and to J. Edgar Hoover. One notices a greater coarseness in both thought and phrasing as Berrigan adjusted his discourse to a much wider audience than he had been accustomed to addressing, and the results of this were predictable in an aesthetic sense even if the writing seemed authenticated by its moral purpose at the time.

One of the exceptions is an essay entitled "The New Man: The Compleat Soldier," which appeared originally in the *Saturday Review* and which dealt with a painful incident that occurred in the Vietnam war. The incident, which Berrigan came across in Daniel Lang's *Casualties of War,* involved a small group of American soldiers who raped and murdered a young woman chosen at random. During the court martial that followed, one of the soldiers admitted to having taken the woman into the bush, where he killed her with his hunting knife, an act that he described as like gutting a deer. Berrigan's response was unexpectedly dispassionate: "Every study of guilt is also a study of innocence."[68]

The focus of Berrigan's attention in the essay is on the one soldier who refused to take part in the rape and murder and who later reported the incident to the authorities:

> He is the near-hero, the near-saint cast up by the
> times, the best we have, gifted with that bare
> minimum of imagination and nerve to see him
> through, a whole skin, something of a whole
> conscience. . . . No war resister he, no great
> questioner, neither mystic, intellectual, nor saint,
> not gifted enough to snatch a girl from violation or
> death. Not heroic enough to die rather than allow a
> crime to proceed to its foul and bloody closure.[69]

For Berrigan the soldier's moral status as a near-hero was
symptomatic of the fatal meekness he believed pervaded the idea of
virtue in modern society.

For this reason he wrote a memorable essay about Dietrich
Bonhoeffer, the Protestant clergyman who had been imprisoned
and hanged for his resistance to Hitler. Reflecting on Bonhoeffer's
and to some extent on his own abandonment of meekness, Berrigan
observed that the "theologian must yet become a Christian, and
after that a contemporary," a process that would turn the "seams of
his mind inside out."[70] Moreover, for Berrigan there was a curious
design, a similitude between Bonhoeffer and Hitler that illuminated
one of the entrenched ironies of history. He outlined the pattern of
Bonhoeffer's fate as the convergence between a tyrant "clever as
only a madman" can be and a recalcitrant resister who was
possessed by a "contrary madness," the two of them channelled by
circumstance - the "tacky wind of chance and mischance."[71] The
word 'tacky' is adroit, a pun on the uncertainty of alternating winds
as well as an expression of contempt for the mindless potency of
chance. As Berrigan's faith in the leadership of both church and
state sank to new lows in the early 1970s, he saw the need for
moral models as greater than ever. What he sought was the

example of people like Bonhoeffer, who, by "imagining the future," helped to "create" it.[72]

While in prison Berrigan read a good deal of poetry, including books by Hart Crane, Gary Snyder, Kenneth Rexroth, Robinson Jeffers, and Emily Dickinson, all poets with whom he felt some affinity. While he believed that poetry was the "primary inevitable response to tyranny," he was puzzled by the way in which the poetry of some writers was at such apparent variance with their lives.[73] Reading Lawrance Thompson's biography of Robert Frost, for example, he was struck with how some of the ugly particulars of the poet's life and character had been transmuted into a "good and great thing for others." Perhaps the poetry, he considered, had been Frost's "salvation," the only way "out of the shell."[74] Berrigan's view that the process of art with its high demand for concentration might serve as a crucible in which the personality of the artist could, even if only temporarily, become morally purified, helped to reaffirm the value of art in his life when he was otherwise preoccupied with social activism.

The new poems in *Selected and New Poems* (1973) are shards of time stretching back to the late sixties, barely rescued moments in a life that was in a process of high acceleration. For this reason they are especially remarkable for their sharply realized clarity and composure. An example is the poem, "Flew to New York," in which Berrigan recounts a furtive trip to the city to perform a baptism, even though his movements at the time had been restricted by a federal prosecutor. Stopping briefly at his apartment, he finds a note and a spring flower left by a friend:

So took up the flower, common as our fate,
tomorrow's
discard. Filled a stem glass,
placed the flower, a prima donna, in a box seat.

> Let tomorrow wane. The flower
> blooms like Tolstoi's ripe riposte,
>   her naked shoulders
> taking time in stride,
>   one white wing, then another.[75]

Through the use of irregular spacing in the final lines Berrigan generates an image of lift-off that was sufficient to raise his own leaden spirit in the period prior to his imprisonment.

In their visual arrangement the poems reflect a freedom and movement that matched the pace of Berrigan's life. In "Autumn, the Streams Are Heavy," for instance, the confluence of rain from above and water from the Cornell gorges below gave rise to the following startling, stanzaic configuration:

> sudden
>
> air   water
>
> conjoin [76]

The emphasis on spacing and movement reflected not simply Berrigan's attraction to open-form poetry but also the fact that he had begun to formulate a theology of movement. In commenting on Pasolini's film, *The Gospel of St. Matthew*, for example, he noted that, as opposed to most sacred art, Jesus was portrayed as "always in motion," thereby epitomizing the kinetic quality inherent in life itself, a "forward movement of awareness, of consciousness, of love" in which the followers of Christ cannot "remain static and hope to grasp what He is about."[77]

During the Cornell years it was inevitable that Berrigan would deal with the university as a poetic subject, and this he does in a sensitive and densely structured poem entitled "The Gorges." Employing the central symbols of water, sun, and light, Berrigan posits absolutes of wisdom both above the earth - where God is pictured in the Greek style as a "waylaying cloud above/waters he struck open" - and below in the still pools of the gorges, whose "cold, untouchable wisdom" is unvisited by the passing sun. The sun, the active principle in the poem, symbolizes the diurnal world of consciousness, which is fertilized by the university - "intelligence, panoply of artists,/genius, entelechy."[78] While bracing and exciting, the intellectual ferment associated with the university is nonetheless depicted as subject to the alternating laws of thermodynamics, which are represented in the poem by the piling of stone upon stone - the venerable university buildings themselves - and by the entropic falling away of water - the cataracts that fed the gorges beneath Cornell.

The speaker in the poem feels himself to be a link between the kinetic world of intellectual endeavor associated with the campus and the ontological pools of absolute wisdom associated with the gorges. He passes through the landscape like a nocturnal animal, moving in "footless" silence over the gorge bridge. The bridge is softly illuminated by the moon, as opposed to the harsh, dissecting light of the sun, which is visualized at one point - in an image that recalls Thoreau - as an axe, a symbol of the shallower and more portentous cerebral activity within the university in its professional and competitive phase. In part the poem mirrors Berrigan's consciousness of his distinctive role at the university, his calling attention to the deeper pools of wisdom that could easily go unobserved amid the burgeoning of ideas within that community. In its elaborate and meticulous interweaving of motifs "The Gorges" is one of Berrigan's most finely crafted poems.

Included in the *Selected and New Poems* was a group of elegiac poems written in tribute to Thomas Merton, the best of which is "Who's Who at the Obsequies." The poem focuses on the relative invisibility of Merton's passing, in contrast to the pomp surrounding the death of Cardinal Spellman, who unlike Merton had supported the Vietnam War and whose funeral was attended by a host of dignitaries, including President Johnson. Present at Merton's funeral in contrast were -

> the shadowed, submerged
> upon whom Kafka's needles
> bear down, write large
> the cuneiform of loss -

> were there. And the four
> ministering spirits of these;
> earth, water, fire, air.[79]

The elemental images of the final lines link the mourners with nature - as was Merton himself as monastic, unaccommodated man.

An elegiac poem about Berrigan's father recalls the death watch kept by his son, who, leaning over his father's bed and "breathing for you/all that night long," became conscious of another watching, the two of them thus "shadows over a fish tank." Then, unexpectedly, the dying man metamorphosed from a "fish" into a "father" before his eyes.[80] Memories of the living father flood the son's consciousness as he stands watch, so that he is able to mentally reconstitute the depleted figure in the bed. Nevertheless, Berrigan's ambivalence about his father provides the poem with some dramatic, unresolved tensions:

> your skinny face puffed out
> yellow as a mandarin's
> your mouth pursed
> your head rolled slightly aside
> (a fallen fruit under a shift of frost.)[81]

The caricature reflects not only the ugliness of death but the harbored, lifelong resentment of the son toward the father. The tone softens, however, in the final parenthetical line with its delicate autumnal images and sibilant sounds.

One commentator aptly characterized the *Selected and New Poems* as "poetry as public record."[82] Of the poems devoted to social themes in the *Selected and New Poems*, "River," written during the months when Berrigan was a fugitive, is one of the most effective. Divided into symmetrical sections, the poem begins with a pastoral scene that appears to uphold the neoplatonic union of the true, the good, and the beautiful:

> My little friend a flutist sits far side of the river
> one knee drawn up, accoutred like Pan.
> Past him and me, cries of the oarsmen, knifing prows
>   shells headlong as hounds.
> Over his head a natural outcropping,
> willow fronds leap as though music were natural
>   urgings, spark in the vein.[83]

Conceding that appearances were against him, the speaker discloses a disturbing, underlying contradiction in the scene. The flutist is not what he seems:

> He plays on a human thigh bone veined with blood.
> There is blood in his hands, venery and stealth in
>   eyes.
> Nine-tenths of the somnolent sun-gazers at ease
>   here
>   will, truth known,
>   hand me over to judgment.
> The big flag above, all but blots out the sun.

A folly. A whore's hips.
The mercy I grasp is
  only partially to grasp
  this noon nightmare,
nightshade held to my lips.[84]

The allusion to nightshade, like the neoplatonism evoked in the poem, recalls Keats. Here, the image is linked to the contrast of night and day in order to evoke the dual themes of blindness and poison, both associated with misplaced patriotism. At the same time the speaker only partially feels the evil before him due to the heightened, compensatory beauty of the scene, again a Keatsian moment. Otherwise, the perception that ordinary, good people could be transformed into monsters by nationalistic fervor (the flag that all but blots out the sun) is a thought that brings Berrigan to his knees. Thus, through poetic metamorphosis, the picture of the preternaturally innocent Pan and his flute degenerates into a scene of "blood" and "venery." With its sophisticated parodying of the conventions of the idyll and its subtle interlacing of images, the poem ranks among Berrigan's best.

Included in the *Selected and New Poems* are lyrics written hurriedly during the trial of the Catonsville Nine, while Berrigan was in a Baltimore jail. The poems were transcribed by fellow prisoner and artist, Thomas Lewis, who then smuggled the sheets out of the prison.[85] The trial poems are suffused with apprehensiveness, exposing Berrigan's private anxiety even while his public pronouncements urged his supporters to surround the trial with vigorous opposition to the timidity of the courts in dealing with the Vietnam war. In the darkness of his cell, for example, he pictured himself as a caged animal by day and an animal preyed upon at night as the moon "striped like a tiger/leaps on us with a cry."[86] Fear reaches its apogee in "The Marshal:"

> I will wear khaki (he grins) and love it
> for years and years
> and play
> night and day
> cops and robbers;
> in dreams, for years
> will scramble the wall like a spider,
> > > fall
> > piecemeal,
> > into my savior's throttling arms.[87]

The Kafkaesque mood of the poem, unsettlingly present in the image of the spider, reaches its climax with the picture of Berrigan as "piecemeal," literally rent into pieces psychologically.

In one of the poems associated with the Catonsville trial, the burning of the military draft files is linked explicitly with Berrigan's earlier trip to Hanoi, a recognition that occurs as the burnt pile of draft documents, the "size of infant caskets," is wheeled into the courtroom. The perception lingers as the speaker, having conflated the images of the charred papers and the scorched Vietnamese children, has a vision of "blackened hands beating/the box of death for breath."[88] The repetition of hard consonants reveals an underlying voltage of anger that acts as a counterpoint in these trial poems to the speaker's pervasive fear and anxiety.

In September, 1972, Berrigan wrote to his friend and fellow protester, Thomas Lewis, that he had broken with Doubleday and that his *Prison Poems* (1973) would be published by a "small resisting press in Santa Barbara."[89] The switch from large to small publishers, which was based on Berrigan's objection to the moral insensitivity of multinational corporations with diverse interests, had a considerable effect on his impact as a writer. From the 1970s to the early 1980s, small publishers often failed to market his books effectively, and as a result there was a shrinkage in both reviews and book sales. In recent years he has returned to a major publisher, Harper & Row, having been reassured about that company's activities.

The conditions under which Berrigan wrote the *Prison Poems* were obviously far from optimal, as he revealed in a sonnet in which he described himself as scribbling lines with difficulty, "lights out, at a barred window./Snow filigrees the April green."[90] The poems, which are tinted by the grey walls of Danbury, give one a convincing impression of the abrasiveness of prison routine. What stands out overall is Berrigan's numbing sense of helplessness, which is particularly acute in his bitter consciousness that the only way prisoners could overcome the lethargy of their days was by going to the prison workshops, which ironically produced cable assemblies for missiles.

Berrigan's candor strengthens the prison poems by bringing out some of the underlying ambiguities of his situation. The sense of alienation he sometimes instinctively felt toward many of his fellow inmates, for example, undercut his hopes for kindling a sense of community within the prison walls:

In the dark movie house
they curse and scream like tartars. Come back
2, 3 times, to snatch
like sticky children,
bobbing big balloons
that wear
smaller balloons in privy places.
They steal food like raping crows.
They steal clothing. They steal
like lice on carrion, blood.
They do not honor the Lord thy God on Sunday

beseemingly. No; snore; fart, turn like stoats
on a picnic spit,
believe in eye-for-an-eye-for-an-eye, would strike
if could, world blind as a crater.[91]

Polarized with the atmosphere of incipient violence in the *Prison Poems* is an entrenched mood of apathy and hopelessness, perceptible, for example, in a poem in which Berrigan reflects on the suicide of a man in the prison hospital. The fact that the suicide took place in prison imbued it in Berrigan's eyes with a note of achievement, a consummation of a collective death wish. The note of dismay in the marrow of these poems is further intensified by the mechanical behaviour of the prison's administrators, "a crowded car-load/of expertise" that "disgorges each A.M./in the compound/running like beetles/each 2 his bureau/briefcases bulging/foreheads furrowed."[92]

While Berrigan believed that the dental and library work which he and his brother performed within the prison was useful, the poems capture the affective dimension of that experience, the disorientation between mind and feeling:

I stand at the dentist's chair
hosing down
the havoc of the pincers
slow   slow
then a wider arc
he draws
the newborn tooth into light of day
Another day
another bloody day
root limb blind as bone
stillborn as a tooth.[93]

One notices an increased freedom in spacing and in the use of sound in comparison with the early poetry. The delayed words in the stanza, together with the harsh consonants, reinforce the bleak imagery and emphasize the painfully slow passage of time.

The sight of nature in these prison surroundings inevitably exposed the buried life. In "Tulips in the Prison Yard," for example, Berrigan wistfully compares his response to the flowers with that of the great Romantic poets: "Yeats, Wordsworth would look once/breathe deeply, sharpen their quills/with a flourish pluck you from time."[94] By way of contrast the tulips at Danbury are not a symbol of perennial freedom, but are "jail-yard blooms," born in prison and destined to die there. Moreover, instead of being an emblem of hope, they are perceived as a harbinger of revolution, a "first flicker in the brain's soil,/the precursor/of judgment."[95] The symbolic import of the flowers, then, is not chiefly that they offer an escape from the dun enclosure of prison but rather that they reveal that even there life could be transformed.

Such a transformation was not to be readily accomplished, however, as can be seen in a long poem reminiscent of Whitman entitled "A Hermit Thrush in Autumn, Over the Wall." In the poem the poignant song of a hermit thrush, unseen beyond the prison wall, elevates the listener's feelings and senses, the music skeining "out & over the wall/like the unwinding/of gold foil from a sage's/ mouth"[96] While many of the Romantic conventions are observed in the poem, these conventions are finally rejected. As the bird metamorphoses into the innocent figure of "Blake's boy," for example, there is a final, devastating change as the boy turns into a victim raped by a motorcycle gang. In a letter to the author about the poem Berrigan added that "of course we were in prison with some Hell's Angels who were scarcely estimable chaps."[97] The poem's orchestrated clashes of imagery, texture, and mood show Berrigan once again aware of the seductiveness of the Romantic imagination and rejecting transcendental release, finally, in favor of the actualities that all too palpably enveloped him in prison.

At the same time, there were moments when he perceived, if not beauty, then a flickering of the human spirit, as in the inmate who fashioned a tiny, exquisite altar or in the newly arrived prisoner who, though hungry, fatigued, and in need of medication headed straight for the prison library:

> I did a double take.
> In the old monastery days the gyrovague monk, on
> > return
> from excursion beyond cloister
> always visited the chapel first, before even
> seeking the abbot's blessing.
> First things first.
> . . . a rare elixir
> of the servant sovereign mind
> even as behind one, time and its termites
> consume bestially.[98]

The image of the "servant sovereign mind" represents an attempt to modulate the celebration of consciousness, to insist on the mind's indissoluble fealty to time while marveling at its occasional ascendancy.

Also opposed to the death of the heart in Berrigan's *Prison Poems* is the stream of images carried by memory, although not all of these images are consoling - as can be seen in the recollection of a dinner in the 1960s attended by the U.S. Secretary of Defense and his wife:

> . . . her husband less admired
> a cost product expert hair slick as a beaver's

cold eyes instantly contracting to
the fleering public glare
              expanding
in the subterranean
warrens where he like a children's
animal tail
              disappeared around
this or that pentagonal corner.[99]

The playful image of the "children's animal tail," an extension of
the beaver metaphor, contrasts the benevolent attitude of the
Defense Secretary with the destruction of children in Vietnam, a
consequence of policies carried out by the Secretary. The metaphor
of the animal tail to describe the elusiveness of politicians refers
not only to their duplicity but to the superficial outlook of those for
whom politics, even when the lives of thousands hang in the
balance, is a but a game or a competition.

     More nourishing memories are to be found in "My Father,"
a long, cumulative poem that includes sections from earlier poems
on the same subject.[100] While the theme of his father's lovelessness
darkens the poem, Berrigan rediscovers in the memory of his father
a tenacity that is his own most pressing need. Over the twelve
sections of the poem he attempts to retrieve the presence of his
father, a large, unresolved force in his life, now potentially
intelligible for the first time in death. Recalling his father's first
scrape with death in 1962, for example, Berrigan is struck by the
old man's command of himself:

He lay there weak as childhood.
They were filling him, an old sack,
with new wine. He took it darkly.
"When the wheat's ready for harvest,

draw it in," all I remember.
Strong enough behind his milky cat's eyes
to spin a trope about death.[101]

This scene, as well as Berrigan's father's final agony, are heightened in the poem by being set within the frame of Berrigan's own ordeal in prison and by the liturgical echoes of Passion week. The gradual overcoming of feelings of rejection opens the floodgates of memory, generating clusters of images that are gratefully received, recollections of life on the family farm, of freezing drives to town in a Model-T, of an unruly goat whom his father named Ursus before selling it off to "metamorphose in paschal stew."

A central symbol in the poem is the firebird or phoenix, which is ostensibly associated with Philip Berrigan but which also comes to represent, by a process of indirection, the fire of all the Berrigans. The phoenix also symbolizes the role of memory in the poem, evoking a feeling of rebirth amidst the taste of ashes. The motif is particularly effective because the phoenix was said to have flown shortly after rebirth to the temple of Heliopolis with the body of its father, which, coated with myrrh, was piously buried there. Although the pattern of memory and rebirth is familiar enough to readers of Romantic poetry, the emphasis here is not on the ecstasy of vision but on moral resolution - the relief that followed the plucking of anger from the heart. Similarly, the poem does not portray the transcending of human relationships but rather the restoring of them.

As in a number of Berrigan's prison poems the structure of "My Father" is rather diffuse. The emotional logic of the collection as a whole gradually emerges, however, even in the long poem about Berrigan's father. If venturing into the painful past yielded the tenuous perception that God's will could be seen in the

Berrigan family history, then presumably God's will was still present in Berrigan's life, even if not altogether manifest. Hence, in a poem about prayer, Berrigan sees the direction of his life as contingent upon a struggle to align his will with God's, a struggle that he describes as "mutually, ritually wounding."[103]

Although Berrigan opened up fresh areas of experience and feeling in *Prison Poems*, the writing shows obvious signs of attrition. From the standpoint of craftsmanship the poems are sometimes desultory and uneven in detail even when their themes and motifs are powerful and moving, as is the case with the poem dedicated to Berrigan's father. As opposed to a journal like *Lights On in the House of the Dead*, where a certain amount of unevenness is to be expected and even adds to the impression of naturalness and immediacy, poetry, particularly lyric poetry, requires a more rigorous and sustained workmanship.

In the poems of the late 1960s Berrigan had demonstrated that topical political and religious themes could occupy an integral place in contemporary poetry without necessarily producing an awkward didacticism. In an essay entitled "Responsibilities of the Poet," Robert Pinsky has argued that while there perhaps should be more contemporary poems devoted to topical social and political themes, nevertheless the poet must turn these materials into art.[104] In the most successful of Berrigan's poems and prose writings composed between 1968 and 1972, ideas and images do not exist as independent materials, but are transformed into art in a suspended solution of thought, feeling, and linguistic form. At the same time, some of the prison poems, not unlike some of the prose pieces in *America Is Hard to Find*, are a disappointment, and illustrate the toll which Berrigan's involvement in social activism finally began to take on his writing.

Notes: Chapter Four

1. William Buckley, Jr., "On the Right," *Ithaca Journal*, Aug. 13, 1970, 7.
2. See Gordon Zahn, "Original Child Monk: An Appreciation," *Thomas Merton: The Nonviolent Alternative*, ed. Gordon Zahn (New York: Farrar, Straus, Giroux, c1971, 1980) xxxvii-xxxviii.
3. *The Geography of Faith* (Boston: Beacon Pr., 1971) 42.
4. "Dan Berrigan with Families in the Underground," *The Berrigans*, ed. William Van Etten Casey, S.J. (New York: Praeger, 1971) 194.
5. *The Dark Night of Resistance* (New York: Doubleday, 1971) 1.
6. *Dark Night* 86-87.
7. *To Dwell in Peace* (San Francisco: Harper & Row, 1987) 251.
8. *Dark Night* 79.
9. *Dark Night* 80.
10. *Dark Night* 84.
11. *Dark Night* 84-85.
12. *Dark Night* 11, 42.
13. *Dark Night* 10-11.
14. *Dark Night* 3.
15. Ibid.
16. *Dark Night* 166.
17. *Dark Night* 17.
18. *Dark Night* 93.
19. *Dark Night* 35.
20. *Dark Night* 141.
21. *Dark Night* 27.
22. *Dark Night* 94.
23. *Dark Night* 123.
24. *Dark Night* 126.

25. *Dark Night* 56-57.
26. *"Now If You Will Please in This Darkness Choose Your Image of the World Inhabit It Walk Within It Peaceably or Run Like Hell The Other Way," Dark Night* 62-63.
27. Ibid. 63.
28. Ibid. 64.
29. Ibid. 64.
30. Ibid. 65.
31. Ibid. 65.
32. Ibid. 66.
33. *Dark Night* 130.
34. "I Am Not Even Sure That the Following Is a Visionary Statement: Decide Please for Yourself," *Dark Night* 133.
35. Ibid. 135.
36. *Dark Night* 13-14.
37. Letter from Daniel Berrigan to Frida Berrigan, April 17, 1971.
38. *Lights On in the House of the Dead* (Garden City, N.Y.: Doubleday, 1974) 272.
39. *Lights On* 245.
40. *Lights On* 10.
41. *Lights On* 243.
42. *Lights On* 61-62.
43. *Lights On* 288.
44. *Lights On* 100.
45. *Lights On* 293-294.
46. *Lights On* 207.
47. *Lights On* 243.
48. *Lights On* 128.
49. For a detailed account of the Harrisburg conspiracy trial see John C. Raines, *Conspiracy: the Implications of the Harrisburg Trial for the Democratic Tradition* (New York: Harper and Row, 1974).
50. *Lights On* 11.

51. *Lights On* 197.
52. *To Dwell in Peace* 263.
53. *Lights On* 16.
54. *Lights On* 99.
55. *Lights On* 30.
56. *Lights On* 214.
57. *Lights On* 289-290.
58. *Lights On* 219-220.
59. *Lights On* 224.
60. *Lights On* 284.
61. *Lights On* 151.
62. *Lights On* 170.
63. *Lights On* 100.
64. *Lights On* 201.
65. *Lights On* 261.
66. *Lights On* 279.
67. *Lights On* 286.
68. *America Is Hard to Find* (New York: Doubleday, 1972) 23.
69. *America* 28.
70. *America* 40.
71. *America* 40.
72. *America* 45.
73. *Dark Night* 8.
74. *America* 162.
75. *Selected and New Poems* (Garden City, N.Y.: Doubleday, 1973) 257.
76. *Selected* 255.
77. Daniel Berrigan and Thich Nhat Hanh, *The Raft Is Not the Shore* (Boston: Beacon, 1975) 138.
78. "The Gorges," *Selected* 254.
79. "Who's Who at the Obsequies," *Selected* 277.
80. "1879 - My Father - 1969," *Selected* 269.

81. Ibid.

82. Fred Moramarco, "A Gathering of Poets," *Western Humanities Review* 28 (1974) 93.

83. "River," *Selected* 287.

84. Ibid.

85. A limited, facsimile edition of the *Trial Poems* was brought out by Beacon Press in 1970. Due to the scarcity of materials in jail Berrigan wrote the poems with popsicle sticks that had been shaped into pens, using a mixture of india ink and cigarette ashed mixed with water.

86. "A Typical Day in the Municipal Zoo," *Selected* 244.

87. "The Marshal," *Selected* 240.

88. "The Boxes of Paper Ash," *Selected* 246.

89. Letter from Daniel Berrigan to Thomas Lewis, Sept. 29, 1972.

90. "O Danbury, to What Shall I Compare Thee?" *Prison Poems* (Greensboro, N.C.: Unicorn Pr., 1973) 22. Unicorn Press moved from Santa Barbara to Greensboro in the early 1970s.

91. "Prisoners: One Only View," *Prison* 78.

92. "8 O'Clock Morning Scene," *Prison* 28.

93. "A Day's Work in the Clinic," *Prison* 103.

94. "Tulips in the Prison Yard," *Prison* 23.

95. Ibid.

96. "A Hermit Thrush in Autumn, Over the Wall," *Prison* 116-117.

97. Letter from Daniel Berrigan to the author, Feb. 11, 1986.

98. "Billy Bones," *Prison* 30.

99. "Memories, Memories," *Prison* 99. Although he doesn't name the Secretary of Defense in the poem, Berrigan is clearly referring to Robert McNamara, who served as U.S. Secretary of Defense from 1961 to 1968.

100. A section of "1879-My Father-1969" from the *Selected and New Poems*, for example, is included.

101. "My Father," *Prison* 47.

102. Ibid. 54.

103. "This Is About Prayer," *Prison* 101.

104. Robert Pinsky, "Responsibilities of the Poet," *Politics and Poetic Value*, ed. Robert von Hallberg (Chicago and London: Univ. of Chicago Pr., 1987) 9.

Chapter Five

THE NUCLEAR SHADOW

Berrigan's writing from the mid-1970s to the mid-1980s is diverse in both subject matter and quality. Some of the prose and poetry is worthy of only a minimum of attention while other writing is of a high standard. In general, he gradually reasserted his identity as an artist following a somber period in which he appears to have had little interest in art and little appetite for life.

On February 24, 1972, Berrigan was granted parole for reasons of health and on the understanding that he would not engage in any illegal protests over the course of the following year. He joyously recorded the moment of his release in a book of meditations published in 1973 under the title, *Jesus Christ*:

> [I] came out of the chrysalis like a blinking new-born paper-winged flyer, wet around the wingpits, into mid A.M. winter light. People were standing knee deep in snow around the flank of the hill, I don't know how many hundreds. My face dissolved like a snowman's under the assault of that affection.[1]

In March and April of 1972 Berrigan recuperated on Block Island off the coast of Connecticut as the guest of William Stringfellow, the Episcopalian lawyer and author whom he had met in the peace movement in the 1960s. He rested up in a small cottage, set apart from the main house, a retreat that he was to return to gratefully over the years. In May, with the reluctant permission of the U.S. government, he travelled to Paris to meet with representatives of the North Vietnamese government and then went on to Cannes for the screening of his play, *The Trial of the Catonsville Nine*, which was well received.

By August, he was back into the thick of things, flying to Hawaii to testify at the trial of James Douglass and others, who had been arrested for pouring blood on secret files connected with the staging of air raids over Vietnam. He was also fasting in sympathy with prisoners at Danbury who were protesting the war, men whom he described in a letter to a friend as having awakened morally while in prison.[2] He also fasted and demonstrated in order to persuade the judge in the Harrisburg conspiracy trial to hand down a long-awaited sentence so that his brother, Philip, might finally be considered for parole. The sentence came down in September, and Philip received eighteen months, essentially for smuggling love letters in and out of prison. The harshness of the sentence caught Daniel by surprise, and cast a pall over his thoughts in late September, as can be seen in a letter he wrote to friends in which he confided dispiritedly to having proceeded for "many years on the simple basis that faith was better than vision, that service of others was better than consolation."[3] In spite of the closeness of the two brothers the relationship had been tested by Philip's secret marriage to Elizabeth McAlister, a former nun, in the spring of 1969. The union had been formalized in January, 1972, at Danbury, and made public in May, 1973. While the violation of clerical celibacy through marriage was not of itself an issue that troubled Daniel theologically, nevertheless he had been temporarily offended by the secrecy of the marriage.

Although Berrigan renewed his involvement in social activism in the fall of 1972, he had come to believe that the clergy should stay out of party politics. Writing to a fellow Jesuit at the time, he contended that priests had "no business in electoral politics."[4] His belief was that the priest should represent an alternative vision, detached from, and thus not obligated to, any party or government. During the 1970s and 1980s Berrigan would move in and out of short academic appointments, having made a resolution not to accept any teaching appointment for more than one semester, thereby leaving himself free to terminate or interrupt his class schedule for the sake of "civil disobedience and its consequence."[5] In spite of these restrictions Berrigan's correspondence at the time makes it evident that he was in considerable demand as a lecturer and that his income, much of which he distributed to those in need, was quite respectable. In the 1970s he reached an agreement with his Jesuit superiors whereby he became free to dispose of his earnings for the "needs of families in the peace movement," and in return he pledged not to ask his order for financial support.[6] Gradually during the 1970s Berrigan loosened his ties with the hierarchy of his order although he maintained a strong attachment to Jesuit traditions and a firm sense of his identity as a Jesuit priest. All the same, he came to feel that many Jesuits were more committed to the professions in which they had been trained than to their roles as priests: "Jesuits are not called just to humanize professional life," he told an interviewer in 1971, but also to "exercise a Biblical judgment upon it."[7]

This prophetic tone intensified as Berrigan devoted an increasing amount of study to the writings of the French Protestant theologian, Jacques Ellul, in the early 1970s. Ellul, the subject of a course given by Berrigan to both Roman Catholic and Protestant students at the Union Theological Seminary in New York in 1972-73, was not a professional theologian but a Professor of History

and Sociology at the University of Bordeaux and a former member
of the French resistance. In books like *The Political Illusion* Ellul
argued that politics was an enclosed system that was essentially
impervious to external values and ethics, a conclusion that further
reinforced Berrigan's wariness about priests in politics. Ellul also
objected to the widespread view that politics was an all-inclusive
activity, characterizing this belief as a contemporary illusion and
calling for a recognition that the individual was not merely a
product of political and sociological currents but an autonomous
center of decision.[8]

In a study of social violence Ellul maintained that the
Christian faith implied "rejection and condemnation of both revolutionary violence and the violence of the established powers."[9] His
focus on the violence carried out by governments struck a respon-
sive chord in Berrigan as did the French writer's realism, which
Berrigan said helped to dispel the "gaseous" influence of Teilhard
de Chardin.[10] Ellul caused Berrigan to review his sometimes
uncritical support for the left - as he conceded in a letter to James
Forest in the fall of 1972: "I am hyperconscious of late of the
strictures which a man like Ellul puts upon those Christians who
have made a great outcry against murder from the right, but who
have embraced a kind of mindless revolutionary violence, blessing
it if only it proceeds from the untainted left."[11]

Berrigan's misgivings were further underscored by reports
in the *New York Times* and elsewhere of eye witness accounts of
political murders by the North Vietnamese and the Viet Cong. In
1973 he and Philip wrote, unsuccessfully, to the Prime Minister of
North Vietnam to express their concern about the reported torturing
of American prisoners of war.[12] In addition, in 1973 Daniel wrote
an open letter in support of political dissidents in the U.S.S.R.[13]
Skeptical about the activities of governments in both East and
West, he turned increasingly to Christianity as a "kind of third eye"

on events. Turning increasingly as well to scriptural writings rather than to traditional theology for moral direction, he confided to Laraine Fergenson in 1974 that he had "made a break with 'formal' religion no less clean than Thoreau."[14] At the same time he announced, paradoxically, that he longed for the kind of church in which he could be "in full communion."[15] Dissatisfied, however, with current institutional Christianity, Berrigan identified in the 1970s and 1980s with early Christianity, which in his view had been animated largely by its martyrs.

On October 19, 1973, Berrigan flew to Washington, D.C. to address a group of Arab intellectuals living in the U.S., an address that was to have a momentous effect upon his role as a public figure and as a writer.[16] Against the background of the war that had broken out between Israel and a number of Arab states, Berrigan described Israel as a militaristic state that had betrayed the moral traditions of its own prophets and the bitter lessons of its own history in ignoring the plight of homeless Palestinians. He further contended that, although many American Jews had opposed the U.S. involvement in Vietnam, official Jewish leadership in the U.S. chose not to criticize the president publicly so as not to jeopardize American aid to Israel.

While Berrigan's fundamental proposals were moderate and constructive and included a *de facto* acceptance of the existence of Israel, the tone of his speech was inflammatory at times, and he drew adverse reaction in the *New York Times* and in many other influential newspapers and journals that had hitherto been supportive. Although he received some support from Jewish intellectuals like Noam Chomsky,[17] he was soon ostracized by many in the media, which inevitably led to a lessening of the media attention given to public demonstrations he was involved in and a reduction in the number of reviews of his books.

Berrigan conceded to an interviewer in the spring of 1974 that he had painted a one-sided portrait of Israel.[18] As a non-Jew he had done the unthinkable in criticizing both Israel and the American Jewish community, although even one of his severest critics admitted that that community was "far less open" to a debate about Israel than was Israel itself.[19] For his part Berrigan was stung by the charge of anti-semitism, particularly in the light of his friendship with Jewish leaders like Rabbi Abraham Heschel. If he had come down hard on Israel, it was in part due to the fact that his moral expectations about that nation and about the Jewish people exceeded those which he had about some of the Arab states. In some respects one might observe the same sort of judgment at work in connection with his vigorous criticism of the United States throughout the 1960s and 1970s. The immediate effect of the furor created by his address was that the judges of the Gandhi Peace Award, alerted by criticism from the American Jewish Congress, set about reconsidering their decision; Berrigan declined the prize before a vote was announced. A subsequent peace prize was offered in 1974 by the War Resistors League, and Berrigan flew back from Paris to accept it, warmed by the fact that Allen Ginsberg, poet and Jew, was to make the presentation.

Berrigan had been visiting with exiled Vietnamese Buddhists in Paris in the winter of 1974 and in the spring he flew to the Middle East to consider the Palestinian problem at close quarters, talking with political leaders and intellectuals in Israel, Egypt, Syria, and Lebanon. In Lebanon and Syria he met with Palestinian leaders Yasser Arafat and Naif Hawatma, and was assured that in the interest of peace they would not authorize further acts of terrorism. On returning to Israel some days later Berrigan felt betrayed on learning that Hawatma's commandos had struck at a schoolhouse in Galilee, killing a number of Israeli children. At a press conference in Jerusalem he and his traveling

companion, Father Paul Mayer, publicly condemned the raid and
the duplicity of Arafat and Hawatma, but also warned against
Israeli reprisals in the form of the "indiscriminate bombing of
refugee camps," which Berrigan declared would be an "equally
barbarous assault on children and non-combatants."[20] In retrospect,
Berrigan has felt that he helped to open a difficult discussion in
America and that the subsequent Israeli invasion of Lebanon in
1982 served to confirm his worst fears.

He came down on the unpopular side of other publicly
debated issues in the 1970s, and in each case lost the support and
friendship of some. Although he stood firmly for women's rights
both within and beyond his church, for example, his opposition to
abortion as a feminist right led to estrangements with some -
although in time it also attracted support from others. On one
occasion an invitation to speak on a panel about the peace issues at
a small northeastern college was withdrawn when his views about
abortion became known to the organizers. Similarly, his public
support of I.R.A. prisoners in Ulster, whom he believed to have
been treated harshly and unjustly, disturbed some observers - even
though he wrote censoriously about leaders of the provisional wing
of the I.R.A. after a trip to Ireland in the mid-1970s.[21] As always,
he went his own way.

In a letter to a friend in 1973 Berrigan referred to himself
as a 'gyrovague,' a term that appropriately sums up his life in the
1970s - as he moved about, incessantly it seemed, both within and
beyond the U.S.[22] Between numerous speaking engagements in
North America and a visit to Europe in 1975, for example, he
taught a course in protest literature at the University of Detroit. The
reading list for this eclectic course included Camus, Melville,
Kafka, Margaret Mead, R.D. Laing, Steinbeck, Doctorow, and the
gospel of St. Matthew. After the mid-1970s Berrigan settled into an
informal, communal arrangement with Jesuit colleagues who were

living on their own in New York in a faded high-rise on West 98th St., a location he has described graphically in a book of reflections entitled *Uncommon Prayer* (1978):

> [I live] amid the wrecks, the hungry, the stoned, the drifters and drunks of upper Broadway. . . . I live among beggars and shopping bag ladies, and those who bed down in the streets. . . . You can find me, one mile distant as the crow flies from the million dollar penthouses of Fifth Avenue, three miles north of the twin World Trade Towers, a bit further from Wall Street. To the northeast of us things are worse: Harlem. And ten blocks due north, presto, another world, the crew-cut, guarded acres of Columbia. I dread it, loathe it, love it.[23]

Berrigan has touched on the matter of his ambivalent relationship with New York in his autobiographical narrative, *To Dwell in Peace*, where he noted that, in contrast to the specious appearance of order in other cities, the "lunacy" of New York was at least "assailable, a mad throat in one's grasp."[24] While the W. 98th St. Jesuits follow their separate occupations each day, they meet at other times for the liturgy and for any joint business, and they have a superior, who nonetheless is expected to recognize the egalitarian nature of the community. The community's mix of individual freedom and attachment to a common tradition appeals to Berrigan.

Softly green because of the profusion of indoor plants, his modestly-furnished apartment is lined with paintings and artifacts, the gifts of friends from across the world. Included on his bookshelves are works of fiction by Dickens and Flannery O'Connor, poems by Wallace Stevens, William Everson, Allen Ginsberg, and an anthology of poetry about the Irish rebellion of

1916 as well as essays by Wendell Berry, Jacques Ellul, Dorothy Solle and a number of books dealing with the threat posed by nuclear armaments. The most well-worn binding is that enclosing the *Psalms*.

Although Berrigan's relationship with the Jesuit community as a whole became more relaxed in the latter part of the 1970s, he found himself on occasion arguing against the support given not only to the Vietnam War but also to controversial, repressive foreign regimes by some of his colleagues. An instance of the tension between himself and his fellow Jesuits occurred in 1976 when he protested the acceptance of an eleven million dollar research grant to Georgetown, a Jesuit university, from the Shah of Iran. Although the protest was unsuccessful and although other such irritants would inevitably arise, Berrigan has continued to be grateful for his life as a Jesuit.[25]

In the fall of 1975 the Berrigans staged an anti-nuclear demonstration on the White House lawn, and in December of 1976 they led a demonstration in front of the Pentagon in commemoration of the death of their mother the week before. On August 6, 1979, the anniversary of the dropping of the first atomic bomb on Hiroshima, Berrigan and ten others were arrested at the Riverside Research Institute in New York - which Berrigan referred to as a Pentagon "think-tank" - for pouring blood over the entrance.[26] In Berrigan's estimation the Pentagon had become not only a threat to the planet, but was virtually indistinguishable from the American economy and by extension from American society, having become the "largest single employer in the world" and having given work to "one of every two engineers and scientists" in the U.S."[27]

Early in the morning on September 9, 1980, Berrigan and a group of religious peace activists, later called the Plowshares Eight, entered a General Electric plant in Pennsylvania and with hammers damaged three nose cones intended for use in multiple-warhead, nuclear missiles which Berrigan has identified as part of a U.S. "counterforce or first-strike policy."[28] In July, 1981, Berrigan and the other Plowshares members were given stiff prison sentences. Shortly afterwards, however, the Superior Court of Pennsylvania, in a ground-breaking decision, reversed the lower court judgment and ordered a new trial, observing that the defendants had not been given an opportunity to argue their case, which was that they acted in a spirit of urgency to protect their country from the inevitable devastation that would result to it because of its commitment to nuclear weaponry. In November of 1985, however, the Supreme Court of Pennsylvania overturned the decision of the Superior Court - although because of legal strategies and delays no final convictions have been meted out.

Characteristically, before proceeding to a demonstration, the Berrigans gather for prayer and then go out as if for a public liturgy. Over the years the principal sign of this liturgy has been the pouring of blood, their own blood, over selected symbols and instruments of war such as the doors of the Pentagon and the tips of nuclear warheads. Against the objections of some in the peace movement, who argue that the pouring of blood carries with it a note of violence and proves to be more confrontational than illuminating, Berrigan's reply has been that the blood helps to give a sense of reality to the apocalyptic armaments hidden under euphemistic phrases like 'national security' and that it symbolizes not only the inevitable fate of the victims of war but the readiness of the demonstrators to risk their freedom and even their lives in protest. Impatient at what appeared to be a lag between worship and conduct, Berrigan expanded the range of the liturgy to include not only the nave but the street.[29]

In addition, Berrigan has striven, in courses taught at Yale and Berkeley, for example, to awaken universities concerning the weapons research facilities in their midst.   He was especially disturbed by the indifference of those in the academic life when he lectured in 1977 at a Catholic university in Nebraska, whose campus was close to the headquarters of the Strategic Air Command, the computerized nerve center of the U.S. nuclear strike force. He recalled bitterly that he "couldn't rouse a cockroach's worth of attention about the blasphemies standing in their silos and hangars, just down the road."[30] In Berrigan's view the complicity of academia in the arming of the nuclear state results from an endemic problem, the tendency of academics to view such matters distantly as if they were "no more than shadows on cave walls," an aspect of what he has termed the "gnostic quest."[31]

For Berrigan, the moral slumbering of many of those in academia is analogous to the pious reticence that has kept religious contemplatives in the West from responding to the moral crises of their societies. Thus, although he praised Thomas Merton's mingling of monastic and social consciousness, Berrigan was frequently disturbed by the social attitudes he encountered on visits to contemplative communities, as on the occasion of a talk he gave to a convent of nuns in New Jersey:

> [Some] were living in some war situation out of their own past or some conception of patriotism that was quite un-Christian. Then I began to notice, every time I went to a monastery after that, there were these same divisions among the monks - the same divisions we had outside. . . .In becoming a monk, one is not always returning to a primitive, fresh understanding of religion. One may well be entering a parallel institution, parallel to the society.[32]

Increasingly disenchanted with the insipid response to the peace issues by Christian officialdom in the West, Berrigan portrayed the church in an evocative set of reflections on the Book of Revelations entitled *Beside the Sea of Glass* (1978) as being dragged along by the state, "its talisman, its bloody good-luck charm."[33] He was equally skeptical about the ability of counter-culture groups to point the way, depicting these groups as searching for a "good life among the ruins," an attempt that he described sardonically in the book, *Uncommon Prayer* (1978), as reaching for a "stirrup cup to extinction."[34] In addition, following his disillusionment with the North Vietnamese, Berrigan became wary about the ephemeral ethics of successful revolutionaries: "From prison to hedgerow to palace," he observed in *Ten Commandments for the Long Haul* (1981), was "by no means the necessary course of revolution, its degradation is by no means inevitable. But such a degradation remains highly likely, as experience shows so bitterly."[35]

Reflecting in part the changing pattern of his own life, Berrigan turned gradually toward a support for small, informal, Christian communities that drew their inspiration from scriptural texts as the vehicle for generating the sort of uncompromising moral critiques that would inevitably contrast with blander institutional responses. His view of these small communities was eschatological, although he has characterized such groups as preserving, not a future sense of the end of things, but rather a sense of present reality *sub specie aeternitatis*. He likened such remnant communities in contemporary society to the monks of the dark ages:

> Irish history has it that during the invasions of the
> early centuries, the monks constructed towers of
> stone, entered them with the book and the cup, and

endured the invasion. The vandals passed through, scorching the earth. The monks descended again to terra firma. The tradition endured. We too may have to think of ways of preserving our simple literacy, our ability to read the story of our origins, against the machine-tooled onslaught of neo-savagery.[36]

In Berrigan's view the remnant communities would inevitably breed martyrs, as did early Christianity, and from them would emerge a consciousness of the moral power of the victim, a lesson brought home to him in reading the life of the Elizabethan Jesuit poet, Robert Southwell, who was executed for his religious beliefs:

He was hanged, drawn and quartered before a holiday crowd. As he was pulled down and the butcher's steel opened his body, a drop of blood struck the face of a youth in the front rank of the crowd. He had come to the unspeakable scene as to a picnic. But the blood of the martyr scalded his soul; a few years after, he died on the same scaffold.[37]

The image of the martyr has consistently appealed to Berrigan, tempering the aggressiveness of his role as a political dissenter. The linked roles of prophet and martyr have suited not only Berrigan's personal spirituality but his conception of how the Christian should deal with the state, moving it toward change but also remaining detached from it in order to properly discern and judge it while accepting thereby whatever resultant suffering this might involve.

Juxtaposed with this rather aggressive religious stance, Berrigan's writings in the 1970s and 1980s have ironically centered on his painful consciousness of the silence of God: "The ultimate scandal of human life is undoubtedly God himself. He is the one who sticks in our throats, he it is who offers no relief, who lets the horror of life rampage onward; the great non-interventionist, the great refuser."[38] Pondering the matter tenuously, Berrigan came at length to the conclusion that, in being stonily silent, God was simply repeating his behavior toward his crucified son and that the existence of that abandoned son was, finally, a reassuring confirmation of the "modesty" of God.[39]

While Berrigan's life and art became more closely intertwined than ever in the 1970s and 1980s, he has characterized his experiences both in and out of prison as lying far from art, a "bathos, a down; the cheap common talk, the fifty basic tired obscenities trotting along, three legs for a mind, a mutt with a bloodied foot."[40] Furthermore, he felt that not only his sense of beauty but his sense of the holy existed within a much narrower range than before within what he called the "narrow breach" - a prison window, a knothole in a wooden cage, the sight of a barely surviving tree undergoing seasons of change; from another window the empty drama of clouds and sunny skies, everything reduced, seen through a burning glass."[41]

The writer encountered in the books produced in the 1970s and 1980s is at once more intransigent and more vulnerable than in the earlier works, more bitter and ironic about the perversity of contemporary culture in the West, but also less and less certain about his own faith. Revisiting biblical sources, he slowly and cumulatively pieced together a theology for the times that stood in ragged contrast with the systematic and analytical theology of his earlier books and essays. The relatively tailored look of the earlier prose and poetry gave way to an eclectic, hybrid style that in some respects resembles that attributed by Berrigan to Peter Maurin, the co-founder of the Catholic Worker movement: "The abbreviated lines stop the eye in its track, get attention; repetition, key phrases, quotes, references to a huge store of authors, living and dead, classics and news stories - everything is useful and put to use, part of the whole, an argument finding its way."[42]

A representative example of Berrigan's prose writing in the 1970s and 1980s is *The Nightmare of God* (1983), which focuses on the Book of Revelations in relation to modern political states. The Book of Revelations appeared to Berrigan as a symbolist parody of humanity's dark psycho-history, "an unclouded mirror of our own voracious souls, a nightmare of appetites on the hoof," our most "secret, guarded, cherished dreams turned inside out."[43] Berrigan perceived the book as God's surrealistic vision of what is to come, a foreshadowing of an orgy of human freedom that would remain unimpeded by divine intervention until the final, all-consuming catastrophe. In this light one can perhaps better understand the apparent and acknowledged irrationality of Berrigan's own quixotic behavior in tilting against the formidable militarism of the modern state. In his view the intractable, paternal managers of the major powers were locked within a collective dream in which unspeakably violent retaliation was readied for those with opposed political ideologies, all within a calming rhetoric of orderly preparedness. Within the unbridled violence of history, however, in Berrigan's view, there had arisen the most curious of all effects, the arrival of a "patient, wise, implacable justice" brought about, as in a Shakespearean tragedy, by the inevitable self-destructiveness of evil.[44]

The fate of the majority in Berrigan's estimation was to remain "morally comatose," unable to identify with the harsh psychological archetypes disclosed in the Book of Revelations and thus doomed to act out a nightmare whose existence they failed to suspect.[45] As has been indicated, however, for Berrigan, the divine vision in the Book of Revelations possesses the relentless realism of tragedy wherein the consequences of evil are not only individual but collective. For this reason Berrigan's purpose is not that the powerful of this world - who embody the collective will - should perish, but rather that they should be converted. The difficulties connected with such a conversion, however, stem from the comprehensiveness of the modern state, which is so encompassing as to be, paradoxically, "all but spiritualized, immobilizing to the imagination."[46] Berrigan's entrenched opposition to many aspects of the modern state - including the impersonality of the welfare state - distinguishes him from thinkers on the left with whom on specific social issues he has otherwise often been in agreement.

In 1975, while he was living temporarily in Paris with a community of Buddhist exiles from Vietnam, Berrigan was struck by the fact that they were always telling stories to one another, and he reflected ruefully that when religion had no more stories to tell it tended to turn, as in the modern instance, to the more arid issuing of "commands and prohibitions."[47] As a result he turned at this time to writing allegories, often based on biblical sources, in order to stimulate the imagination of readers so that, as he put it, they might paradoxically become capable of "imagining the real world."[48]

In *A Book of Parables* (1977) Berrigan experimented with allegorical writing with uneven results. The best of the tales, "The Patience of Job in Detroit, Michigan," grew out of his experience of living in a black ghetto while he was teaching at the University of Detroit in the spring of 1975. The story was based in part on his caring for his landlord, who was dying of lung cancer while continuing to chain smoke, an old Greek who had to bear not only the eating away of the cancer but the harassment of his two uncaring, black, adopted sons. As with Job, the landlord, overwhelmed by misery, hovers near despair, never quite succumbing, his head tossing "balkily, sick and starved, all but transparent, a grave heavy with Easter seeds."[49] While the narrative situation is made interesting enough, a richer, underlying current focuses on the coming of death as a dramatic point of interplay between two worlds, one eerily "indistinct, evanescent," the other "hard and clear and infinitely beloved, the crawl space of the land animal."[50] In its unsentimental poignancy and imagistic vividness the story anticipates Berrigan's superb studies of the dying in *We Die Before We Live*.

Another literary hybrid, *The Discipline of the Mountain* (1979), is an amalgam of prose and poetry loosely based on Dante's *Purgatorio*. Dante provided Berrigan with an allegorical scenario involving the viewing of life as a contest of moral forces. Furthermore, from an aesthetic point of view, Berrigan was attracted by the idea of knitting images of the past into those of the present. In a review essay written in 1964, for example, he praised poems by Allen Tate and Robert Lowell in which features of the classical world had been attached to the "brusque arm of the living." In reading Lowell's "Falling Asleep Over the Aeneid," he wrote, "one awakens treading the coals of our own burning cities; and the circles of hell are contemporary city planning at its worst."[51] In a similar vein, in a letter written in 1978, Berrigan explained that he saw Dante's *Purgatorio* as a "master metaphor for *this world*."[52]

In order to fashion his personae, Berrigan inserted himself into the ascent of the seven-storey mountain in the *Purgatorio* in the company of both Virgil and Dante. As Virgil had been to Dante, a "loving adversary, a friend who will tell the truth," so would Dante be to Berrigan.[53] Overlooking some obvious differences between the medieval and contemporary worlds, Berrigan stressed that Dante, like himself, had lived in an age of

violence, and, like himself, had lived in exile. The poem is thus a
sort of Socratic dialogue between Berrigan and Dante as to how
each perceived the presence of evil - with Dante being portrayed as
someone who viewed evil as essentially personal while Berrigan
perceived it from the point of view of a later age as both
institutional and personal. Nevertheless, because of his largeness of
vision, Dante is identified as quite properly a modern as well as an
ancient spirit:

> soul of wit and fire benign quicksilver
> but stern too a face the dead put on
> soul's final form [54]

While analogies between Dante's world and the nuclear
age are thematically explored, with Berrigan using the frame of the
Purgatorio somewhat loosely as a principle of narrative unity, the
writing is often simply jarring without being either heightened or
distinctive, particularly in the prose commentaries. The most
successful writing in *The Discipline of the Mountain* is to be found
not in the prose sections but in the poetic cantos, which exhibit
great freedom of imagination - as in the canto on sloth:

> I saw
> hands of scholars boneless as ribbons
> Saw faces of monks whose boredom
> death lifted like death masks
> Now they ran eager on the spoor of life.[55]

As is apparent in this mordant imagery from *The Discipline
of the Mountain*, there were important changes in the tenor of
Berrigan's writing from the mid to the late 1970s. While, for
example, he became absorbed by the literary journey toward God

in scripture and in Dante, he found himself less and less certain about the immanence of God in the world. In an Alexandria, Virginia, jail in 1977, for example, following a Pentagon protest, he wrote in *Beside the Sea of Glass* (1978): "Grant us at least the presence of your absence. Let us taste that void, at the heart of the raucous yelling of prisoners, the void between the bars, between the hours that hang around like days, the days that stand like years."[56] The blessing of God, he noted bleakly in *A Book of Parables*, "rightly understood, often arrives in the form of a curse."[57] The imagery in *A Book of Parables* mirrors the prevailing mood of joylessness, as in the meditation on Psalm 130, whose dolorous sounds Berrigan described as "a stroke of acid along the crystal."[58] While overwhelmed by a sense of the absence of God, Berrigan became himself more and more uneasy with the "kind of view that reduces the experience of God to one's neighbor,"[59] disdaining the tendency among many contemporary religious thinkers to reject transcendentalism.

The search for God took the form of a review of his own experience, as can be seen in *Portraits: Of Those I Love* (1982), a retrospective gallery that included Berrigan's mother and aunt, Thomas Merton, Dorothy Day, Peter Maurin and John McNeil, the American Jesuit who has been an advocate for Catholic homosexuals. Although the prophetic voice surfaces in a final self-portrait, the book as a whole exhibits a noticeable change in mood in comparison with the previous decade, and nowhere is this change more apparent than in the chapter devoted to the dying woman simply called Christina, a piece of writing that is noteworthy as well for its narrative value.

Berrigan first visited Christina, a painter of Hispanic background, after having been startled by her letter to the *Catholic Worker* in 1978 in which she announced her impending death. In spite of her suffering she had delayed going into a hospital in order to remain at home where she could care for her infirm husband. In visiting her, Berrigan became acutely conscious of the strength possible in someone who was confronting death, as in Christina's exhausting effort to make her words clear and exact while under the "hammer of pain."[60] Nevertheless, it was the physical weakness of the dying woman which permitted the combative side of Berrigan's nature to relax. Heightened by the woman's struggle with death, he became absorbed by her "classic face, vulnerable and strong-boned," somewhere between "adamant and eggshell."[61]

Berrigan's meetings with Christina followed a ritualistic order, which was imposed so that the woman could deal in a dignified manner with the ravages of the fatal growth within her:

Ring the buzzer, open the door, twenty steps down the Tom Thumb corridor, up the blind stair, cross the court. Her door is ajar. "Come in, Daniel." There are flowers to be unwrapped and admired and put in place. Her walker must be shifted to one side. She arranges herself on the bed, a minimal shift of position will be required of her poor bones for an hour or so.

I move the table to one side and pull up a chair (the only chair). It is like tea time Behind the Looking Glass. The precision of each move, the inching of furniture to left or right, banishment of impediments to speech and sight - there is economy here - of time and place. The grave is narrow, the time short.[62]

After some time Christina consented to being moved into a hospice, her bones by that time having become, according to Berrigan, "flimsy shells strung to one another" in a body with "hardly more breath than a tucked blanket." With convincing deftness Berrigan delicately paints the coming of death, the elegiac mood slowly alternating with that of reprieve during the cycles of rallying consciousness and ever more final sleeps: "Slack jaw, pallor, remoteness, feverish dew of hand and brow." The word "dew" exquisitely asserts the primacy of the dying woman's spirit against the collapse of matter, the two linked antithetically in symbol and in fact - as when her "withered arms went up" in acknowledgement of flowers received, "a Spanish gesture, grand and baroque."[63] The visits conclude with a final running of her hand over Berrigan's face with a touch "lighter and more exacting than any I have known" - as though "in her blind journey she were memorizing the outline of a life she must say farewell to."[64]

Berrigan's writings about the dying are as freshly observant, as sensitive and discriminating, as any that come to mind, equaling at times the power of Tolstoy's tale about Ivan Ilych. In *We Die Before We Live* (1980) Berrigan offers portraits of the dying patients he visited at St. Rose's Home on the lower east side of Manhattan in the late 1970s and early 1980s. The home was a hospice run by an order of nuns founded by Rose Hawthorne Lathrop, the daughter of Nathaniel Hawthorne. Berrigan's interest in this work had been kindled in part by his search for God. He had determined that he would seek signs of the spirit, if not of God directly, precisely at that point where life was most assailed.

The dying presented Berrigan with various sets of dualities. Some persons died better than they lived, some apparently worse; all became involved, consciously or not, in rites of compensation, as does Berrigan himself in joining his strength with that of the dying. Often, to his delight, a remarkable, compensatory strength is discovered in the poor, who with little to lose more easily slip their "moorings" to the "mainland."[65] Furthermore, due to the role of Berrigan as narrator and observer, the polarities of his vision are added to those of the dying person. The chapter about Oscar, the dying thief, is an example:

> See him, if you will, sneaking on rubber wheels into a cubicle; the curtains drawn seemly, the breath labored, the hour short. There, in the awesome space between one shudder and the next, Oscar extracts unto himself some trifle or not so trifle, lifting a limp hand or wrist to expedite matters, transferring hegemony of ring or watch unto himself.[66]

Rather than portraying Oscar simply as a comic antihero who moves surreptitiously through the hospital stealing from his fellow patients, Berrigan relates him to the book's implicit theme of compensation, not only by showing him giving away his ill-gotten goods, but also in revealing that Oscar's bizarre thefts are an expression of his resistance to death. Seen in such a light, Oscar's value becomes transformed. Similarly, while Sulkey, the old Jewish man in "Three Who Went in Style," sorely tests the charity of those attending to his needs, Berrigan again perceives a compensatory virtue in this otherwise unlovable man: "If God were an old Jew dying of cancer, he'd quite possibly look like this one," demanding "plenary service like this one. He'd go out like a peacock, tail flaming."[67]

In their journey to the unknown, Berrigan noticed, the dying, like the old deaf man who patiently knits a white scarf to be used by someone who will survive him - or the former contractor who constructs an elaborate doll's house - make a bridge for themselves, planting themselves on this side through some such gesture before launching out. In the hollow between what Emily Dickinson has called the heaves of storm, Berrigan watches the dying creep towards death, "these damaged bodies, a beggar's opera, a procession out of Bosch or Bunuel," scrawling in the dust a rueful message about the "seducing illusions of youth and health and sexual prowess."[68]

The dualistic pattern which underlies the structure of *We Die Before We Live* relates not only to the attitudes of the dying but is seen to be implicit in the body itself in its macabre, contrapuntal dance with mind, as is evident in Pete's death. He lay there, Berrigan writes, a reminder of the stench of death, a rebuke of the "olfactory lie" promoted by contemporary mortuaries: "Were we captive among the flowers, was the Big Embalmer approaching with his sweet talk, his needle, to plunge it deep, deep, to the joining place of marrow and spirit, to make of us his chemical darlings, his amortized, smiling, odorless tribe?"[69] With a merciless vividness Berrigan records the triumph of death over the body - as in the brain tumor that resembled a "terrible red potato" ready to split into "two livid parts" so that it "literally" fumed. With unflinching aptness he describes a similar growth in another patient, a sea captain, whose protruding tumor, swathed in bandages, looked like a "grotesque tea caddy."[70]

Parrying the humiliation inflicted, not by death, but by the process of dying, some of the dying men observed by Berrigan unexpectedly took control of their bodies in order to hasten the end. An old man warns Berrigan off, for example, when offered companionship: "It was as though he were swinging a censor of hot coals and incense as they do in the Greek mass to create a sacred circle." Racing to the finish, the man goes up in a "conflagration, no debris."[71] The man becomes one of many observed by Berrigan who fashion an unrepeatable work of art out of their dying. If the dying reach an uncanny physical resemblance to one another, "more alike than the newborn," according to Berrigan, "one saffron, one used parchment," a contrary solidarity develops in which the dying and those who walk to the end with them confront the darkness shared.[72] The unity achieved is evident in the scene in which Berrigan dredges up from his own life recollected images of the migration of Canada geese over a Wisconsin lake that helped to revive both his own spirit and that of the dying man he attempted to comfort. At the end of the interview the man spread his hands, Berrigan noted in pleasure, "like a man illustrating flight."[73] Similarly, there is the orderly observed by Berrigan who patiently trims the fingernails of a doomed man, an "invisible gesture" in its apparent futility, it would appear, but a graceful bow in the direction of life.

Within the recesses of Berrigan's consciousness there emerges a further dualistic irony, a "surreal clarity of understanding" vouchsafed by the rarity of his contact with the dying and on the other hand a lingering, melancholic sense of the silence of God.[74] That silence is nowhere more painfully felt than in the chapter entitled "The Child." There, a comatose, cancerous boy sleeps on towards death with no hoped-for awakening to assuage the grief and bewilderment of the onlooker. Without resolving the enigma of the boy's suffering and death, Berrigan, breaking the silence of God himself, so to speak, changes the shape of his narrative from a realistic format to a dreamscape in which the child undergoes a final apotheosis.

The motif of silence, like everything else in *We Die Before We Live*, is associated with an Emersonian, compensatory law so that the stunned narratorial silence surrounding the death of the comatose child is complemented by the deliberate silence of the consciously dying: "Mainly, the dying are wrapped like a chrysalis in the silence before the journey. I don't mean coma, but an intense musing, a withdrawal enforced by pain or entered by choice."[75] For many, Berrigan brings out, death is an antechamber of unpracticed concentration, experienced with or without pain, a surrounding space that is a "heart of silence."[76]

Occasionally, the silence is cut open, as in the case of a policeman who, no longer able to deny his dying, helplessly succumbs to tears. The sight ironically makes Berrigan ecstatic:

> I stood there appalled, flooded with joy. I was witnessing a great violation in nature; in the nature of stone, say, or of bronze. Such a transformation, transfiguration, as would imply not only that dead matter lived, but that the bronze or stone had renounced the form in which it had been cast, renounced the limit imposed by its maker. [77]

The scene illustrates what Berrigan had come to the dying to witness, the resurgence of the soul from beneath the debris of the ego. Here at least, with death a breath away, the living gave evidence of the existence of the soul as well as, in some cases, of its failure.

The distinctive character of these finely-wrought portraits issues from Berrigan's patience, precision, and composure in recording the encroachment of death. His astringent writing style was well suited to his studies of the dying, and although these writings are among the least known of his works, they represent a literary harvest of high quality. In them he regained an important principle of balance, which allowed him to see, in practice if not always in theory, that the pain and defeat of death are only significant when set against a life whose value can be celebrated. It is this latter quality that had been lacking in some of the prose writings of the 1970s, as has been noted, and that had blunted their effect. In *We Die Before We Live* Berrigan returned to the high road of both art and religion.

Following a lapse in his arrangement with St. Rose's Home early in 1984 Berrigan began to visit with patients who were dying of AIDS at St. Vincent's Hospital in Greenwich Village. In *To Dwell in Peace* he has recounted the history of his acquaintance with homosexuals at Cornell and at Danbury prison. He went on to describe a talk he gave at Berkeley to the gay fellowship of the Unitarian-Universalist Church in which, while committing himself to the dignity of homosexual people, he admonished that community to avoid becoming too self-absorbed and instead to become more aware of the poor and of the nuclear arms race. The homosexual patients dying of Aids, however, were another matter, and, faced with the concreteness of their serial ordeals, Berrigan found himself wondering who in witnessing these deaths could "waste a thought on an abstract good?"[78] A particularly moving section of *To Dwell in Peace* is the account of the young artist, Douglas, whom Berrigan visited in his final months of life and who made him aware of the compensatory power of art in offsetting the ravages of time and disease:

> There we sat, young Lazarus and I, in a commu-
> nion of grief. The afternoon sun fingered the room,
> the artifacts scattered about like a noble flea
> market, all created by the dying man and his spas-
> modic, doomed genius, all up for the cruel disper-
> sion time wreaks. Ars longa, vita brevis. Indeed.
> Time was scattering us. He to the four winds; and I
> - I must find reason (or abandon reason) to hope
> on, walk on, go through those motions that signify
> or simulate life. And which was the harder
> summons I could not tell.[79]

The symmetrical dance of opposites here - the living man envying the dying man, for example - creates subtle interstices in which the filaments of life and death commingle ironically. The excerpt reveals as well that the vocation of art, which for Berrigan particularly meant poetry, had survived the years of militancy: Ars longa, vita brevis.

In 1984, a volume of Berrigan's poems entitled *May All Creatures Live* was published privately in a small California town by an attorney named Harold Berliner. Berliner, a supporter of the peace movement, had met Berrigan when the latter taught at Berkeley in 1973. Although the collection is not widely available and is thus not well known, it is important in that it contains a valuable selection of Berrigan's poetry from 1973 to 1983. In general, the poems help to fill out our view of Berrigan in the 1970s, something that he recognized himself in a retrospective essay published in 1982 in which he referred to his poems as a "kind of dark bulb of existence," a "perennial root that, in spite of all, keeps coming up and up."[80] In the same essay he announced that he relied upon poetry as a way of submitting his anger to a "strict discipline" and spoke of it as a means of survival.[81]

Such poetry as he produced in the mid and late 1970s was written hurriedly on planes or added to copies of letters to friends, with some of it appearing eventually in journals scattered across North America. During the 1970s Berrigan participated in poetry readings at the Folger Library in Washington in a series that included James Merrill and Allen Ginsberg. He felt that he had kept up with recent trends in poetic form, sufficiently at any rate to be able to say in a review written in 1977 that contemporary poetry reflected its time, "which is to say, anything goes."[82] At the same time, he complained about the loss of moral energy in contemporary verse,[83] and he was especially critical of the poetry coming out of academia, which he referred to as more "stifled, monkishly

cloistered," and "ingrown," than that which had been produced by
the truly cloistered, Thomas Merton.[84] He told an interviewer in
1974 that he refused to be "possessed" by writing, illustrating the
sort of balance between life and writing which he approved of by
referring to Marianne Moore's giving up of many years of her
writing in order to care for her invalid mother.[85]

He incorporated some of his views about the ideal balance
between art and life in a poem in *May All Creatures Live* entitled
"Come Now, Choose:"

> The eye regards the
>   heart, a western view
>   The heart regards
>   the eye, the Chinese
>   say
>   and the great world
>   between -
>   both
>   known by
>   caliper and transfus-
>   ion
>   rigor and gift.[86]

The cascade of isolated syllables, symbolizing the cost of choosing
between eye and heart, reaffirms Berrigan's dual commitment to
contemplation and action.

Berrigan incorporated his belief about the social and
political import of poetry in a number of poems in *May All
Creatures Live*, as in the following lines:

> When the poet recanted
>   they hacked off his fingers

and gave him a signet ring

The poet recanted.
They tore out his tongue
and crowned him their laureate.[87]

Berrigan believed that academic poets in particular risked being emasculated by the state which employed them, a compounding of a moral danger already implicit in their physical remoteness. In spite of his reservations about cerebralism, however, his response to the life of the mind and to art in *May All Creatures Live* is one of celebration, as can be seen in poems like "A Visit to the Book of Kells and A Walk in the Park." Berrigan had also developed into a more reflexive poet than he had been, as is evident in "Salvation" in which he postulates skeptically the ambiguities of his relationship to his reader, a thematic preoccupation of American writers during the 1960s and 1970s. Beginning with a conventional, reassuring statement about the community of poet and reader, Berrigan proceeds to subvert that convention by picturing confusion as the likely effect of the reading experience. In a similar vein the poem, "Apologia," offers a seriocomic review by Berrigan of his own work:

What I offer is
spontaneous
life, soap,
operas, death
& above all & so to speak
mystical effluence [88]

A modernist skepticism is also present in "Ignorance Is Like a Sourdough Starter." In a letter to the author Berrigan has explained that the word "ignorance" in the poem really means a kind of humility, "at once modest and yeasty, that I consider a prelude to such knowledge as ends up not inert."[89] In a more precise sense the poem is a candid reflection of Berrigan's plunges into social action, which were sometimes taken with a minimum of knowledge but which were followed by a rising of consciousness as mind interacted with event and as inert knowledge sprouted into deed. Stylistically, the poem is typical of the poems in *May All Creatures Live* for its provocative imagery and phrasing. An example is the depiction of the sterile knowledge that Berrigan associated with much academic poetry as unleavened dough, a "death's head" that "squats/stares at the phantom tit."[90]

In a few of the poems Berrigan considered his tattered relationship with the Catholic church. In "O Catholic Church," for example, he pictures himself as a trapeze artist performing under the "tent's navel," but nonetheless anchored by the church. Though his tone is conciliatory here, he objected to the church's bureaucratic heaviness, its compulsion to regiment every detail of its religious vision instead of

. . . a word
from a starry mouth
heard softly here and there
with authority too

- a forefinger pointing
- a voice saying 'north'

We could infer the other directions.[91]

Although most of the poems in *May All Creatures Live* are terse and relatively unadorned, some are more subtle in tone and more elaborate in structure than others. "Life and Death and Everything in Between," for example, is unusually formal and visionary, a forerunner of the poems in *Block Island*. Moreover, while there is sexual imagery in the poem, it is presented reverently and delicately - in contrast to the directness of poems such as "Ignorance Is Like a Sourdough Starter." Set in a graveyard in the Maryland hills, the poem focuses on a "rangy cedar" tree which has a large hole through its "tegument and heart" and which stands on "dead feet" with only a "topping frond/like a green cap/tossed in air." Approaching the tree, the speaker, who sees it as a "transfigured woman's body," has a vision of a "roseate child weaving flowers." He then kisses the tree hole, "that cervix/that burning glass," and then has a second vision:

> A dead woman, upright
> her eyes dread
> draws the living child to breast
> and backward sinks
> the green earth closing over. [92]

While there are personal associations embedded in the text - the coincidence of the dead woman and Berrigan's recently deceased mother, for example - the poem's power derives from its originality, its evoking of the beneficent interfusion of life and death through carefully modulated language involving the interweaving of pastoral and sexual motifs.

Noticeably in these poems from the 1970s the beauty of nature became a consolation when Berrigan had become increasingly conscious of aging, partly due to the accelerated attrition experienced in the resistance movement, as is evident in poems like "Birthday" and "Alone." As his personal vitality ebbed, he clung to signs of vitality in the world at large, and this accounted in part for

a gradual shift in mood from the somber, apocalyptic scenarios of
the 1970s to the nurturing landscapes of the 1980s. Nevertheless,
even in these landscapes, death hovers, though with an oddly reassuring quality, as can be seen in poems like "Ambition" and
"Consolation," where Berrigan initiates a colloquy with the dead,
"filling you in/like winds in empty/branches like stars/in wintry
trees."[93] The analogies are apt; like the wind in the branches and
the stars seen through the winter trees, the voices of the dead,
though marginally perceptible, are a felt presence. No one was
more poignantly present to Berrigan than his mother, who died in
1975 and who is the subject of a sequence of poems in *May All
Creatures Live*. The best of these, "The Ring," is similar in some
respects to James Merrill's oedipal lyric, "The Emerald," in
Braving the Elements. In "The Ring" Berrigan relates how he
began wearing his mother's wedding ring after her death, hoping
that he "who never married" would be changed by her womanhood,
which he must "borrow from the dead/and from little children," the
tenderness and "long loneliness/that are her planet's/ring of
light."[94] The phrase "long loneliness," the title of Dorothy Day's
autobiography, links Day symbolically and psychologically with
Berrigan's mother. With its measured serenity and elegiac sublim-
ity the poem conveys a new mildness that betokens the poetry to
come.

Stylistically, most of the poems in *May All Creatures Live*,
unlike "The Ring," exhibit the serrated imagery that is the hallmark
of Berrigan's art. An example is the succinct rendering of
Darwinian naturalism through the image of "the goose's blood/on
the fox's grin" in the poem "Spirit Explained To a Child."[95]
Equally incisive in both picture and sound is the metaphor of the
eye of a dying gull as "a diamond on a pivot."[96] Berrigan is most
effective when the ideas and motifs in his poems are condensed,

producing a stab of recognition, as in the image of the spoor in his poem about the California dream:

Incurably blond, gigantic
landsmen take to the surf -
the skiffs head in like hounds
landward, on the spoor
of pure catastrophe. [97]

The most successful poems are those in which Berrigan combines this sort of compressed irony with an exuberant play of language - as in "Jerry, Carol and I Make the Grand Tour." Set in Cambridge, the poem projects its central conceits of heat and cold both through the perambulations of the touring friends in the narrative foreground and also through the sense of the past, the terror caused by Henry VIII, whose sexual appetite ("hot forensic jewels") was in reality ruthlessly "cold." The logic behind the metamorphosis from heat to cold in describing Henry's sexuality pivots on the speaker's announcement in the middle of the poem that he associates "cold with hell."[98] The speaker moves sure-footedly toward a concluding contrast between the sort of calculating lust symbolized by the Tudor king ("an icy blade to a stone block") and genuine love ("though sharp as asp/the sword/no edge." Exhibiting a fine union of intelligence, control, and high energy, the poem reflects the recovery of Berrigan's poetic powers following the earlier, somewhat disappointing volume of *Prison Poems*.

The poems in *Block Island* (1985) grew out of Berrigan's use throughout the 1970s and 1980s, as was indicated earlier, of a cottage owned by his friend, William Stringfellow. The island off the coast of Rhode Island in Long Island Sound served Berrigan as a haven from the stress of life in Manhattan and as a location in which to write. Relaxed and affectionate in tone for the most part, the untitled poems in *Block Island*, which were written at various times, flow easily into each other. Sharing a single location and cast of characters, the poems offer an unhurried and undated view of experience.

Rustic and wind-blown, life on Block Island is portrayed as elemental and domestic, a change from Berrigan's highly socialized existence on the mainland. The mood of the poems, which develops cumulatively, alternates between a mournful feeling of loss and a modest assertion of survival. Death occurs as naturally and implicitly on the island as life. At one point, Anthony Towne, the writer who shared Stringfellow's house on Block Island, dies alone - with Stringfellow away in Canada at the time and Berrigan teaching at Berkeley. Upon their return the two bury the ashes of their friend beneath a huge rusting anchor, both of them shivering under a "driving downpour, prayer books dissolved/to illiterate oatmeal."[99] Similarly, the death of Katherine Breydert, longtime resident of Block Island, physician to the poor, and artist, is part of Berrigan's elegiac tapestry.

John Leary, Harvard graduate and member of the Catholic Worker movement, dead at the age of 24, is commemorated in the image of the scarlet sumac plant, whose appearance Berrigan compares to a "swipe of blood," and yet (in recognition of Leary's work among the indigent) he calls it a "near tree," as well.[100] Considered together, dead friends form a company so numerous that they populate the house at meal time, departing afterwards "down cliffside," turning "in farewell."[101] The intermingling of life and death, so characteristic of the mood of these poems, is sustained through an underlying, autumnal rhythm: "Autumn thrums the life span's/abrupt quietus."[102] In another poem we are reminded that although it is a "honeyed autumn time," under the fallen leaves a "shadow whispers: ruin, shortly, begin."[103]

In a similar mood, suspended between sleep and non-sleep in his cottage at night, Berrigan sees a form sitting in "shadow," a "birth/or death watch," which then "vanished." He remains puzzled, uncertain of what he has seen, the "death watch of my father" or "fields of new children," apparitional "pods of autumn", perhaps, "seeding spring."[104] The motifs of life in death, death in life, were heightened by the fact that while he wrote within the dispensation of timelessness bestowed by the island, Berrigan awaited the final judicial decision on his action as a member of the Plowshares Eight group, a decision that he believed could entomb him for the rest of his life.

The metaphysical calm of the poems in *Block Island* derives partly from the simplicity and limpid depths of the perspectives offered by the island, as in a view of the distant stillness of a cargo ship. Similarly, life on the mainland, though never really forgotten, feels remote, so much so that the sorting of his mail feels to Berrigan like "tugging distant nets ashore."[105] In like vein and recalling the village landscapes of Robert Frost, Berrigan focuses on the way in which the manner of the islanders, reserved and taciturn, creates a space both within and between individuals which complements that which exists under the canopy of the sky. An example is Berrigan's passing of Anthony Towne on the road; no hands are lifted in greeting as Towne gazes straight ahead, "forefinger barely lifted from wheel's round."[106]

Meditative and emblematic, the *Block Island* poems are suffused with an engaging freshness and tolerance. If the theme of the absence of God had been a source of quiet anguish in some of the writings of the 1970s, here it becomes a source of humor, as in the poem in which God appears as an old, possibly cantankerous, cosmic homesteader who blinks, stands, and "goes unsteadily to the porch" where he "relieves himself ecologically."[107] The whimsy has its serious side in the sense that nature, though perceived as an incomplete reflection of its creator, nonetheless conveys an impression of the divine mind: "For the sea, for God, speech is act."[108] The impression would serve as a kind of creed.

As if righting an imbalance in the activist writings of the 1970s, the poems in *Block Island* lean towards the contemplative. Berrigan's perception of Anthony Towne, for example, approvingly emphasizes Towne's retreat from society, his resolve, like a "Stonehenge circle, simply/to be."[109] Similarly, although in slicing "country apples" Berrigan recalls that that was what he had been doing when arrested by F.B.I. agents on Block Island in 1970, his attitude is not one of painful remembrance but of grateful survival, captured in the image of the deep dish pie with its "Resurrected apples." [110]

Providing a further structural unity to the sequence are the recurring motifs of sea, bird, and house, the latter being the most prominent and elaborate symbol. The house is not only important as a symbol, though, but also as a literal reality, a stable residence among people whom Berrigan thought of as a family, a refuge from a nomadic life in which the nearest a "Jesuit knows/of dwelling place" is the communal "long house."[111] Living on Block Island recalls primal images of the family homestead in Ely, Minnesota, where Berrigan's father and his sons every October packed the foundation with banks of dry foliage against the extremity of the coming cold and where in winter he listened to wolves howling at the moon.

A more personal memory connected with wolves surfaces when Berrigan recalls his older brothers hoisting him into the dark of the wood shed:

> Blinded, I sensed a hairy phiz
> pushed against mine. Little boy's
> eyes cleared, through darkness stared -

baleful moons, a stark suspended
timber wolf, frozen, eye to eye.
Screamed and screamed! [112]

Released temporarily from the demands of the peace movement,
Berrigan's mind turned inward, at night becoming "a hot
pot/constantly stirred, fumes intense, voices/grandiloquent."
Moreover, the poems show Berrigan sending down imperishable
roots into the soil of the island:

I summon compassion,
the undefeated faces of the subway run
wishing them solitude, this house, cliff,
wild roses, blackberries, scoured pines
the panoply, the subtle dance
self's truth emerging like a headland
when morning fog uplifts a seventh veil.[113]

In Whitmanesque fashion the boundaries of self and non-self dis-
solve across the elements from which the house is made and to
which it will return. As can be seen in the image of the ocean,
which furrows in a "boundless brow," the streaming of consciousness from sea to house to mind is remarkably unfettered.[114]
Released from the need to actively shape reality in the light of
social goals sought, Berrigan's mind slipped into a more passive
mode in which the ordering of things could be accomplished by
others, even by the rustic house itself:

The little house
all eyes, saw for me. I peered through windows
that colored nothing dank or rosy, saw
a waxy bush billowing like a sail; or hunched

> face downward, a buffalo riding storm.
> No. A mere bush, no burning bush. [115]

Implicit in the rejection of the biblical burning bush is a sense of release from the pressure of an allegorical reading of the world and a resting instead against the concreteness of being.

Berrigan extracted from his sojourns on Block Island a sense of well-being that allowed the house and island to pass for an experience of heaven:

> Be not astonished
>   if, on stroke of midnight,
> stroke of noon -
>   table, porch, fundament, roof
> pots and pans, with great clatter
>   levitate in the blue.
>   Dumb clapboards strike alleluia!
> Blue nail heads burn like glass!
> Shingles - feathers of birds of paradise!
> an angel's shoulder nudges the house, no weightier than
>   balloon and basket - up, up
>   into the Presence. [116]

The irregular, shifting lines, which mimic the loosening and rising parts of the house, reflect the sustained airiness of *Block Island*. Even the elegiac passages are infused with a lightness of touch that keeps afloat the pervasive theme of a community of the blessed. The experience amounted to a curious personal actualization of Berrigan's earlier theology of history. What he had not foreseen in the 1950s, however, was that the experience of a new heaven, new earth, would be fleeting and rare rather than the expansive alteration of history he had envisaged, fresh from his reading of Henri de Lubac and Teilhard de Chardin.

From the vantage point of the 1980s, with the mass movements of the 1960s and early 1970s well behind him, Berrigan came to believe more firmly than ever in the small community, whether on Block Island, in front of the Pentagon, or in the barrios of Central America. In the case of Latin America, liberation theology had given rise to small Christian groups called base communities that had begun to proliferate. With this in mind Berrigan lined up a trip to El Salvador and Nicaragua in 1984, writing to James Forest that he had been invited by Jesuits who, due to their involvement in social change, had for years been the targets of numerous, sometimes successful, death threats sanctioned by governments in the region. He told Forest that he wanted to see how the people of Central America, including the Jesuits, lived with death, feeling once more that he required an alternative view of the church in society to the relatively comfortable situation which obtained in the U.S.[117]

While visiting the region, Berrigan kept a journal, subsequently published as *Steadfastness of the Saints* (1985), in which he recorded his impressions of the quotidian ordeal undergone by the peoples of El Salvador and Nicaragua. The book is a narrative documentary, rather similar to *Night Flight to Hanoi* in structure, containing incident and dialogue interspersed with observation and reflection. The disparate elements of the book are held together by Berrigan's nomadic and ongoing quest of the heroic church.

The initial scene of departure from the United States is ironically illusory, Berrigan soon discovers, since the U.S. is conspicuously entrenched in the area he will visit. The American embassy in El Salvador is described as a walled fortress of "gargantuan height, breadth, and width, a hideous parody of Pauline cosmology," an architecture designed, Berrigan observes, like that of ancient Rome, to project an image of unassailable power among "impoverished clients and vassals."[118] The images introduce the U.S. as the protagonist fueling the turmoil in El Salvador and Nicaragua, and thus serve to knit together the two major sections of the journal. In the final analysis, therefore, Berrigan's Central American journey became one more chapter in the moral exploration of his own society.

But only in part. The blatant openness of the violence in El Salvador, for example, left no doubt that Berrigan had entered a different world, leaving little for his mind to do but record in stunned silence the officially sanctioned death squads in their armor-plated cruisers, "nosing about in traffic, ominous and swift as sharks on the prowl," their interiors invisible, "no glimpse even of a set of brows or of weaponry or a blurred terrorized captive."[119] Complementing these agents of fear are the streams of victims, including the mothers of the disappeared who search endlessly through albums of the mutilated and the dead.

The spirit of resistance in these societies is represented literally and metaphorically by what Berrigan calls steadfastness, the controlling motif of his journal: "Persecution is the clue, the bloodshot clue."[120] As was true at its beginning, Berrigan notes, the church's proper destiny in the modern world is to be persecuted. One can infer from all of Berrigan's writings that it was not his view that the church should seek persecution, but rather that, if it is performing its appointed task in the world, it will assuredly be persecuted.

The major symbol of steadfastness in the El Salvador segment is Archbishop Oscar Romero, who had been assassinated while saying mass a few years prior to Berrigan's visit. While the murder of the bishop, who had spoken out against institutionalized injustice in El Salvador, was generally viewed as having been officially sanctioned, Berrigan's attention was drawn not to the murderers but to the victim. If outrage at the powerful had characterized Berrigan's writings in 1970s, the spiritual majesty of the individual became his thematic preoccupation in the 1980s. Winged in death as it had been in life, the spirit of Romero is revealed in San Salvador's unfinished cathedral, which he had intended to remain uncompleted until every citizen of El Salvador was decently housed and which thus became a daily reminder to those in the ornate presidential palace that faced it of ills that had not been remedied. Festooned with messages and plaques, Romero's tomb reminded Berrigan of that of Thomas a Beckett: "We knelt there like Chaucer's motley pilgrims, at our Canterbury shrine, this uninviting impregnable tomb, imbedded like a time capsule in our mad century."[121]

Alternating with the theme of steadfastness is that of patience, a virtue that amidst the inefficiencies of Central America is quickly acquired. Waiting endlessly on the streets of Managua for a taxi or a bus to come along, for example, Berrigan feels the force of the tropical sun, a "hammer of bronze," upon him. On the other hand, the experience of waiting impresses upon him that waiting has in effect been his life's work, "almost a vocation." Thus, his task in Central America is accepted as spectatorial, the opening of a "third eye on this third world."[122] Waiting in the antechamber of the Department of Justice in San Salvador for a never-to-be-granted permission to visit political prisoners, Berrigan endures the hollow courtesies of a "vermicular" public official with a patience that surprises even himself. As in the Block Island poems he is all eyes, absorbing, weighing, setting out his perceptions in unhurried sequence. The measured pace and reserve differ greatly from the urgent and decisive perceptions that had characterized the earlier journal, *Night Flight to Hanoi*. There, he had felt under pressure to act, whereas in *Steadfastness of the Saints* his primary task is simply to understand. For this reason his assessment of the political and social situation he is confronted with is more judicious than in *Night Flight to Hanoi*, just as his perspective is a little more distant and reticent, a reticence based upon an increased skepticism about political and ecclesiastical parties of all stripes.

Thus, although appalled at the institutional cruelty that pervaded life in El Salvador, Berrigan remained as skeptical about the mingling of clerical and secular life in the Nicaraguan cabinet as he was about the theology whereby certain priests in Central and South America, like Camilio Torrez in Colombia, had taken up arms. In Nicaragua, Berrigan didn't conceal his disapproval of Ernesto Cardenal, Minister of Culture in the Sandanista government, priest, poet, and former student of Thomas Merton's at the Abbey of Gethsemani in Kentucky. In spite of Cardenal's protestations about his ability to serve God and man in political office, Berrigan judged that the priest had been swallowed by the politician.

Berrigan's steadfast saints are invariably those who stood apart, like the Lutheran pastor in El Salvador who had been tortured and imprisoned for speaking out on behalf of the poor. As always, Berrigan was struck by the oddness of the marks of authenticity in the saint, in this case a curious flatness in speech that contrasted with the grim details of the pastor's prison ordeal. Judging by the man's tone, Berrigan noted, his story might have been one of "statistics, births, marriages, deaths in safe beds, of old age and tired hearts. He was a very connoisseur of understatement, the dispassion of the survivor whose world must, for sake of sanity, be presented as bound by fairly normal routine."[123]

Berrigan's style in *The Steadfastness of the Saints* is spare and modest in comparison with the eruptiveness of his writing in the late 1960s and 1970s. Much of the writing exhibits an attractive, understated concreteness - as can be seen in the following description of peasant life in war-torn Nicaragua:

> A child sleeps in its hammock in the shed. Now the
> young mother takes up an ax, starts splitting wood
> in the torrid noon. The sun strikes off her blade.
> The wood makes a fire that makes the noon meal.
> It is all simple and primitive and direct, as though
> some new beginning of things were being under-
> scored in an exhausted and depleted world. [124]

What stands out is Berrigan's pleasure at existence itself, the pale satisfactions of the survivor. Furthermore, whereas in the earlier work he turned to analogies and symbols, here literal realities are illuminating enough - since in the volatile, surreal societies of El Salvador and Nicaragua event and symbol had become one. This much, at any rate, is implied in his description of a refugee camp on the edge of San Salvador where the misery of hundreds was bared to the sun, offset only by the "crepuscular light" within the interiors of some crude shacks. There was a single spigot of water, Berrigan points out, for 900 people, and yet piled against the northern fence of the camp was a mound of boxlike objects, concrete sinks sent by the wife of a chief of state, a heap of "inspired useless junk."[125]

Less censorious and barbed than *Night Flight to Hanoi*, *Steadfastness of the Saints* exhibits a convincing visual objectivity. The faces of the Nicaraguan soldiers are sketched as bewildered and forlorn in contrast to Berrigan's censorious descriptions of the military throughout the 1970s.[126] Similarly, government helicopters in El Salvador, alternately dropping explosives and ferrying the wounded, are described in language both more restrained and impartial than in earlier writing. A similar objectivity can be seen in Berrigan's view of the peasant populations in Central America. While fundamentally in sympathy with these exploited peoples, he was struck by the contrast between their rudimentary housing on the one hand and the array of cheap electronic gadgets within, to say nothing of the garish statues in the churches, clothed in "bizarre finery" and exhibiting a fixated stare behind glass, "deterrent dolls of heaven."[127] Occasionally, the effect is bilious enough to provoke mirth, as in the cathedral in northern Nicaragua where the statues are said to resemble performers in an "*opera bouffe*, frozen in untamed fortissimos."[128]

Berrigan's commitment to the poor on the one hand and his detached consciousness that a certain amount of ugliness and absurdity are an inevitable aspect of poverty strengthen his journal, which places pointed descriptive detail convincingly against a backdrop of tempered realism. The change in Berrigan's tone is evident in the internal landscape as well, as can be seen in his dreams, which are benign in comparison with those described in the writings of the early 1970s. An example is the dream of the plummeting airplane that metamorphoses into a feather, a dream that is in sharp contrast with that of the fatal airplane crash which was chillingly recorded in *Lights On in the House of the Dead* in the early 1970s.[129]

In the spring of 1985 Berrigan was approached by film director, Roland Joffe, to be a consultant for a film which Joffe was preparing to shoot in South America. The film, *The Mission*, which later won a number of awards at Cannes and at the Academy Awards in Los Angeles, was about a Jesuit mission territory in 18th century Paraguay in which the Indians were organized into a thriving agricultural and manufacturing cooperative in which they were protected from the slave traders.[130] A crisis developed when a boundary change involving Portugal and Spain threatened the autonomy of the mission settlements and the freedom of the

Indians. The screenplay by Robert Bolt is a partly fictional account of how the Jesuit missionaries reacted to the closing of the missions by their superiors, who were in turn under pressure from the Portugese not to interfere with the boundary change.

Berrigan accepted the invitation to assist in the making of the film and flew off to Colombia where most of the filming took place. He was attracted by the story of the ill-fated, South American missions, and as in his earlier journey to El Salvador and Nicaragua he again found himself in pursuit of the heroic archetype that had initially drawn him into the priesthood. In this respect he was heartened by the sight of contemporary Jesuits working in the barrios of Colombia in spiritual continuity with their courageous predecessors who had come out from Europe in the 17th and 18th centuries. Other signs of continuity were less consoling. There were the sporadic signs of violence and of the presence of the police state in modern-day Colombia that recalled the rapaciousness and oppression of the past. There was the class structure which underlay the abject state of the Colombian poor and of the Indians, a situation ironically perpetuated by the film-makers, Berrigan noted with chagrin, who hired and displaced hundreds of Colombians, including a small tribe of Indians, without having any particular interest in the long-term effects of this dislocation. Berrigan's reservations about being part of the film are contained in an interesting journal which he kept of his four months in South America, which was published in 1986 under the title, *The Mission*.

Ambivalence lies at the heart of this journal, just as it had pervaded *Steadfastness of the Saints*; the resulting braiding of antithetical observations and attitudes, however, reveals Berrigan near the top of his form as a writer. While Berrigan found himself repelled, in touring the old Colombian seaport of Cartagena, by vestiges of the Inquisition, he was also visited by the perplexing thought that if the past had been barbarous and cruel, it had nonetheless exhibited a religious certainty that contrasted with contemporary conundrums about the existence of God - a state of affairs that Berrigan believed had the effect of precluding the experience of God.[131] Rather like the narrator of Hawthorne's *Scarlet Letter*, Berrigan envied the sanguine decisiveness and energy of the past while trembling at its benightedness and narrowness. In a similarly ambivalent vein, while he acknowledged the social discernment of the liberation theologians whose views underlay much of the church's resistance to oppressive governments in Central and South America, he was dismayed by the tendency of some liberation theologians to become so mesmerized with sociological analysis and class conflict that they lost touch with the biblical roots and insights that had made the role of the church historically distinct.

The Paraguayan mission seemed to Berrigan to be an exception to the spiritual darkness of both past and present as well as being a model of the sort of small community that could be set against the alienating structuring of modern societies. Throughout his stay in South America, though, he was troubled by a proliferation of doubts that centered on the relationship between art, history, and religion. While offended by the extravagant display of consumer goods which the film company thrust upon the third world Colombians, he nevertheless hoped, though without much confidence, that the finished film itself would prove to be a counterweight that would allow the human soul to "shine through."[132]

On the other hand he feared that the very splendor of the film, set amid exotic scenery, might so arouse the senses as to inhibit a genuine contemplative response to the film's moral themes. On the whole he found himself remaining doubtful about even the most morally impeccable works produced by the cinematic "dream factory."[133] On the set Berrigan perceived that film was not only an art form but also an arm of technology and, as such, something to be wary about: "The cameraman thinks only of his machine, its function, placing, focus, switch. He stands or sits on his platform, moving the great orb about ponderously, a lesser god monitoring a greater."[134] The actors, though, were a different matter, and Berrigan gained a renewed respect for their calling during the filming, terming it an ascetic vocation in its demand for concentrated effort:

> . . . the actor thinks only of his part; there is, according to his fiction, no eye upon him. His own eye has buried itself in dreams, like a bird of paradise asleep; and therefore in its dream most acutely awake. His soul is sewn, as his frame is, into a costume; within it, life is savage, extravagant, or slowly and somberly, flowing. Then it is done, the big Eye turns off indifferently; it has seen all it is pleased to see. The actor collapses in a canvas chair; he is once more a mere mortal. [135]

Berrigan worried about whether the actors in *The Mission*, who were not especially knowledgeable about the film's historical subject, would be able to mime the "incandescent spirits" of the 18th century Jesuit missionaries.[136] Opposed to the success of the film in this respect was not only an initial ignorance by the cast about the spiritual attitudes of the distant figures who were the subject of the film, but a tendency in the actors, Berrigan observed gloomily, to interpret behavior exclusively in psychological rather than in spiritual terms. Nevertheless, as the film proceeded, Berrigan observed with hope an enlarged moral consciousness in the principal actors as they brushed both against the spiritual depths of their tale and against the harsh realities of life in the third world.

While he was concerned about the spiritual authenticity of the film, Berrigan appears less concerned in his journal about historical accuracy. He accepted the screenplay's unhistorical inclusion of an Indian Jesuit superior of the mission, for example, on the grounds that, even if no Indians in the 18th century settlement had become priests, a good many did so in subsequent centuries. He also persuaded the director of the film to alter the ending so that the Jesuit martyr who protests the eviction order issued by his superiors is killed while walking openly in religious procession rather than being a passive victim within a blazing church - as the script had dictated. Wanting to point up the active role of the pacifist, Berrigan felt little compunction about altering the film's ending since he was essentially intent upon shaping a contemporary morality play rather than offering a strict dramatization of recorded history.

On the other hand, he objected to others connected with the film tampering with its historical accuracy when the effect interfered with the symbolic tableau which he himself had in mind. An example is the film's opening, startling image of a Jesuit, stripped and tied to a wooden cross, who is sent hurtling over an immense waterfall. Though many Jesuits had been martyred in the Paraguayan missions, there had been, according to Berrigan, no instance of the sort that was proposed, and he recoiled from the violence of the scene, regarding it as a sop to commercialism.

Increasingly in *The Mission* journal, Berrigan concedes the manipulative nature of the project in which he had involved himself as well as the probable futility of such an attempt to reconstitute the past. In a scene involving five Jesuits praying around a campfire, for example, he points to the difficulty of remembering that were three stages to be considered in recalling such a scene from the past. In the first stage, that of literal history, only the event itself is remembered - "firelight, the sound of water bickering and sliding along, the light of fire on the faces." In the second stage, that of collective myth, the news of the missionaries who were martyred for resisting the disbanding of their mission, spread to Europe, and the lives of the Jesuits assumed an aura of "purity and heroism, a kind of transfigured distancing in contrast to the banality of life in the temperate zone of Europe." The third stage is that of art, specifically the film which Berrigan was working on, in which skill and technology brought "romantic yearnings to an apogee. Shades of Rousseau and the Frenchman in Tahiti and the libertine in Montmartre and the Dutchman on the Côte d'Azur!"[137]

History, Berrigan implies, as well as the art based upon it, have always lent themselves to an ongoing process of assimilation whereby the felt collective psychological needs of the audience prepared the artist to mix historical ikons on his palette until the selected hues matched the point of view of his own generation. At the same time, Berrigan's dry allusions to the "libertine in Montmartre and the Dutchman on the Côte d'Azur" indicate that he was not satisfied with this way of assimilating history into art even if in retrospect it seemed an inevitable process.

What Berrigan as a consultant attempted to have come out of the film and in fact has attempted to have come out of his writing as a whole was an image of reality that both included the modern sensibility and yet indicated alternatives to that sensibility, not merely within the flux of history but from a viewpoint partially external to history. Instead of the conventional mingling of fact and wish fulfillment in art, therefore, fact could be joined, as in the film's changed ending, to a view of what modern audiences and readers *should* wish for in their collective myths. In this instance, as well as elsewhere in his writings, Berrigan appears tacitly to subscribe to Ezra Pound's view that all art is didactic, that some art is simply didactic in a deeper manner than other art.

Didacticism has not proven to be a problem in Berrigan's work as long as any didacticism that had seeped in has remained supplementary to the act of imaginative fusion that produced a successful poem, essay, or journal. While Berrigan's reflections about art, history, and religion form an engrossing intellectual core in the case of *The Mission*, for example, the strength of this journal is to be found in the way in which the eye of the artist, seeing the world anew, alters and heightens our perceptions of a world we thought we knew. These comments about Berrigan as artist are especially appropriate in the sense that *The Mission* journal is very considerably about art. The antitheses that shape the journal's contents, for example, take on an unforeseen value as art when they form part not only of a set of ideas but of a dramatic encounter with the past in Berrigan's pilgrimage to the site of the original 18th century Paraguayan mission of San Ignacio. At this point the book rises from its bed of images and ideas to crystallize with unusual eloquence Berrigan's nostalgic search for religious heroism from within an antiheroic period:

> One stone column along a row had been entirely enveloped over the years in a living tree, like a body of stone wrapped in folds of wooden raiment. I glanced through a natural cleft in the wood and felt along with my hands; and indeed the heart of the tree was stone. We walked diagonally across the sward toward the church portal. The broken archway loomed up before us, wine red and the lucent green of the lawn. Indeed it was as though the wine of life had petrified there, falling and tumbling. [138]

Corollaries to such evocative stimuli from the past are found in the forms of primitive life that survive in the present, as is seen in Berrigan's startled encounter with a large sloth, which he saw draped over the shoulder of the Dutch ambassador's wife at the Cartagena airport:

> The creature clung to her like the newborn; its head turned ever so slowly over her shoulder, regarding us with mild wonderment. The great arms and legs were covered with the softest silvery fur. It looked out on the world, blinking slowly, as though clearing cobwebs from the mind, or as though it could scarcely credit what it saw, this world of nonsloths walking rapidly into the rear end of an iron bird. [139]

Vividly complete in itself as anecdote, the incident also amplifies the journal's themes of initiation and adaptation, capturing in particular Berrigan's sense of strangeness about the climate, vegetation, and customs of the world he had entered as well as his awareness of how strange he in turn appeared to the Colombians and Paraguayans.

The chief protagonists and symbols in this drama of cultural interface are the Indians, whose image, set against that of the modern world, forms a parallel to the historical juxtaposition of past and present that has already been discussed. The Indians were interesting to Berrigan because they offered a rare alternative to the cultural monopoly created by the success of the West. In this respect they differed from the rest of the Colombian and Latin American population, which for the most part struggled in the wake of western capitalism. In the Indians who had been transported to take part in the film, Berrigan perceived a physical and mental health, together with a social equilibrium, that distinguished them from the bulk of the Colombian poor. As well, the Indians seemed aloof and even slightly bemused at their affluent visitors from the north. Berrigan concluded that there was something "almost monastic" about them, something "stable, benign, playful, mindful, ungrabbing, direct in look and speech" and that their treatment of the Americans and Europeans involved in the film was marked by a respect that brought out the best they in turn could muster of their own "dignity."[140]

While aware, as was indicated earlier, of the dangers of being Rousseauistic, Berrigan could not deny the testimony of his own eyes, as in his consciousness of a continuous "hum" of low voices that pervaded life in the Indian community, the "swish and buzz of brooms sweeping the fallen leaves, the birdlike counterpoint of the children's treble - the variety and subdued consonance of a human hive," a "sweet undercurrent" that went on from dawn to dusk.[141] While the word, "hive," distances Berrigan's view of the Indians, he is attracted to the "consonance," a voluntary process, that he perceived as underlying the harmony of Indian life. At the same time, he felt as excluded as he was fascinated by the Indians, whose way of life represented an integral, closed system in contrast to his own nomadic, inquisitive lifestyle.

Nevertheless, the complaisance, modesty, and confidence of the Indians produced a ferment in Berrigan's imagination, giving rise to a fresh perception of the ego as a "conscious bowl or vessel" which, though desiring to be filled with the images and experiences of this world in order to create its identity, needed to be deliberately and repeatedly emptied so as to make possible a detachment from the self and from the menu of experience. The alternative, Berrigan wrote, was to remain stuck in the world "up to one's neck," like the characters in Samuel Beckett's plays, whom he perceived as unable to imagine another world beyond the "glutted ego."[142]

Less obsessively individualistic than people in the industrialized West and more humble in the presence of nature, the Indians had achieved a balance between self and non-self that seemed to Berrigan to have had a beneficial effect on the stability of their community. Nonetheless, conceding that western medicine had enhanced the rate of survival of the Indian children even within the short span of the film's production, Berrigan found himself characteristically stretched between his culture and that of the Indians, trying to learn from them while perceiving that he could never be like them, stopped at the perimeter of their world by what he termed their - for lack of a better word - innocence. Nevertheless, struck by the Indians' unashamed awareness of their difference from others, even in the face of obvious condescension, Berrigan resolved to continue "tipping the bowl" of his ego over in future when confronted by figures of power for whom he would then play "the idiot, the inarticulate," if not quite the innocent.[143]

Relaxed in mood and yet bristling with provocative and original conceptions and images. the *Mission* journal revealed Berrigan as having moved out of the thematic impasse of the 1970s where, stung by the draconian treatment by civil and legal authorities of himself and of the other war protestors, he had, without perhaps fully realizing it, slipped into a despondency about human blindness and perfidy. The prophetic tone of Berrigan's writings had modulated through the 1970s and 1980s from a vision of apocalypse to one of survival. The nuclear sword of Damocles that hung over the writings of the 1970s continued to hang by a hair over the writings of the 1980s - although a change in perspective had occurred as the aging Berrigan became more interested in and consoled by the fundamental values of existence. Rather than prophesying the end, he had become curious about and grateful for the underlying rhythms of life that might, if he could make them audible enough for contemporary readers, slowly turn humanity toward the heart of being and away from its unconsciously willed self-destruction.

Notes: Chapter 5

1. *Jesus Christ* (Garden City, N.Y.: Doubleday, 1973) unpaginated.
2. Letter from Daniel Berrigan to Nita Regnier, Aug. 25, 1972.
3. Letter from Daniel Berrigan to William and Margaret Farmer, Sept. 28, 1972.
4. Letter from Daniel Berrigan to Rev. James Hietter, S.J., Oct., 1972.
5. *Ten Commandments for the Long Haul* (Abingdon: Nashville, 1981) 126.
6. Letter from Daniel Berrigan to the author, Feb. 11, 1986.
7. "Daniel Berrigan, S.J." *The New Jesuits*, ed. George Riemer (Boston: Little, Brown, 1971) 44.
8. Jacques Ellul, *The Political Illusion*, trans. Konrad Kellen (New York: Vintage, 1972) 224.
9. Jacques Ellul, *Violence: Reflections from a Christian Perspective*, trans. Cecilia King (New York: Seabury, 1969) 145.
10. Letter from Daniel Berrigan to the author, Feb. 11, 1986.
11. Letter from Daniel Berrigan to James Forest, Sept. 15, 1972.
12. See "On the Torturing of Prisoners," *Fellowship* 39 (Sept., 1973) 4-5.
13. See "An Open Letter to Political Prisoners in the U.S.S.R.," *WIN* 9 (June 28, 1973) 9. See also "Slave Camps and Tiger Cages/Letter to Leonid Brezhnev," *Village Voice*, Oct. 5, 1972, 74-77.
14. Quoted in Laraine Fergenson, "Thoreau, Berrigan, and Transcendental Politics," *Soundings* 65 (Spring, 1982) 110.
15. Quoted in *The New Jesuits* 47.
16. For a review of the controversy surrounding Berrigan's speech see *The Great Berrigan Debate* (New York: Committee on New Alternatives in the Middle East, 1974). An edited transcript of Berrigan's speech entitled "Responses to Settler Regimes," was published in *American Report*, Oct. 29, 1973, 5, 16-17.

17. See Noam Chomsky, *Peace in the Middle East?* (New York: Pantheon, 1974) 167-180 and *The Fateful Triangle: The United States, Israel and the Palestinians* (Boston: South End Pr., 1983) 4, 148.

18. Harriet Shapiro, "Berrigan in Crisis," *Intellectual Digest* 4 (May, 1974) 10.

19. Paul Cowan, "The Moral Imperialism of Dan Berrigan," *Village Voice*, Jan. 23, 1974, 23-24.

20. The press conference statement was made on May 19, 1974, and was published as "In War, Truth is the First Casualty" in *Fellowship* 40 (June, 1974) 12.

21. See *Ten Commandments* 40.

22. Letter from Daniel Berrigan to James Stevenson, July 3, 1973.

23. *Uncommon Prayer* (New York: Seabury, 1978) 125-126.

24. *To Dwell in Peace* (San Francisco: Harper & Row, 1987) 306.

25. See "Anniversary Poems: Report from the Empty Grave," *Thought* 57 (March, 1982) 74-75.

26. Letter from Daniel Berrigan to James Douglass, Sept. 25, 1979.

27. "The Time Bomb That Makes Daniel Berrigan Tick," *U.S. Catholic* 45 (July, 1980) 9.

28. *Portraits - Of Those I Love* (New York: Crossroad, 1982) 148.

29. See Berrigan's article, "Linking the Altar to the Pentagon," *I.F.O.R. Report*, July, 1979, 7-8. See also "Morality: What Are We, the Church, to Do?" *National Catholic Reporter* 13 (April 8, 1977) 12-13.

30. "Star Wars: Cruel Fantasy," *Sojourners* 6 (Sept., 1977) 34.

31. *Ten Commandments*, 128, 58.

32. *Raft* 100-101.

33. *Beside the Sea of Glass* (New York: Seabury, 1978) 64.

34. *Uncommon* 135.

35. *Ten Commandments* 41.

36. *Words* 28-29.

37. "Introduction," *The Cell* by Horst Bienek (Santa Barbara: Unicorn, 1972) iv.

38. *Uncommon* 21.

39. *Portraits* 145.

40. *Jesus Christ* unpaginated.

41. *Glass* 99.

42. *Portraits* 65.

43. *Uncommon* 39.

44. *Nightmare* 114.

45. *Nightmare* 111.

46. *Nightmare* 89.

47. "Daniel Berrigan, S.J.," *Contemporary Authors: Autobiography Series*, I, ed. Dedria Bryfonski (Detroit: Gale, 1985) 54.

48. *Consequences: Truth And...* (New York: Macmillan, 1967) 21.

49. *A Book of Parables* (New York: Seabury, 1977) 88.

50. *Parables* 87.

51. "The Season of Youth," *Today* 19 (May, 1964) 30.

52. Letter from Daniel Berrigan to George Lawlor, ca. June, 1978.

53. *The Discipline of the Mountain: Dante's Purgatorio in a Nuclear World* (New York: Seabury, 1979) xiii.

54. *Discipline* 3.

55. *Discipline* 60.

56. *Glass* 68.

57. *Parables* 74.

58. *Uncommon* 131.

59. "The Eucharist and Survival," *Seeds of Liberation*, ed. Alistair Kee (London: SCM Press, 1973) 88.

60. *Portraits* 35.

61. *Portraits* 33.

62. *Portraits* 44.

63. *Portraits* 48.

64. *Portraits* 48-49.

65. *We Die Before We Live (New York: Seabury, 1980)* 7.
66. *We Die* 55.
67. *We Die* 46.
68. *We Die* 41.
69. *We Die* 52.
70. *We Die* 28, 31.
71. *We Die* 32.
72. *We Die* 27-28.
73. *We Die* 28.
74. *We Die* 24.
75. *We Die* 73-74.
76. *We Die* 87.
77. *We Die* 125.
78. *To Dwell in Peace* 325.
79. *To Dwell in Peace* 328.
80. "Anniversary Poems" 75.
81. Ibid.
82. "The Seventy Times Seventy Seven Storey Mountain," *Cross Currents* 27 (1977-78) 386.
83. "Daniel Berrigan, S.J.," *Contemporary Authors* 54.
84. *Portraits* 28-29.
85. Shapiro 8.
86. "Come Now, Choose," *May All Creatures Live* (Nevada City, Ca: Berliner, 1984) 46.
87. "I Hope and Pray This Doesn't Happen to Me," *Creatures* 88.
88. "Apologia," *Creatures* 14.
89. Letter from Daniel Berrigan to the author, June 7, 1986.
90. "Ignorance is Like a Sourdough Starter," *Creatures* 59.
91. "O Catholic Church," *Creatures* 22.
92. "Life and Death and Everything in Between," *Creatures* 51.
93. "Consolation," *Creatures* 13.
94. "The Ring," *Creatures* 20.

95.   "Spirit Explained To a Child," *Creatures* 47.
96.   "A Dying Gull on the Beach," *Creatures* 56.
97.   "You Might Call This a Love Poem," *Creatures* 61.
98.   "Jerry, Carol and I Make the Grand Tour," *Creatures* 63.
99.   *Block Island* (Greensboro, N.C.: Unicorn, 1985) 9.
100. *Block* 56.
101. *Block* 18.
102. *Block* 91.
103. *Block* 90.
104. *Block* 57.
105. *Block* 48.
106. *Block* 15.
107. *Block* 35.
108. *Block* 26.
109. *Block* 7.
110. *Block* 17.
111. *Block* 6.
112. *Block* 82.
113. *Block* 13.
114. *Block* 1.
115. *Block* 14.
116. *Block* 45.
117. Letter from Daniel Berrigan to James Forest, June 4, 1984.
118. *Steadfastness of the Saints* (Maryknoll, N.Y.: Orbis, 1985) 29-30.
119. *Steadfastness* 11.
120. *Steadfastness* 44.
121. *Steadfastness* 68.
122. *Steadfastness* 118, 120.
123. *Steadfastness* 27.
124. *Steadfastness* 116.
125. *Steadfastness* 10.
126. *Steadfastness* 55.

127. *Steadfastness* 62-63.
128. *Steadfastness* 92.
129. *Lights On in the House of the Dead* (New York: Doubleday, 1974) 154.
130. For a historical account of the Paraguayan mission that provided the basis for Bolt's screenplay, see Philip Caraman, *The Lost Paradise: the Jesuit Republic in South America* (New York: Seabury, c1975).
131. *The Mission: A Film Journal* (San Francisco: Harper & Row, 1986) 110.
132. *Mission* 93.
133. *Mission* 151.
134. *Mission* 45.
135. *Mission* 45.
136. *Mission* 46.
137. *Mission* 119.
138. *Mission* 153.
139. *Mission* 61.
140. *Mission* 128.
141. *Mission* 70.
142. *Mission* 67.
143. *Mission* 67-68.

Chapter Six

PLACING THE WRITER

As was true of his friend, Thomas Merton, Berrigan's life and writings are so completely intermingled that any attempt to separate the two for the sake of analysis runs the risk of being shallow and tedious. In the tradition of Thoreau, whom he greatly admired, Berrigan's life has, almost from the beginning, flowed into the writing, which in turn has clarified both for himself and others the direction in which that life had been moving. Moreover, just as it would be absurd to focus merely on the formal aspects of Thoreau's writings, which draw much of their value from the configuration of his life, so too with Berrigan, more than with most contemporary writers, one has to relate the man to the writing and both to their time in order to determine his significance. Nonetheless, in the case of a writer like Berrigan, whose involvement in high-profile, topical issues has been so pronounced, one has to guard against assigning value to the writing on the basis of either sympathy with or antipathy toward the social movements with which he has associated himself.

As a protagonist in the anti-war movement Berrigan's achievements both as a writer and as an activist have been formidable. As Charles Meconis has demonstrated in his excellent study of the Catholic Left, Berrigan had a considerable influence not only upon the anti-war protest and the American withdrawal from the Vietnam war but also upon the official teaching of the American Catholic hierarchy on the issue of war.[1] His influence can be seen in the episcopal letter, *The Challenge of Peace*, which was published in 1983 and which, though it accepted the policy of deterrence and the theology of the just war, questioned the application of that theology in the case of a nuclear war since such a conflict would be difficult to contain. In addition, the bishops asserted the rights of conscientious objectors, and supported the activities of those committed to non-violence as an alternative to deterrence. The imprint of the Berrigans and of the American Catholic peace movement in turn upon the American hierarchy becomes especially apparent when *The Challenge of Peace* is compared with statements by the bishops of France and England during the 1980s in which a traditional morality of war is upheld and largely advocated.

In addition, as was evidenced by the international impact of the trial of the Catonsville Nine as both event and play, Daniel Berrigan demonstrated how a small and apparently powerless group could focus public attention on a particular issue in a manner that would shape the outcome of that issue, and while Berrigan's attempts at using society as a public theater have not been so successful of late, the techniques he used in 1968, drawing on the examples of Gandhi and Martin Luther King, continue to play an influential role in American social and political life.

As a writer Berrigan continues to have a significant, if not uncontroversial, effect on the role of the clergy and on the Jesuits in particular. In his life and in his writing, drawing on his early exposure to the French worker priests and to the Catholic Worker movement, he redesigned the role of the American priest by locating that role not in the isolation of the rectory or classroom but in the human community at large. Partly through Berrigan's influence, the number of priests and nuns who have emulated the worker-priest model, including the Jesuits who make up Berrigan's own community in upper west Manhattan, has grown significantly in recent years. Not unaware of the notoriety of his reputation as a cleric in some quarters, Berrigan, in a recent letter to the author, passed on the waggish remark of a colleague about his small acting role in the film, *The Mission*, that if he couldn't be a Jesuit, he "might as well play one."[2]

Pointing to the model of early Christianity in many of his writings, Berrigan has repeatedly questioned ecclesiastical habits of thought that had supplanted in some quarters the informal, communal, and ascetic patterns of the first Christians. In spite of his increasingly direct reliance upon scripture rather than upon theological tradition and in spite of his past skirmishes with ecclesiastical authorities, Berrigan has remained grateful for his identity as a priest. On the other hand, rooted ideologically in the American tradition of dissent, he has insisted on his right to shape both American religion and society according to his own lights without in any way abandoning his underlying commitment to both church and country. Nevertheless, seeing that his church had, over the decades, wrapped itself in the national banner, he determined to free it so that it might criticize American society according to its own perceptions and ethical canons - the third eye which he believed Christianity as a sort of meta-culture brought to bear on human affairs.

While consciously adhering to the origins of the Christian tradition, which involved small and often isolated communities that encouraged the sharing of possessions and that stood in spiritual opposition to the prevailing order, Berrigan has implicitly contributed to the current protestantizing of the Catholic church in the United States. He has done so in part by asserting the primacy of the individual conscience, an idea that had been given cautious approval by the Second Vatican Council but which has been downplayed by Rome in recent years. He has encouraged his fellow Americans to behave in religious matters as they have been educated to behave in political matters.

His approach toward episcopal authority since the mid-1960s has been to regard that authority with what he has called the critical 'glance' of Christ, as he put it in *To Dwell in Peace*. It must quickly be added, however, that that glance has inevitably reflected Berrigan's own interpretation of the scriptural writings, without reference, for the most part, to other authority.[3] Nonetheless, in spite of the feelings of separation from institutional Christianity which Berrigan has expressed throughout the 1970s and 1980s, he has frequently, in both his poetry and prose, reaffirmed his identity as a Catholic and as a Jesuit priest. Similarly, while at odds with institutional politics in the United States during his lifetime, his identity as an American has been firmly and warmly adhered to throughout his life.

Such complexities of mind and bearing, which are part of Berrigan's value as a writer, were touched on by the psychiatrist, Robert Coles, some years ago in introducing a published colloquy between Berrigan and himself:

> A man of culture and refinement, he has lashed out at the academic and artistic world. A man versed in logic, and in many ways an obvious rationalist, indeed a skeptic, he can become all of a sudden mystical. I never wanted to "analyze" his personality, but its complexities kept appearing and never quite resolved themselves; I suspect they will grow and grow, and become the full-blown paradoxes that significant lives so often present to us.[4]

Embedded like a thorn in the bosom of his church and of his society, Berrigan continues as a writer to provoke controversy in a number of areas, from his denouncements of American foreign policy in Latin America and of the U.S. commitment to a strategy of nuclear stalemate to his outspoken statements on behalf of the terminally ill AIDS patients he has visited over the years in New York. In a recent letter to the author, for example, he dwelt on the difficulty of providing comfort not only for the dying person with AIDS but for the family members, many of whom had been alienated from homosexuals by what Berrigan has termed a harsh, "local" Catholicism.[5] On a number of issues, then, Berrigan's writings have made room for a new model of the priesthood in which essential orthodoxy may coexist, however tensely and precariously, with an aloofness and even at times a contempt for the trappings and traditions of American Catholic culture.

As a spiritual writer Berrigan has evolved through a number of distinct stages.[6] Stimulated by the writings of the German theologian, Karl Rahner, in the 1940s and by the French theologians, Henri de Lubac and Teilhard de Chardin, in the 1950s, he at first espoused a triumphant Christianity in which God was portrayed as wedded indissolubly to his creation and through his incarnated son to human history, gradually and perceptibly drawing humanity through the church toward the ideal, divine idea of the world. The tone of these early writings is confident and in harmony with the solid, formal arrangement of their reasoning and imagery.

In the essays and journals of the 1960s Berrigan turned increasingly toward the third world where, in the light of the apparent acquiescence of the church toward blatant social injustices in some of the developing countries, he began to doubt the creative, historical thrust of institutional Christianity. What brought the issue to a head was his horrified perception of his own country's and church's complicity in the tragedy of the Vietnam war and in the massive social suffering experienced by the peoples of Latin America.

These experiences gave rise to an individualized, though still modestly confident, view of the possibilities of Christian action. The writings of the 1960s attest to Berrigan's increasing alienation from conventional theological analysis and to his growing reliance on the New Testament and on the first-hand experience of contemporary Christians like Dorothy Day, Dietrich Bonhoeffer, and Thomas Merton in grappling with the application of Christianity to the social order. As the journals make evident, Berrigan relied more and more upon his own experience and consciousness as he came to perceive Christianity as a laboratory experiment in which in each generation new materials formed part of religion's evolving relationship with the larger society.

As both a poet and a prose writer in the late 1960s, particularly in the years at Cornell when his books sold widely, Berrigan both altered the social thinking of his church regarding war in general and the Vietnam conflict in particular, trenchantly inserting the views of religion, for a time at least, into the mainstream of American political thought. In an age in which interest in religion has been clearly on the decline, Berrigan made the relevance of religious consciousness to the temporal world in the late 1960s both apparent and urgent.

Through his writings in the 1970s and 1980s Berrigan made himself accessible to those who had become alienated by either secular or religious institutionalism, producing a moral agenda that appealed, potentially at least, to a universal readership, a quite different audience from that which he addressed in the 1950s in a voice that was distinctly clerical. At the same time, Berrigan's theme from the beginning has been that the interests of religion, when properly considered, are those of humanity itself. For this reason he was frequently cutting about the tendency of some involved in religion, such as the prison chaplain in *Lights On in the House of the Dead*, to seek the interests of religion first.

Berrigan's moral outlook can be distinguished from the programs of political parties and movements on the left in that he has consistently drawn on biblical insights in order to illuminate the chronic human malaise that he sees as underlying contemporary culture, including contemporary religious culture. He has been skeptical about the ability of political thinkers and social planners to cope with this social malaise on a structural basis without there being an accompanying moral and psychological transformation both in the planners and in society in general. He has been especially persuasive in linking the current, widespread infatuation with technology to the growth of passivity in the population at large and to the corresponding acceleration in the arms race by governments, noting discerningly in *The Nightmare of God* that the problem was not simply that modern nations had the nuclear bomb but that the "Bomb has us."[7] Collectively, Berrigan argues, we think in an exclusively technological way about armaments and national security, and thus cannot free ourselves from the political and psychological cul-de-sac in which we find ourselves.

While Berrigan's thinking about war may seem ingenuous to some observers, others, like the respected political scientist, Anatol Rapoport, have underlined the futility of a merely technical approach to arms negotiations, and have cast doubt on the wisdom of placing national security in the hands of a scientific establishment. The reason, Rapoport has noted, is that in such conflicts only "relative strength counts, and this does not necessarily increase with technological potential and strategic cleverness, because the opponent is impelled to make similar gains." Even though international negotiations conducted on moral principles inevitably appear ingenuous to pragmatists, Rapoport adds, in a historical perspective it would appear that "great, irreversible changes in the human condition have been brought about by the accumulation of such acts."[8]

In bringing religious consciousness into harmony with the ecological concerns being expressed by a number of intellectuals during the 1960s and 1970s, Berrigan indicated a further new alignment for American Catholicism. In the 1970s, as has been seen, when Berrigan felt bereft of an awareness of the intervening presence of God in the world, he turned increasingly to creation for reassurance, as in the Block Island poems, and the thought that nuclear warfare might obliterate that residual trace of God's presence became particularly unbearable.

Berrigan's somber view of contemporary culture, which derives from a biblically reinforced perception of perennial evil, surfaced in the courses which he gave at Cornell in the late 1960s, which were grounded in apocalyptic scriptures and Greek tragedies. Humanity's only chance against an automatic institution-alizing of its fundamental disposition toward evil, he has contended, is the existence of individuals with a modest courage to dissent that hovers somewhere between purposeful action and a sense of the absurd. Hence the ubiquitous mood of irony that pervades Berrigan's writings during the 1970s and 1980s. The irony has been fortuitous in creating a critical distance both between himself and the conventional beliefs and practices of his faith and between himself and the religion which a number of his contemporaries have made of art. The distance thus created has made possible the antithetical play of mind that has characterized Berrigan's poems, prose writings, and journals since the late 1960s.

Both skeptical and quixotic, Berrigan has argued that the resistance communities of which he has been a part and about which he has written so extensively undermine by their very exis-tence the technological hegemony of power and pleasure that has pervaded contemporary culture. Moreover, beneath the common-sense assertion of the moral superiority of some aspects of technology over others in twentieth-century culture, Berrigan has perceived an underlying hatred toward an imperfect world by modern technologists and thereby an implicit disdain for the alleged divinity that might have created such a world. It is this aspect of technological culture that Berrigan has most vigorously responded to, his sense that the imperfection of the world - which as an artist he has depicted as often paradoxically intermingled with its beauty - is a symbol of humanity's essential incompleteness, which instead of inviting disdain, should become the foundation of an international, vulnerable consciousness of interdependence rather than of a promethean competitiveness.

As an essayist Berrigan has evolved, as has been seen, through a number of styles, from the relatively erudite and formal manner of the 1950s and early 1960s to the semi-poetic, autobiographical, rather omnivorous style of the later work. During the later phase, fragments of Berrigan's life and reading melted into open-ended streams of prose in which he attempted to register the changing configuration of his experience of dissent. In these elliptical narratives would emerge, he implicitly came to believe, a sense of direction for the morally sensitive at a time when both religious and secular institutions in America had failed to provide adequate understanding of some crucial ethical issues. Nevertheless, aware of the pitfalls of narcissism, Berrigan has frequently viewed even these issues in the depths of his essays, poems, and journals with a satiric eye, showing himself as capable in his best writing of self-doubt as of moral passion.

The most profound and moving prose writings are those in which Berrigan chose to confront the very imperfections of a world whose metaphysical rightness, all the same, he has repeatedly attempted to justify. His incisively compassionate studies of the severely ill, for example, particularly in *We Die Before We Live*,

brought Berrigan face to face with the darkness of his God, a God
who seemed prepared to allow an innocent child to sink into death
after prolonged pain and a lengthy coma for a reason so mysterious
that the consciousness of the observing priest all but dissolves at
the thought of it. Similarly, in journals like *The Dark Night of
Resistance* and *Lights On in the House of the Dead*, Berrigan
confronted both the absence of God and the desert of faith with a
chilling sense of vertigo. Wedded to irony as the only serviceable
idiom in such a universe, he plunged ahead in the certainty that if
God had remained absent for him, he had been no less absent for
his incarnated son.

If there are times, especially in the writings of the 1970s,
when one wonders whether or not Berrigan had transferred some of
his anguish concerning the absence of God into a rage directed
against mankind, such is not the case with the three works
mentioned above. What gives these books authority and makes
them cling to memory is their dramatic depiction of a mind
careening downward from ledges of assurance that had marked
earlier conviction. Only irony, it would appear, a quality that
Berrigan eventually ascribed to God, allowed him to keep some
measure of equilibrium. For Berrigan, irony is not only the mind's
response to disappointment, but the striated pattern of being itself -
not just a sign of the mind's resiliency, but also and preeminently a
pointer to ultimate truth, however dimly perceived.

If Berrigan's writing can be said to be characterized by one
attribute in particular, that attribute is movement. The prose and
poetry, which have registered major changes in his thought and
experience, have also led readers on a ceaseless physical journey
across the face of the earth. In this respect Berrigan has much in
common with American authors of the 19th and 20th centuries,
including Beat poets like Allen Ginsberg with whom he has felt a

particular affinity. In other important respects, however, he has been at odds with most contemporary poets, including the Beats.

In some ways, for example, Berrigan may be considered a poet whose view of art stretches back to the Renaissance, where poetry was assumed to be a proper vehicle for truth - especially moral truth. Thus, Berrigan would not be in complete agreement with critics like Helen Vendler who have questioned that anyone "except believing Christians" could now read the 17th century poet, George Herbert, with delight if "truth of doctrine and ideological relevance were the chief basis of aesthetic response."[9] In opposing the present, majority view that only beauty finally counts in art, Berrigan - in harmony with poets like Ivor Winters, perhaps - would argue that the contents of a poem are as crucial to its success as its form and that while commonplace and vulgar sentiments are obviously not the stuff of art, nevertheless the moral significance of a work of art is an important part of its value. In this connection, in his study of recent American poetry, Paul Breslin rejects the wrong-headedness both of the sort of protest poetry that too easily ignores the demands of form and the sort of reflexive poetry that attends to little other than form.[10] While Berrigan perceives the narrowness of contemporary poetry to be related to the philosophical assumption that neither moral knowledge nor moral control are possible, he contends that both are possible, however imperfectly, and has dedicated his poetry and life to the achievement of both, offering his own moral peregrinations as a point of departure.

Unlike William Carlos Williams, who argued that there were no ideas but in things - or Archibald MacLeish, who wrote that a poem should not mean but be - Berrigan not only reasserts a rational and ethical basis for poetry, but assumes that poets should have an influence upon conduct. In this respect he again expresses his traditionalism, in contrast to the sort of position taken by writers like Saul Bellow:

> Romantic poets and other edifying theorists of the
> nineteenth century had it wrong - poets and
> novelists will never be the legislators and teachers
> of mankind. That poets - artists - should give new
> eyes to human beings, inducing them to view the
> world differently, converting them from fixed
> modes of experience, is ambition enough, if one
> must offer a purposive account of the artist's
> project.[11]

For Berrigan, the relationship drawn by Bellow between art and the
building of consciousness would be regarded as perceptive but
incomplete. In the tradition of Thoreau and Dickens, Berrigan is an
artist who has sought not only the awakening of the mind but the
altering of behavior. That such an enterprise has not appealed to
contemporary poets and artists in general does not demonstrate that
it is a purpose that is incompatible with poetry or art, particularly if
one takes into account the poetry of earlier centuries in which some
measure of didacticism appeared to fit comfortably.

    While Berrigan, as has been pointed out, bears some
relationship to nineteenth-century American writers like Thoreau in
his combining of transcendentalism and political dissent, he has
less in common with the late Romanticism represented in much
recent poetry. Following the example of Wallace Stevens, most
contemporary American poets have abandoned the early Romantic
connection between imagination and reality. Steeped in intellectual
and moral relativism, Stevens concentrated on the drama of
perception as the sole subject matter left to the poet outside of the
authority of science, and thus severed the connection between
perception and what was assumed to be external reality. For this
reason, most contemporary poets influenced by the empiricism of
imagism and by the relativism of Stevens, have avoided using

poetry as a medium of ideas about reality, moral or otherwise. While poetry has always been subjective, it has become increasingly reflexive and solipsistic in the twentieth century.

While the Beat poets have clung to an earlier American Romantic tradition, they too have tended to emphasize consciousness rather than reality as the object of the poetic quest, even though like Berrigan they created poetry that was anti-academic, improvisational, and politically subversive. The emphasis by the Beats on consciousness rather than on external reality was recently reaffirmed by Allen Ginsberg in an article entitled "Poetry or Fiction?" Poetry, Ginsberg points out, involves selecting the "disparate and contradictory" elements in the mind, the "confusions and discontinuities of consciousness," and assembling these in an order which will produce for the reader the "sensation of consciousness."[12]

Epistemologically, Berrigan has more in common with poets like T.S. Eliot, the early Robert Lowell, and Robert Frost. Frost in particular, while far from immune from the skepticism of the age, grounded his poems in the fullness of experience rather than exclusively in consciousness, and exhibited an implicit belief in the correspondence between the mind and the external world; this was why he was usually careful to silhouette, usually humorously, subjective flights by those in his poems. Thus, although Berrigan was influenced by twentieth-century movements like imagism, philosophically he may be said to represent an earlier phase of American writing in which, in however attenuated a fashion, reality was assumed to be at least generally knowable as opposed to the contemporary depiction of perceptual knowledge in poets like Ashbery, for example, as merely provisional.

Allowing for some notable exceptions during the 1960s, the limitations of an almost exclusive preoccupation with consciousness by modern poets were pointed up by W.H. Auden in his dramatic poem, *The Age of Anxiety*, in 1947:

> To refuse the tasks of time
> And, overlooking our lives,
> Cry - 'Miserable wicked me,
> How interesting I am.'
> We would rather be ruined than changed,
> We would rather die in our dread
> Than climb the cross of the moment
> And let our illusions die. [13]

In a similar mood the poet, Wendell Berry, has convincingly depicted the majority of contemporary poets as having made a hermetic religion of their art, "a religion based not on what they have in common with other people, but on what they *do* that sets them apart." In this way poetry serves not as a connection between the poet and the experience of others, but rather becomes a solipsistic "seeking of self in words."[14] For Berry this modern tendency represents a regrettable betrayal of the traditional use of words as indicators of experience shared by the poet and the reader, words whose meanings generally originated in society before being taken up by the poet. Another ill effect of this use of words, Berry argues, is the draining of the moral implications of words and of the "consequences of these, both practical and spiritual."[15]

Apart from the practice of contemporary poets, twentieth-century philosophical thought in general has tended to empty the traditional conception of the good of any precise significance, replacing this terminology with the notion of value, even though, as the philosopher, George Grant, has observed drily, no one has been "able to tell us what a value is."[16] For this reason as well, Berrigan's poetry appears to go against the grain. As Wendell

Berry's analysis implies, however, Berrigan may be doing art a service in the long run by helping to recall it to some of its earlier fullness and richness.

Berrigan is distinctive in recent American writing for uniting the roles of observer and actor, even though, as he has mentioned in his autobiography, *To Dwell in Peace*, he has had at times the sense of being broken into two, into the "private and public halves of a person", as though in a nightmare a "guillotine" had fallen on him, "not across his neck, but down the length of his being."[17] Much of twentieth-century American literature has been characterized by a cleavage between the roles of observer and actor, a thematic offshoot of the Romantic passion for consciousness, which condescendingly relegated the sphere of action to the uncultivated. In recent American literature the gap between the sensitive, ineffectual observer and the coarser, vigorous actor has been enlarged by the fact that American writers, especially poets, have been lodged in academia and generally in possession of a relatively narrow range of experience, a fact that has caused Berrigan to measure carefully his involvement in university life.

As a writer Berrigan is distinctive for his lifelong attempt to balance his participation in thought and action. Tucked away in the leafy surroundings of Le Moyne in the 1950s and early 1960s, for example, he nonetheless immersed himself in controversial social reform, finding himself in time carried rapidly toward a more aggressive activism by the Vietnam war, which intensified, beyond even his own expectations, his involvement in political activity:

> Vietnam was, for many of us, a line drawn in earth
> and time. The "before" was the entire weight of our
> prior lives, the numbness of spirit with which we
> turned to the question of violence, the cultural and
> religious suppositions that left us infants in a dark

> wood. Then we crossed over - afoot or crawling,
> hesitant, dragging a great weight of the past. . . .
> And from thenceforth, life in America, in the
> church, in our families (in the Jesuits), could never
> be as it was. [18]

While writers like T.S. Eliot, Thomas Merton, and Robert Lowell
had created a place for religious poetry in the twentieth century,
Berrigan has been distinctive, not only in advocating the sort of
balance of contemplation and action already discussed, but in
demonstrating the creative windfall that such a balance brings to
the artist. In a little known article published in the 1960s entitled
"Sacrifice and Modern Man" Berrigan argued that even the learned
needed to have the "power of their minds released by immersion in
a dramatic action."[19]

In retrospect, it can be said that Berrigan's writing did
benefit from his turning to social action in the 1960s - up to a point.
The best of Berrigan's writings were published when the contemplative and active parts of his life were on a relatively even keel in
the late 1960s. If the early theological writings, which were intellectually challenging, had revealed an engaging, contemplative
mind, those of the later period, particularly the 1970s, appear at
times largely to be footnotes to a life of action. It was in the late
1960s that Berrigan seemed to reach a pivotal stage in his life and
writing when the social activist and the writer not only nourished
each other but when Berrigan's faculties and energy were at their
peak.

In assessing the writings of the early and mid 1970s, one is
forced to recognize the debilitating effects of Berrigan's prison
experience. In the late 1970s to mid-1980s, on the other hand, the
writings, both prose and poetry, regain some of the equilibrium of
the late 1960s in atmosphere and outlook, if not in energy. In the

narrative sketches about the dying, the Latin American journals, and the poems written on Block Island, Berrigan emerges as an attractive and interesting persona, a warrior worn smooth by time and experience, whose consciousness is nonetheless easily kindled by memories of past battles and present adversaries - the military, the docile and complicit universities, and the overweening bureaucracies, all of whom contributed to the anesthetizing of the individual conscience.

Berrigan's apocalyptic vantage point, which is highly visible in the prose and poetry of the 1970s, though less obtrusively present in other of his writings, has been a stumbling block for some readers. In a review of Walker Percy's novel, *The Thanatos Syndrome*, Terrence Rafferty has voiced the sort of objection which many readers feel toward apocalyptic writing - which Rafferty calls "ahistorical":

> The apocalyptic imagination is innocent of the kinds of fine distinctions a cultural critic has to make. It's all marking time until the end, the fiery climax, the series finale, with events in the lapse-time between the original sin and the last judgment erasing themselves continually as we formulate and reformulate their meaning, until all that's left of them is a blinding-white constant significance - the last word.[20]

While there is some truth in Rafferty's observations about apocalyptic writing in general, Berrigan has repeatedly called attention to inconsistencies in ideologically abstract readings of history, whether secular or religious. For Berrigan, while the end is normative, it is also existential, and is thus dependent upon the evolution of both matter and culture. While Berrigan's faith in the

progress of cultural evolution has sagged in recent years, he has
never abandoned his belief that human experience, in all of its
ramifications, has value simply as human experience. Indeed, his
principal quarrel has been with those who, in the name of morally
constrictive ideologies, have sought to narrow the range of human
consciousness and action.

If some of Berrigan's contemporaries, as was suggested
earlier, had fashioned a religion out of art, Berrigan has shown
convincingly how art could be made out of religion in a century
when such an attempt might otherwise have seemed merely
anomalous. Because of the extraordinary composition of Berrigan's
life with its juxtaposition of identities - iconoclastic priest, ironic
poet, political dissenter, and contemplative nomad - Berrigan has
been able to make accessible to the contemporary sensibility what
it feels like to be reflectively and courageously religious in a
predominantly non-religious culture:

> Let us imagine, as the gift of religion to the world,
> five minutes of consciousness. The *sight*, that is,
> which we go to the theater to see, the voice we
> hearken to, when we read great poetry, or listen to
> Brahms or Cage or the Beatles. The mind at work
> in John's gospel; come, be healed, or be reborn, or
> raised from the dead. To taste; in the biblical sense,
> to pluck the world, and find it unpoisoned.[21]

Composed in 1968 for a lecture that he had been asked to
give, the words are vintage Berrigan. It was because of his
passionate love of the world that he had sprung to its defense
against those who would plunder it and exploit its peoples. The
angry lines and biting caricatures in his writing came from a poet
and priest who has felt himself to be on the ramparts of the world,

threatened not by legions of devils but by large, impassive organizations with potentially apocalyptic powers. The best of Berrigan's writings are the polished mirror of a conscience affronted by the threat to humanity posed by these diffused organizations, a likeness unlike that produced by any other twentieth-century writer.

Notes: *Chapter Six*

1. Charles Meconis, *With Clumsy Grace: the American Catholic Left, 1961-1975* (New York: Seabury, 1979) 144-152.
2. Letter from Daniel Berrigan to the author, June 7, 1986.
3. *To Dwell in Peace* (San Francisco: Harper & Row, 1987) 144.
4. Robert Coles, "Introduction," *The Geography of Faith* (Boston: Beacon, 1971) 32.
5. Letter from Daniel Berrigan to the author, June 7, 1986.
6. For instructive analyses of Berrigan's theological development see Robert Ludwig, "The Theology of Daniel Berrigan," *Listening* 6 (Spring, 1971) 127-137 and Paul Weber, "Daniel Berrigan: Political Theology in the Post-War Years," *Chicago Studies* 12 (Spring, 1973) 77-90.
7. *The Nightmare of God* (Portland, Ore: Sunburst Pr., 1983) 2.
8. Anatol Rapoport, *Strategy and Conscience* (New York: Harper & Row, 1964) 284.
9. Helen Vendler, *The Music of What Happens* (Cambridge, Mass. and London: Harvard University Pr., 1988) 4.
10. Paul Breslin, *The Psycho-Political Muse: American Poetry Since the Fifties* (Chicago and London: Univ. of Chicago Pr., 1987) xv.
11. Saul Bellow, "Foreword," *The Closing of the American Mind* by Allan Bloom (New York: Simon and Schuster, 1987) 17.
12. Allen Ginsberg, "Poetry or Fiction?" *Margin* 2 (Spring, 1987) 22.
13. W.H. Auden, *The Age of Anxiety: A Baroque Eclogue* (London: Faber and Faber, 1947) 123.
14. Wendell Berry, *Standing by Words* (San Francisco: North Point Pr., 1983) 7.
15. Berry 96.
16. George Grant, *Technology and Justice* (Toronto: Anansi, 1986) 41.
17. *To Dwell in Peace* 347.

18. *Steadfastness of the Saints* (Maryknoll, N.Y.: Orbis, 1985) 35.
19. "Sacrifice and Modern Man," *Sponsa Regis* 32 (Nov. 1960) 73.
20. Terrence Rafferty, "The Last Fiction Show," *New Yorker*, June 15, 1987, 92.
21. "A Modest Proposal." Unpublished typescript, dated January, 1968.

SELECTIVE BIBLIOGRAPHY

WORKS BY DANIEL BERRIGAN

Poetry

Time Without Number. New York: Macmillan, 1957.
Encounters. Cleveland: World Publishing, 1960.
The World for Wedding Ring. New York: Macmillan, 1962.
No One Walks Waters. New York: Macmillan, 1966.
False Gods, Real Men. New York: Macmillan, 1969.
Selected and New Poems. Garden City, N.Y.: Doubleday, 1973.
Prison Poems. Greensboro, N.C.: Unicorn, 1973.
May All Creatures Live. Nevada City, Ca.: Berliner, 1984.
Block Island. Greensboro, N.C.: Unicorn, 1985.

Play

The Trial of the Catonsville Nine. Boston, Beacon Press, 1970.

Prose

Books

The Bride: *Essays in the Church*. New York. Macmillan, 1959.
The Bow in the Clouds: *Man's Covenant with God*. New York: Coward-McCann, 1961.
They Call Us Dead Men. New York: Macmillan, 1966.
Consequences: *Truth and...* New York: Macmillan, 1967.
Love, Love at the End. New York: Macmillan, 1968.
Night Flight to Hanoi. New York: Macmillan, 1968.

259

No Bars to Manhood. Garden City, N.Y.: Doubleday, 1970.

The Dark Night of Resistance. Garden City, N.Y.: Doubleday, 1971.

America is Hard to Find. Garden City, N.Y.: Doubleday, 1972.

Jesus Christ. Garden City, N.Y.: Doubleday, 1973.

Lights on in the House of the Dead. Garden City, N.Y.: Doubleday, 1974.

A Book of Parables. New York: Seabury, 1977.

Beside the Sea of Glass. New York: Seabury, 1978.

Uncommon Prayer. New York: Seabury, 1978.

The Words Our Savior Gave Us. Springfield, Ill.: Templegate, 1978.

The Discipline of the Mountain. New York: Seabury, 1979.

We Die Before We Live. New York: Seabury, 1980.

Ten Commandments for the Long Haul. Nashville: Abingdon, 1981.

Portraits: Of Those I Love. New York: Crossroad, 1982.

The Nightmare of God. Portland, Ore.: Sunburst Press, 1983.

Steadfastness of the Saints. Maryknoll, N.Y.: Orbis, 1985.

The Mission. San Francisco: Harper & Row, 1986.

To Dwell in Peace. San Francisco: Harper & Row, 1987.

Articles

"Faith and Poetry." *America* 70 (1944): 353-354.

"Forgotten Splendor." *America* 70 (1944): 605-606.

"The New Poetry." *Modern Humanist* [Weston, Mass.], 8 (Autumn, 1951): 1-14.

"Sacrifice and Modern Man." *Sponsa Regis* 32 (Nov., 1960): 72-83.

"The Catholic Dream World and the Sacred Image." *Worship* 35 (1961): 549-560.

"The Spirit of Modern Sacred Art." *Liturgy for the People.* Ed. William J. Leonard. Milwaukee: Bruce, 1963. 147-167.

"The Season of Youth." *Today* 19 (May, 1964): 29-30.

"The Council and the Priest." *Perspectives* 9 (March-April, 1964): 52-55. Written under the pseudonym of John Winter.

"The Mission of the Church." *Perspectives* 9 (Sept.-Oct., 1964): 137-143.

"The Eight Hundred Years of Notre Dame." *Critic* 22 (June-July, 1964): 30-38.

"The Other World and Poor America." *A.I.D. Dialogue* 2 (Jan.-Feb. 1965): 1-6.

"Russian Journey." *Critic* 23 (June-July, 1965): 52-56.

"Reflections on the Priest as Peacemaker." *Jubilee* 13 (Feb., 1966): 22-29.

"Africa: A People's Art." *Jesuit Missions* 41 (Jan.-Feb., 1967): 22-27.

"The Tension between Art and Faith." *Critic* 26 (Aug.-Sept., 1967): 11-12.

"The Modern Concept of Missio." *Jesuit Spirit in a Time of Change.* Ed. Raymond Schroth. Westminster, Md.: Newman Press, 1968. 203-220.

"Diary from the Underground." *The Underground Church.* Ed. Malcolm Boyd. New York: Sheed and Ward, 1968. 50-62.

"Values and the University." *Katallagete* 2 (Fall, 1969): 27-29.

"Foreword." *The Politics of the Gospel.* By Jean-Marie Paupert. New York: Holt, Rinehart, and Winston, 1969. vi-xviii.

"The Breaking of Men and the Breaking of Bread: An Introduction." *Prison Journals of a Priest Revolutionary.* By Philip Berrigan. New York: Holt, Rinehart, and Winston, 1970. xi-xix.

"Notes from the Underground." *New Blackfriars* 51 (1970): 454-461.

"Star Wars: Cruel Fantasy." *Sojourners* 6 (Sept. 1977): 34.

"Introduction." *The Cell.* By Horst Bienek. Santa Barbara: Unicorn, 1972. i-iv.

"The Brotherhood of Prisoners." *Commonweal* 99 (1972): 476-478.

"Responses to Settler Regimes." *American Report* 29 (Oct. 29, 1973): 5, 16-17.

"On Celebrating Our Defeats." *New Politics* 11 (Winter, 1974): 26-30.

"*Ezra Pound: The Last Rower.*" *Critic* 35 (Fall, 1976): 76-80.

"The Seventy Times Seventy Seven Storey Mountain." *Cross Currents* 27 (1977-78): 385-393.

"Swords Into Plowshares." *Catholic Worker* 46 (Oct.-Nov., 1980): 1, 3-4.

"After the Deaths of Dorothy Day and Thomas Merton, the Bishops Spoke for Peace." *Cross Currents* 31 (1981-82): 387.

"Anniversary Poems: Report from the Empty Grave." *Thought* 57 (March, 1982): 74-83.

"Thomas Merton on Peace and Nuclear War." *Cistercian Studies* 17 (1982): 366-372.

"The Hope that Hopes on." *Katallagete* 8 (Spring, 1983): 35-39.

"The Peacemaker." *Thomas Merton, Monk: A Monastic Tribute.* Ed. Patrick Hart. Kalamazoo, Mich.: Cistercian, 1983. 219-227.

Interviews

The Geography of Faith. Boston: Beacon, 1971.

Absurd Convictions, Modest Hopes. New York: Random House, 1972.

The Raft is not the Shore. Boston: Beacon, 1975.

"Daniel Berrigan, S.J." *The New Jesuits.* Ed. George Riemer. Boston: Little, Brown, 1971. 34-64.

Shapiro, Harriet. "Berrigan in Crisis. *Intellectual Digest* 4 (May, 1974): 6, 8, 10, 68.

"Daniel Berrigan and Hans Morgenthau Discuss the Moral Dilemma in the Middle East." *Progressive* 38 (March, 1974): 31-34.

"Father Dan Berrigan: The Holy Outlaw." *Christianity and Crisis* 30 (1970): 184-193.

"The Push of Conscience." *Sojourners* 10 (June, 1981): 20-23.

SECONDARY SOURCES

Books and Dissertations

Bannan, John and Rosemary. *Law, Morality and Vietnam.*
Bloomington and London: Indiana University Press, 1974. 124-230.

Bianchi, Eugene. *The Religious Experience of Revolutionaries.* Garden City, N.Y.: Doubleday, 1972.

Curtis, Richard. *The Berrigan Brothers.* New York: Hawthorn, 1974.

Bloom, Allan. *The Closing of the American Mind.* New York: Simon and Schuster, 1987.

Breslin, Paul. *The Psycho-Political Muse: American Poetry Since the Fifties.* Chicago and London: Univ. of Chicago Pr., 1987.

Cargas, Harry J. *Daniel Berrigan and Contemporary Protest Poetry.* New Haven: College University Press, 1972.

Casey, William Van Etten, ed. *The Burden of the Berrigans.* New York: Praeger, 1971.

Chomsky, Noam. *Peace in the Middle East?* New York: Pantheon, 1974. 167-180.

Deedy, John. *'Apologies, Good Friends': An Interim Biography of Daniel Berrigan, S.J.* Chicago: Fides/Claretian, 1981.

Friday, Robert. "Rhetorical Analysis of Daniel Berrigan's Defense at the Trial of the Catonsville Nine." Ph.D. dissertation. Univ. of Pittsburgh, 1983.

Gray, Francine du Plessix. *Divine Disobedience.* New York: Knopf, 1970.

Halpert, Stephen and Murray, Tom. *Witness of the Berrigans.* Garden City, N.Y.: Doubleday, 1972.

von Hallberg, Robert, ed. *Politics and Poetic Value.* Chicago and London: Univ. of Chicago Pr., 1987.

Hughes, Catharine. *Plays, Polemics and Politics.* New York: Drama Book Specialists, 1973: 83-90.

Klejment, Anne. *The Berrigans: A Bibliography of Published Works.* New York: Garland, 1979.

McNeal, Patricia. *The American Catholic Peace Movement 1928-1972.* New York: Arno Press, 1978. 241-299.

Meconis, Charles. *With Clumsy Grace: The American Catholic Left, 1961-1975.* New York: Seabury, 1979.

Nelson, Jack and Ostrow, Ronald J. *The FBI and the Berrigans.* New York: Coward, McCann, 1972.

Oddo, Thomas C. "The Monk and the Activist: A Comparative Study of the Spirituality of Thomas Merton and Daniel Berrigan." Ph.D. dissertation. Harvard, 1979.

Raines, John C., ed. *Conspiracy: The Implications of the Harrisburg Trial for the Democratic Tradition.* New York: Harper and Row, 1974.

Vendler, Helen. *The Music of What Happens.* Cambridge, Mass. and London: Harvard Univ. Pr., 1988.

Zinn, Howard. *The Politics of History.* Boston: Beacon Press, 1970. 223-237.

Articles

Bellow, Saul. "Foreword." *The Closing of the American Mind.* By Allan Bloom. New York: Simon and Schuster. 11-18.

Cameron, J.M. "What is a Christian?" *New York Review of Books* 13 (May 26, 1966): 3-4.

Chomsky, Noam. "Daniel in the Lions' Den: Dan Berrigan & His Critics." *Liberation* 6 (Feb., 1974): 15-24.

Cowan, Paul. "The Moral Imperialism of Dan Berrigan." *Village Voice* 31 (Jan., 1974): 22-23.

Day, Dorothy. "Dan Berrigan in Rochester." *Catholic Worker* (Dec., 1970): 1, 6.

Day, Dorothy. "The Berrigans and Property Rights." *Fellowship* 37 (May, 1971): 25.

Fergenson, Laraine. "Thoreau, Daniel Berrigan, and the Problem of Transcendental Politics." *Soundings* 65 (Spring, 1982): 103-122.

Ludwig, Robert. "The Theology of Daniel Berrigan." *Listening* 6 (1971): 127-137.

Mayer, Paul. "Voices of the Middle East." *WIN* 10 (Dec. 5, 1974): 12-19.

Moramarco, Fred. "A Gathering of Poets." *Western Humanities Review* 28 (1974): 83-84.

Patton, John H. "Rhetoric at Catonsville: Daniel Berrigan, Conscience, and Image Alteration." *Today's Speech* 23 (Winter, 1975): 3-12.

Percy, Walker. *"The Bow in the Clouds."* *America* 106 (1962): 772-773.

Ruether, Rosemary. "Ruether's Open Letter to Daniel Berrigan." *National Catholic Reporter* June 5, 1968: 4.

Semmer, Robert F. "The 'Why' Behind Civil Disobedience at Catonsville." *Cornell Law Forum* 21 (Fall, 1968): 5, 18.

Sax, Joseph. L. "Civil Disobedience: The Law Is Never Blind."
    Saturday Review 51 (Sept. 28, 1968): 22-25, 56.
True, Michael. "Poetry and the Vietnam Vortex." *Cross Currents*
    26 (1976): 251-256.
Wain, John. "Art, Play and Protest." *New Republic* 162 (June 20,
    1970): 23-25.
Weber, Paul J. "Daniel Berrigan: Political Theology in the Post-
    War Years. *Chicago Studies* 12 (Spring, 1973): 77-90.
Zahn, Gordon. "The Great Catholic Upheaval." *Saturday Review*
    54 (Sept. 11, 1971): 24-27, 54, 56.
Zinn. Howard. "The Prisoners: A Bit of Contemporary History."
    The Politics of History. Ed. Howard Zinn. Boston, Beacon
    Press, 1970. 223-236.
Zwisohn, Van. "Daniel Berrigan: Walking to Prison." *Parnassus* 3
    (1975): 243-258.

INDEX

267

About the Author

Ross Labrie teaches American literature at the University of British Columbia in Vancouver. He is the author of *The Art of Thomas Merton* (1979), *Howard Nemerov* (1980), and *James Merrill* (1982) as well as of a number of articles on modern American literature.